Education in a Globalized World

Education in a Globalized World

The Connectivity of Economic Power, Technology, and Knowledge

Nelly P. Stromquist

ROWMAN & LITTLEFIELD PUBLISHERS, INC.
Lanham • Boulder • New York • Oxford

ROWMAN & LITTLEFIELD PUBLISHERS, INC.

Published in the United States of America
by Rowman & Littlefield Publishers, Inc.
A wholly owned subsidiary of the Rowman & Littlefield Publishing Group, Inc.
4501 Forbes Boulevard, Suite 200, Lanham, Maryland 20706
www.rowmanlittlefield.com

Estover Road
Plymouth PL6 7PY
United Kingdom

British Library Cataloguing in Publication Information Available

Library of Congress Cataloging-in-Publication Data

Stromquist, Nelly P.
    Education in a globalized world : the connectivity of economic power, technology,
and knowledge / Nelly P. Stromquist.
        p. cm.
    Includes bibliographical references and index.
    ISBN 0-7425-1097-2 (cloth : alk. paper) — ISBN 0-7425-1098-0 (pbk. : alk. paper)
    1. Politics and education—Cross-cultural studies. 2. Education—Economic
aspects—Cross-cultural studies. 3. Globalization. I. Title.

    LC71 .S87 2002
    379—dc21

                                                                        2002001826

Printed in the United States of America

♾™ The paper used in this publication meets the minimum requirements of
American National Standard for Information Sciences—Permanence of Paper
for Printed Library Materials, ANSI/NISO Z39.48-1992.

Contents

Preface   vii

Acknowledgments   xi

Introduction   xiii

1   Theorizing Globalization   1

2   The Twinning of Ideas and Material Conditions: Globalization,
    Neoliberalism, and Postmodernism   19

3   Educational Impacts of Economic and Cultural Globalization   37

4   Consequences of Communication Technologies on
    Culture and Education   63

5   Transnational Corporations and the Creation of
    New Values and Citizenship   83

6   The University as the Spearhead of Globalization   103

7   Gender within Globalized Education   133

8   Agency and Resistance in the Globalization Era   157

9   Reframing the Future   177

Appendix A   189

References   195

Index   213

About the Author   221

Preface

The world is changing rapidly and greatly, not the typical intergenerational change we have witnessed in the past but a change so profound and encompassing that we have never seen its likes before. We face a momentous time in which we are present at the creation of new values, new organizational procedures, and new ways of relating with other human beings. Some take all these developments for granted as part of normal evolution. Others assert that little is new under the sun and that we are seeing manifestations of trends present since the fifteenth century with the discovery of America and the beginning of mercantilism. Yet others prefer to consider current developments for the profound impact they appear to portend and as the prime ground for discussion of specifically what the changes imply and what consequences they will bring to different groups of people and countries.

Globalization (which we define in chapter 1) is often presented as the correct way to achieve progress and modernization. In this approach, which is endorsed by governments, the media, and the business sector, emphasis is given to the virtues of globalization as represented by the speed of communications, the density of social networks, the diffusion of new ideas, the interdependence of groups and communities, and the creation of more efficient institutions (Held 1995). In contrast, the darker side of globalization—which covers a more complex set of interrelated processes, many of them represented in the substantial concentration of economic power in the hands of few institutions and countries, the increasing poverty and exclusion of large numbers of people in developing countries, and the challenges they face given the reduced role of the state and the emergence of an aggressive global market—has received secondary attention in the literature.

By now, the phenomenon of globalization has inspired many books; amid this abundance, there have been three emphases: its economic and technological features and to a lesser extent its cultural attributes. I do not seek to compete with previous studies. I wish to contribute to the debate by highlighting the *interconnectedness* between economic and technological globalization and cultural and educational manifestations. I wish also to compare views from the North with those from the South so as to clarify the particular, differential consequences of globalization. My intention, therefore, is to provide a more balanced and empirically valid theory of globalization than is usually presented in the more ideological versions of globalization.

Globalization brings to the fore the area of education. Globalization promotes not only the expansion of education but also its importance in everyday life in terms of both material production and life success. In my view, educators, perhaps more than any other professionals (excluding those perhaps in social communications), need to become highly conscious of the role that ideology and certain other forms of knowledge play in shaping our contemporary world. They also need to become more aware of both intended and unintended consequences of the numerous innovations in formal and informal education.

Since countries are not equal, the study of a globalized world calls by its very nature for investigations of linkages between center and periphery and thus for research on countries, institutions, and social groups that is comparative. The specialization of comparative and international education acquires new relevance and is the object of heightened expectations in this era of change. I agree entirely with the observation by Marginson and Mollis (2001) that comparative education has not engaged in sufficient "theorization of the changing global/national relationship," including challenges to the parameters of the specialization itself. It is my ambitious purpose to contribute to some of the prerequisite reflective thought by putting under a closer lens not only higher education—the level most examined to date—but also primary and secondary education. An analysis of the strong interaction between economics, technology, and culture shapes my writing. Gender issues, which are still central sources of inequality in all human societies, have been taken up in every chapter of the book; in addition, they are discussed in a specific chapter. This special focus is present in this work because the attainment of the world's "improvement" must perforce traverse through the paths of gender sensitivity and gender transformation.

I have attempted to engage in a constant effort to bring both positive and negative views of globalization into discussion. But my analysis does not end in neutral or ambivalent conclusions. I present the evidence and pass on definite judgment while admitting that the available evidence is incomplete (even though it keeps arriving daily, especially through the media and the Internet). Some might consider it risky to pass on judgment while data are still accumulating. I do not, for if we were to wait until all necessary evidence is amassed, the world would simply pass us by on others' terms.

The book is directed toward social science researchers and educational policymakers in hopes that they will understand better the linkages among multiple domains and layers of our contemporary world. It is aimed also at advanced undergraduates and graduate students concerned with ongoing social changes and willing to accept the obligation to know about them and act accordingly. If the general public were alerted to the impacts documented and foreseen in this book, that, too, would not be a bad thing.

Acknowledgments

Who can claim to be a globalization expert? The study of globalization calls for multidisciplinary knowledge. Moreover, the areas under its reach are so encompassing and so constantly unfolding that for any one person to have complete knowledge is virtually impossible. When I started to work on this theme, I did so much more out of curiosity than competence. My first book on the subject, edited jointly with Karen Monkman (*Globalization and Education: Integration and Contestation across Cultures,* 1999), derived from a western regional meeting of the Comparative and International Education Society held in 1996, at which time we wanted to explore the concept of globalization by zeroing in on its educational impacts. The production of the book put us in contact with a group of scholars throughout the world who had examined globalization on a firsthand basis.

The joint editing of that book marked for me the beginning of a persistent interest in globalization. This second book, an adventure into the information and knowledge contained in libraries, cyberspace documents, and various primary sources, appears at the request and extraordinary trust of Dean Birkenkamp, my editor at Rowman & Littlefield. Dean found my first writings to be useful and challenged me to expand on the subject and produce a book that would be easily accessible to college students.

At my place of work, the University of Southern California, I was truly fortunate to have the assistance of Andrew Chlebek, then second-year doctoral student, an indefatigable Internet surfer and sleuth of globalization articles and events. His own interest was piqued by the material he came across, and he eventually selected to do a dissertation on this topic. Commentaries from colleagues, particularly Raymond Morrow, Steven Klees, and Rolland Paulston, were of much help in improving analysis and conclusions. I wish to express special thanks to Dean Karen Gallagher and Professor Lawrence Picus of the Rossier School of Education for enabling me to participate in the First World Social Forum, held in Porto Alegre, Brazil (January 2001). In an ocean of people from all walks of life committed to social justice, I gained a deep sense of how crucial it is to pursue and reach alternative social agendas. A semester's sabbatical was also instrumental in affording me the extended time needed for concentration and sense making. My husband, Eric, as in all my previous work, demonstrated great patience with my time allocations and granted me clear and precise editorial assistance.

The comfort of the Bellagio Study and Conference Center in Italy, graciously provided to scholars by the Rockefeller Foundation, was of immense help in the completion of this manuscript. During one month of sunny weather, the incomparable scenery of the lakes of Como and Lecco (against the background of the Alps) and genial companions, constructive thought came in heavy doses and was constantly augmented and challenged through conversation with other residents.

Finally, my thanks to Alison Sullenberger and Terry Fischer, production editors, and to Bruce Owens, who copyedited this book.

Introduction

This book has descriptive and explanatory aims. It seeks to provide a sense of major developments associated with globalization that are affecting all levels of education (from primary to university) in various parts of the world, comparing and contrasting conditions between the First and the Third World. Being multidimensional, globalization touches economic, technological, political, and cultural dimensions. In other words, as certain goods circulate widely throughout distinct societies, new dynamics develop between the consumer and the object consumed. As technology expands into more areas of life, economic production is affected, creating in the process new cultural ways of relating to technology and environment. This book explains unfolding events and practices by tying them to the intention of specific actors who are convinced of the merit of their new visions and actions. Not everyone is an equal player in the globalization process, and some of the previous power structures (e.g., the state, international financial and development agencies, and the private sector) have not decreased in importance but rather modified their functions.

While the interactions and synergic dynamics that constitute globalization are many, we seek to highlight how education and culture are transforming as a result—sometimes gradually—but often this transformation is rapid and more comprehensive. The new globalization era is full of promises for individuals, institutions, and countries. Among these promises is education— as advanced skills and sophisticated knowledge (heavily weighted in favor of science and technology) are deemed essential to the construction of the "knowledge society" and countries and regional blocs are positioned as competitive entities that will enter the global market with (it is hoped) superior strengths and abilities. So, education as a *means* to succeeding in a globalized world is now given great importance, even to the extent of exaggerating its potential to create wealth, independent of other factors of production and regardless of other international/global parameters and contexts.

At the same time, education has become the key *venue* to support globalization. All processes of social transformation require simultaneous ideological support. That education has become the primary site for the creation and transmission of such ideologies can be seen worldwide in (1) the adoption of economistic values and the naturalization of new objectives and concomitant practices in schools and universities, (2) the priority assigned to certain subject matters and fields of study over others, and (3) the disregard, and sometimes plain erasure, of certain knowledge, particularly that which might contest points 1 and 2. We concur with the assertion of the United Nations Development Program (1999a) that culture is the ideological battleground of the modern world system. The globalization process in education is accomplished paradoxically via both centralization and decentralization mechanisms. Notable among decentralization strategies is the privatization of education (along with other social services), linking thus the goals of profit and knowledge. Centralization appears through competition at all levels (individual, institutional, national, and regional)—competition that, through comparisons seeking to identify those that excel, sets uniform criteria for judging all performance.

The process of globalization today links the economic and technical power of certain groups with the knowledge and skills that are produced in schools. Many educational policies reflect the will of outsiders, particularly international financial institutions and business groups. Consequently, the study of globalization requires that we undertake a political and economic analysis of schooling and knowledge in order to grasp what forces account for the nature and order of educational institutions, to gain an understanding of who benefits and who does not, and to predict what further manifestations we will see. Critical theorists have been advocating this direction for a long time; today it becomes more necessary than ever.

Michael Apple, in his classic *Teachers and Texts* (1986), warns against falling into economic reductionism but argues that there is "a very real set of connections between schooling and economic, cultural and political power" (7–8). His examination of micro-level events in U.S. schools enables him to grasp the subtle and recurrent practices of schools and classrooms; simultaneously, his consideration of higher-level players permits us to understand how events take the form they do and, more importantly, have the outcomes they do. If Apple's work on teaching and curriculum is ambitious, a book on globalization and education results may be even more ambitious: While the economic and power and cultural connections are clear, not all necessary data are there, certain processes involving important negotiations or decisions are not public knowledge or easily retrievable, and comparisons cannot always or easily be made across countries either because of the absence of parallel studies or because different contexts may preclude reliable comparison. Despite these difficulties, some trends are tangible and some outcomes undeniable.

SOURCES OF DATA

This book builds on a variety of sources. Some derive from secondary sources in the form of journal articles and books dealing with globalization. Some are government policy documents and official statistics on the distribution of wealth and education and documents produced by international development agencies. A large set of the information comes from Internet materials, particularly those produced by civic groups responding to issues of globalization. The mass media, primarily in the form of newspapers, provided additional pertinent information.

Most of the available evidence exists at the national level. As Beaverstock et al. (2000) remark, the majority of socioeconomic data are state produced and state referenced. While data on globalization should include transstate events, processes, and statistics, much of the available information on globalization exists at a unit of analysis that is not always the most relevant to detect globalization forces and measure their impacts.

The available evidence has yet another important characteristic. Many pieces of data central to an assessment of the features and consequences of globalization are not publicly available. Privatization and competition—values highly inherent to globalization—foster secrecy. An immense layer of processes and motivations remains submerged and impervious to datagathering efforts. In several cases, construction and extrapolation from partial documents and studies become necessary to produce comprehensible accounts as well as to portray a "full picture."

METHODOLOGY

The evidence and its interpretation are very much dependent on which discipline is being applied. Cultural studies emphasize sense making based on images and texts, political scientists are particularly attuned to issues of power, sociologists see broader changes in groups and are perhaps more sensitive to the identification of commonalities, and anthropologists often tend to see more diversity at micro levels and thus question the homogenizing effects of globalization. While globalization is being examined from multiple perspectives and many assessments of its processes and consequences exist, we feel that any conclusions about it become more definite and even consensual when there is a concrete referent, be it indigenous groups, the environment, or women. In our case, the key referent is education, both in institutional forms (schools and universities) and in more diffuse ways (i.e., through the mass media).

Previous—and still valid—works on education, notably those by Martin Carnoy (1974; *Education as Cultural Imperialism*) and John Meyer and Michael Hannan (1979; *National Development and the World System*), have made it demonstrably clear that external forces have deep repercussions on education. In the first work, the influence of colonialism on schooling was explored; in the second, changes in technology and communications were traced to the internationalization of the labor market. In both studies, education was found to function within a transnational context.

In this book, we are not making the claim that through globalization a large number of impacts are being felt on education and culture for the first time. External influences on education are a dynamic with a long trajectory. What we show is that new transnational social actors have positioned themselves with explicit voice and power in the arena of education. We show also that new technologies of communication are not only influencing education but also contributing to its redefinition.

Our account is based on a combination of quantitative and qualitative data. Where statistical indicators exist, we use them. Narratives of discrete events are presented; trends are also considered. For the most part, the analysis builds on the connection between specific agents and events. We differentiate between processes of adaptation/accommodation and imposition and—probably to the horror of postmodernists—contrast situations and consequences between industrialized and developing countries, women and men, and the powerful rich and the powerless (disenfranchised) poor. Binary analysis, or comparing opposing tendencies, is not very popular these days, yet it offers here the distinct advantage of rendering concise and parsimonious—and still real—what could otherwise be lost in an amorphous set of discrete and insignificant elements. Moreover, though fine gradations exist for almost every phenomenon we know, it is also the case that polarization of processes and outcomes tends to characterize conflictual developments.

REALITIES IN OUR CONTEMPORARY WORLD

It might be instructive to begin our discussion of globalization with some understanding of how specific groups within countries and the countries themselves fare in the various available indicators of well-being. Perhaps because of their relative ease of formulation, indicators of quantitative nature predominate over those that might better describe the more diffuse situations affecting knowledge and cultural changes.

Statistics regarding wealth (or lack thereof) are simply mind blowing. People today live better and longer than people in previous centuries, reflecting advances in nutrition, health, housing, and knowledge, to mention but the most fundamental. In the large scheme of things, the twenty-first century is a much more desirable time than many others in history. In the past, there were kings and queens but also large segments of extremely poor people. Today, we have a middle class, with true signs of steady progress in the material conditions of humanity. We are reaching constantly higher levels of technological development and, with it, improved conditions in basic areas of life.

At the same time, we are experiencing considerable poverty, with large segments of the global population facing lives below the satisfaction of basic needs (Townsend 1993; United Nations Development Program 1998). There are also enormous levels of economic and social inequalities across countries and within countries. These inequalities do not necessarily bother some people: For them, the inequalities are temporary and justified in terms of their contribution to worldwide economic growth and the achievement of economic justice tomorrow (Thurow 1980).

In terms of income distribution, the world is becoming more unequal; the first quintile (the top 20 percent) has become a more exclusive First World "club" in 1999 than it had been in 1965. According to Arrighi and Silver (2000), the only two First World countries that were not in this "club" in 1965 (Portugal and Greece) had joined it by 1990, but three Third World countries in it had descended (Argentina, Venezuela, and Trinidad and Tobago) as well as two Second World (socialist) countries (Poland and Yugoslavia). Arrighi and Silver also note that the ascent to the first quintile of countries by former Third World nations such as South Korea, Taiwan, Hong Kong, Singapore, and Saudi Arabia have been more than counterbalanced, in terms of population, by the descent of Argentina, Venezuela, and Trinidad and Tobago.

Income levels are widening between central and developing countries. According to the United Nations Development Program (1999a, 3), income differentials between rich and poor countries presented an eleven-to-one ratio (i.e., individuals in rich countries earned on the average eleven times more than those in poor countries) in 1913. These differentials increased to thirty to one in 1960, rose to sixty to one in 1997, and became seventy-one to one by 1997. Since the differentials grew considerably at some time during the 1970s, they are linked to globalization, which indisputably has benefited many people around the world but has also widened the gap between wealthy and poor countries.

Concentration of wealth at the individual level has also grown rapidly. It is estimated that the 200 richest people in the world more than doubled their

net worth between 1992 and 1998, reaching a total of more than U.S.$1 tril-
lion. And, if we were to use a finer cut, we would find that the assets of the
top three billionaires are more than the combined gross national product
(GNP) of all least-developed countries and their 600 million people (United
Nations Development Program 1999a, 3).[1] The profusion of gated communities and condominiums secured by guards throughout the entire world is
"emblematic of large spatial patterns of segmentation and separation, certainly by social class and often by race" (Mittelman 2000, 240). Studies by the
United Nations led it to conclude that globalization amounts to a profound
transformation of national economies. The immense wealth that is being created is accompanied today by an increasing share of workers without contracts (United Nations Development Program 1999a, 37). This new wealth
coexists also with fewer instances of free provision (medical, legal, educational, and so on) to the poor. And the poor are being defined as incompetent, under the assumption that one becomes primarily what one is capable
of accomplishing. A recent speech by Kofi Annan, current secretary-general
of the United Nations, gives particular concreteness to the disparities in the
world today:

> Imagining the world really is a "global village," then 150 inhabitants live in an
> affluent area of the village, about 780 in poorer districts. Another 70 or so in a
> neighborhood in transition. The average income per person is US$6,000 a year,
> and there are more middle-income families than in the past. But just 200 dispose
> of 86 percent of all the wealth, while nearly half of the villagers are eking out an
> existence on less than US$2 per day. (Annan 2000, 14)

The North

The accumulation of wealth by richest countries is reflected in their GNP
per capita and in the expansion of social security and welfare expenditures.[2]
It is further reflected in their growing share of world export markets, foreign
direct investment, and information (world telephone lines and computers).
Countries in the Organization for Economic Cooperation and Development
(OECD), with only 19 percent of the global population, have 71 percent of
global trade in goods and services. Naturally, their consumption levels are
also high: They use up 80 percent of the world's resources.

Among the richest countries, the greatest beneficiary of the new wealth
is the United States. In April 2001, the U.S. government announced a
U.S.$281 billion surplus for the fiscal year, certainly a sign of wealth and
prosperity.[3] In this country, 3 percent were millionaires in 1990; by 1999,
there were 14 percent. According to the 1999 U.S. Census report, one of
every ten households has an annual income of more than U.S.$100,000,
and this type of household is the fastest-growing category. Unemployment,

one of the greatest scourges of the new economy, has not hit the United States, where, apparently, globalization has restructured occupations but has not reduced the total number of jobs (Graham 2001). But the globalized economy is one that simultaneously upgrades and downgrades labor. About half a million Americans are displaced by imports each year. Of these, about one-third will be reemployed with no lifetime earnings loss, one-third will experience moderate lifetime earnings reduction, and another one-third will experience severe reductions (Graham 2001). According to the 1999 U.S. Census report, more than thirty-two million people live below the poverty line, and more than half of all households own stock in the United States, but the top 5 percent of equity owners hold about 80 percent of all stock value, and 1 percent holds 50 percent of it (cited in Will 2001).

Despite rhetoric favoring a totally free market, farmers in developed countries receive considerable state support. In 1999, Norway granted average agricultural subsidies of U.S.$34,000 per farm, Switzerland U.S.$33,000, Japan U.S.$26,000, the United States U.S.$21,000, the European Union U.S.$16,000, and Canada U.S.$9,000 (*The Economist,* 2001, 45).

Arrighi and Silver (2000, 4), citing Milanovic, who examined income distribution of individuals for 1988 and 1993 from household surveys of ninety-one countries (adjusted for differences in purchase power parity), state that world inequality increased very rapidly during that period. They found that inequality *between* countries accounted for three-fourths of world inequality while *within* country inequality accounted for the remaining one-fourth during that period.

Thanks to their wealth, industrialized countries are able to engage in a great amount of investment in education, with an average of 20 percent of GNP spent on schooling, on-the-job training, and research and development in the early 1990s (Davies and Guppy 1999, citing Drucker 1993).

The South

One hundred developing countries, totaling 1.6 billion people, experienced economic decline between 1965 and 1998; in almost half, the average incomes are now lower than in 1970 (United Nations Development Program 1996).

There are large areas of the world with people living in conditions of chronic malnutrition (defined by the World Food Program as "not having enough food to provide the nutrients for active, healthy lives"). Of the 830 million such people, 791 million are in developing countries. Considering the distribution of this malnutrition by region, sub-Saharan Africa accounts for 180 million, or one-third of its population. In Asia, there are 525 million, or 17 percent of its population; and in Latin America and the

Caribbean, they number 53 million, or 11 percent of its population (Wren 1999).

According to recent UN sources (United Nations Development Program 1996, 1999a), standards of living conditions have fallen significantly in forty-eight developing countries. Between 1965 and 1988, the number of rural women living below the poverty line increased by 47 percent; the corresponding figure for men was less than 30 percent. In sub-Saharan Africa, per capita income in 1999 was lower than in 1970. During the 1990s, the external debt faced by this region became greater than its entire production. Since the poorest 20 percent of the world's people share only 1 percent of the world trade, little benefit has accrued to them from globalization (Bakker 2000).

Developing countries have not been doing well for various reasons. Multinational institutions prefer to give explanations based on internal factors, such as national corruption or, plainly, high levels of incompetence. However, it is well known that the ability to generate wealth has been affected by conditions in the global market. Excluding energy, the price of raw materials fell relative to finished goods from 1947 to 1978 (Thurow 1980). More recent data (Arrighi and Silver 2000) indicate a continuation of this trend. As Ehrenreich (2001) reminds us, people in industrialized countries foster the exploitation of people in the Third World by setting costs of primary products and wages at very low prices."

Conditions in some of the poorest countries are dismal and appear to be beyond a market solution. In the case of sub-Saharan Africa as a region, to achieve a 6 percent rate of growth (the rate necessary to start reversing negative trends), the external resource flow into the region would have to increase by up to 150 percent in the short run. At present, very few commercial firms want to invest in that part of the world.

The poverty of the Third World results in low investment in public education and great distinctions in access and quality of education between the poor and the rich. On the average, annual per capita expenditures in basic education in the South hover at about U.S.$100 compared to about U.S.$5,000 in the North. And this differential investment has been rapidly growing. In 1960, OECD countries spent fourteen times more in basic education than in developing countries; in 1980 the differential was twenty-two times more, but by 1990, OECD countries; were spending fifty times more (Heyneman 1997, 502). Not surprisingly, cross-national comparisons of student performance show low performance among students from developing countries. With decreased state engagement in public education, most children of the poor are provided low-quality services, while the more wealthy can afford a higher-quality private education, resulting in an ever widening gap in educational attainment between the rich and the poor within countries. In India, youths between fifteen and nineteen years of age from the richest 20 percent of households completed an average of ten years of schooling; children from the poorest 40 percent of the households have on average no schooling (World Bank 1999b, 31). In Brazil, only 15 percent of the fifteen- to nineteen-year-olds of the poorest households have completed primary school (World Bank 1999b). In addition, poor children experience much more repetition than those in other social classes; repetition is highly predictive of school withdrawal.

THE EMERGING KNOWLEDGE SOCIETY

One of the strongest assertions made by advocates of globalization regarding contemporary society is that the world is moving toward becoming a "knowledge society," a claim that seems to imply that (1) high knowledge will be needed at all levels of economic activity, (2) individuals and countries can "make it" by relying solely on the acquisition of knowledge and skills, and (3) no impediments exist to the acquisition of such knowledge.

Yet we have evidence that between 40 and 50 percent of the jobs in the new economy will not require university training but rather some type of work-based technical or trade credentials. New economy sectors such as aerospace, information technology, technological maintenance, animation, film, and tourism are some of the areas for which such training is needed. Data for the state of California, one of the economic epicenters in the globalized economy, show that there is a greater number of workers earning poverty-level salaries than a decade ago, the result of more than two-thirds of the job growth during the past ten years in the state going to lower-paying employment (*San Francisco Examiner,* 2000).[4] The globalized economy will need individuals with highly advanced knowledge, but it will also need persons with skills appropriate for labor-intensive jobs. An important dynamic that globalization will create will be the demand for a relatively small number of university-trained graduates while ensuring that there will continue to be persons with lower levels of education and that they understand their situation as part of a fair process that allows the success of only those who are most meritorious.

The current prevalence of an international discourse on the "knowledge economy" may not be simple coincidence. Today, the discourse emanating from official institutions in the North does not call for understanding the economic plight and exclusion experienced by much of the Third World but rather seeks to depoliticize issues and events. Concentrating attention on "knowledge" takes away consideration of conflict and controversy in economic, political, and cultural arenas. International organizations today also avoid the term "developing countries," preferring instead to use the term "emerging nations," which presupposes ascendancy through certain means, in which education figures prominently.

Those in the education field are faced with three challenging questions: How can we apply the theory and knowledge of unfolding globalization developments to create an understanding of new educational phenomena? How can the field of comparative education help us sharpen our understanding of globalization? What kinds of responses to the effects of globalization can we provide as educators?[5] Regarding the first question, we should examine how economic and technological dimensions are woven to create new educational objectives and cultures. We should also consider the implications posed by the state as it shifts from provider of goods and services (schools, teaching, and credentials) to buyer of goods and services produced in the private sector (Santos 1995). In attempting to answer the second question, a comparative approach would help us locate points of commonalities in educational objectives, content, and practices between countries and to discover to what extent convergence emerges. As we analyze convergence (or divergence, when this is the case), we should be constantly cognizant of whether it is the product of conscious adaptation, blind imitation, or pressure to conform. And the most fundamental question in the comparison would be the extent to which societies are moving toward more fair arrangements in the distribution of knowledge and rewards. Seeking an answer to the third question would enable us to adopt a well-justified ethical and political position.

NOTES

1. Thurow (1980) observes that the calculation of the GNP per capita may be simple but that it is very difficult to make precise standard-of-living comparisons among nations. "In each country, individuals naturally shift their purchase toward those items that are relatively cheap in that country. Tastes, circumstances, traditions, and habits differ. Individuals do not buy the same basket of goods and services. What is a necessity in one country may be a luxury in another. Health care may be provided by government in one country and purchased privately in another" (5).

2. Rudra (2000, 9) found that rich countries increased social and welfare expenditures from an average of 12 percent of the gross domestic product in 1972 to 16 percent in 1995. In contrast, developing countries had gone from spending 3 percent to 2.5 percent in the same period.

3. Because of taxation changes, the government revenues became lower for 2001, estimated now at U.S.$158 billion instead of the original U.S.$281. The estimate of a U.S.$3.4 trillion surplus over ten years has not yet been modified.

4. In the Silicon Valley of the United States—unquestionably the heart of the technological revolution so integral to globalization—seven of ten new jobs earned less than U.S.$10,000 in 2000. The majority of these jobs are filled by African American and Hispanic minorities. As a country, the United States has seen the emergence of the "working poor"—people whose salary does not allow them to live comfortably.

Many menial workers earn an hourly wage of U.S.$7, or U.S.$13,000 a year. Assuming a family of three (one adult and two children), an income of US.$.30,000 would be needed for decent living (Ehrenreich 2001).

5. I owe the identification of the first two queries to Gita Steiner-Khamsi of Columbia University when she used them to orient the presentation of participants in a panel she organized on "Globalization and Education" at the annual conference of the Comparative and International Society in Washington, D.C., in 2001.

1

Theorizing Globalization

As we embark on an examination of globalization and how it influences education, we must attempt first to formulate a theory to ground the various observations and assertions that will be made. A theory of globalization must define its characteristics, seek to understand the forces that produce the dynamics and interrelated effects of globalization, and then assess its outcomes not merely on economic productivity and the accumulation of wealth but especially on social outcomes, specifically, who benefits and who does not. Given the pervasiveness of globalization, its dynamics should be analyzed not only in terms of origins and features but also in terms of its *distributive* consequences (Petras 1999).

Globalization is a multidomain, multilevel phenomenon. The complex reality that is, and that is produced by, globalization needs several axes and layers to analyze it. In this chapter, we introduce key actors in this emerging reality—some of them enforcers of globalization, others reacting to its effects. We also bring into the discussion the tensions generated by opposing interests and perceptions, such as the relative strengths of the global and the local; the connections between these two levels; the trends toward convergence and divergence in economic, technological, and cultural practices; and the tensions between concentration and dispersal of power. Since our focus is education (defined in its broader sense), a key concern as we attempt to theorize globalization centers on the identification of its consequences on *knowledge production and transmission*.

DEFINING A MULTIFACETED PHENOMENON

There are a large number of studies focusing on globalization, and they differ either because they perceive the nature of the global situation in distinct ways or because they concentrate on a particular set of consequences. Many studies of globalization emphasize its technological features, paying a great deal of attention to the way it is comprising time and space and reconfiguring social relations (Castells 1996, 1997; Featherstone et al. 1997; Friedman 1999; Harvey 1989; Robertson 1992) or to the way its processes are creating widespread flows of people and ideas and thus creating new and hybrid forms for culture that articulate the local with the global (Appadurai 1990, 1996; Castells 1996; Cvetkovich and Kellner 1997; King 1991; Lash and Urry 1994). A few look at its sociopolitical impacts, primarily on developing countries, by and large the losers of globalization (Giddens 1990; Mittelman 2000). Many discussions of globalization, however, slight the antecedent and concurrent political forces shaping it (except for works by Amin 1997; Arrighi and Silver 2000; Petras 1999; Veltmeyer and Petras 2000).

Some of the debate on globalization is due to the emphasis on its treatment either as economic globalization (in which the historical trajectory of this process goes back many centuries) or as technological globalization (in which case attention is paid to the recent information revolution via the use of computers and satellites). Thus, the debate centers on whether the phenomenon of globalization is old or new. In my view, the current globalization is a process that builds up on previous relations of social and economic asymmetry. Yet to call it "old" is to miss the complex set of relations and consequences it is creating in various areas of social life. Some technological tools are not only new but constantly changing. They are affecting production, information, consumption, and culture in unprecedented ways, from finances to migration, from identity to knowledge, from business to language. Power has existed since time immemorial; the configuration and use of power under contemporary globalization is new because it touches the entire world and even defines it.

Different analysts of globalization have come up with distinct explanations of what globalization is and what forces produce it, depending on their disciplinary lenses. To state the obvious, accounts by cultural analysts and anthropologists emphasize the role of cultural influences, explanations by political scientists pinpoint the growing political influence of economic actors, and analyses by economists tend to focus narrowly on material growth and the technological contributions to it.[1] In general, researchers from cultural studies and anthropology tend to perceive much greater diversity and local responses in the globalization process than political scientists and sociologist would tend to see.

Describing studies that specifically focus on globalization and schooling, Tikly (2001) categorizes them into two types: those that consider the impacts of globalization on education provision and those that probe the links between education, skills formation, and the global labor market. In his view, the first type reports on the negative impacts of economic measures on school enrollment and quality; the second type highlights the contradictions between the negative effects of economic austerity and strategies to invest in human resource development. There are, however, a number of studies that consider the global connections between education and economic power (Fischman and Stromquist 2000; Pannu 1996; Watson 1998), noting the connections between discrete economic actors and educational and cultural consequences.

It is not our intention here to review existing theories of globalization but rather to present a framework for how we approach it and to apply that framework to the analysis of education. As others, we recognize that the intense and constant movement of goods, jobs, and capital that constitutes globalization creates political, environmental, and cultural consequences. In other words, globalization has multiple dimensions—economic, technological, and political—all of which spill into culture and affect in all-encompassing ways the kinds of knowledge that are created, assigned merit, and distributed.

Appadurai's globalism rejects center-periphery frames, arguing that there is no single organizing principle. However, Appadurai does seem to prioritize cultural aspects since he sees deterritorialization and reterritorialization as the two strongest features and outcomes of globalization. We disagree with this position, asserting instead that economic forces dominate, greatly aided by simultaneous technological developments. Jenson and Santos (2000) propose the following definition of globalization: "a process by which a given local condition or entity succeeds in traversing borders and extending its reach over the global and, in doing so, develops the capacity to designate a rival social condition or entity as local" (11). This definition captures elements of power in the border crossing of the globalization phenomenon, yet it does not identify sources of power. In our framework, globalization is not a decentered phenomenon but rather has definite points of origin: It is a process initiated by advanced industrialized countries and pursued through both formal and informal means. A case in point of the globalization phenomenon is migration. While it is a feature of globalization, it is not one of its causal pillars but rather an outcome of the overall change process by which populations (both skilled and unskilled in the South) move to the North in search of better economic opportunities. We also posit a strong connection between the new understandings and practices promoted through globalization and the benefits accruing to those who promote them. In other words, what we call "globalization" has a number of controlled and intended features (e.g., regulations governing the importation of some products, the advocacy of decentralization, and the emphasis on accountability) and perhaps just a few entirely random outcomes.

It is exceedingly difficult to pinpoint the starting force in the globalization phenomenon. Did triggering technologies come first? Did firms in central countries press for economic liberalization policies, thus bringing greater cross-border exchanges? Did noncommunist central countries see the opportunity to assert the capitalist model as the only one? Or was globalization perhaps unleashed by unexpected and simultaneous discoveries and practices? We leave these questions to contemporary historians, noting that perhaps globalization has been characterized by many simultaneous events that have often resulted in circular causation.

IDENTIFYING THE UNIT OF ANALYSIS

Globalization implies both global processes and global outcomes. Therefore, it is clear that traditional ways of looking at social and economic phenomena, which have emphasized the nation-state as the key unit of analysis, remain limited. Here we share Wallerstein's concern for the appropriate level at which to aim our explanations. Wallerstein (1999), one of the earliest proponents of world-system theories, asserts that major social and economic outcomes in the prevailing capitalist system are the product of actions that transcend the nation-state and are all embedded in a strong historical context. Further, Wallerstein shuns the common understanding that modern life is composed of the three relatively autonomous spheres of politics, economics, and culture, asserting, on the contrary, that these domains interact with each other in strong and unavoidable ways.[3] We agree with this view. As de Oliveira (1996) notes, today's globalization seeks the union of science and industry; the apoliticization of unions; the organizational fragmentation in the production process; the globalization of cultural, information, and business networks; and the unification and standardization of pleasure and consumption Even though mostly economic aspects are discussed in the proliferating trade agreements among nations and contracts with transnational corporations, the interconnections among various dimensions of contemporary life are evident, as globalization processes entail also the creation of identities of a broad set of social actors and territorial spaces (be they changes in cities or the increased density of cyberspace).

The selection of the proper unit of analysis is fundamental. Were explanations of developments to concentrate at the personal level, events and outcomes would be perceived as if autonomous individuals were the prime movers behind globalization tendencies. As several scholars note (e.g., Petras 1999), this unit of analysis would obscure the role of economic influences and weaken the identification of adverse social consequences. It would also underestimate the centrality of institutional power.

Agreeing that globalization dynamics have to be seen as larger than the nation-state produces two consequences for our work: (1) It obligates us to consider institutions that operate beyond national borders, and (2) it causes us to view events and trends in most countries as linked to initiatives begun in central countries. The adoption of such initiatives in the rest of the world is assumed to occur in some cases through persuasion and in others through imitation.

DYNAMICS ACTIVATED BY GLOBALIZATION

A phenomenon whose impact has been compounded by technological advances (in production, communication, and transport), globalization results in the ability of core countries to impose new practices that bring all countries into conforming with capitalist economic systems. The conjunction of a myriad technological inventions and a single economic model has been greatly aided by the demise of the Soviet bloc. When the other prevailing form of economic organization (i.e., central planning) fell into disrepute, the gates were opened to a flood of market-based ideas and hopes.

Innovations in communications are giving people greater and more immediate access to information. Previously remote and exotic areas of the world have become easily accessible through more rapid and cheaper forms of transportation. Many goods have attained levels of mass production through the use of machines and equipment that make it possible to segment production and yet obtain high precision and quality in the final product, and advanced biological technologies have increased yields of agricultural products. Media expansion in television, journals, and newspapers ensure that goods and services are well advertised, and increased levels of consumption follow.

Advances in quantity and quality at first sight make it appear that worldwide we have attained a high level of progress and that we are moving toward new horizons of abundance. Unfortunately, it is becoming clear that along with the growing wealth in the highly industrialized countries, there is emerging a growing gap between the First and the Third World.[4] Some argue that the existence of a gap is not important; switching to the metaphor of a pie, they advance the argument that as long as the pie gets bigger, everybody will get a slice bigger than before. But it is not demonstrably clear that bigger pies result in bigger slices for all.

What in the view of an increasing number of observers becomes problematic is that with the arrival of greater levels of production and trade, new values have also emerged—values that are making individuals throughout the world much more interested in personal material success than in values that promote sensitivity to the needs of others and the protection of the small planet on which we live. Today, with the fall of the Soviet Union and the drastic changes in the makeup of eastern Europe, the enemy is not out there but perhaps rather within us in the form of excessive consumption, individualism, and competition—the three dominant traits of our times. There are many groups that feel this is an exaggeration, that better times are here now, and that whatever inequalities and disadvantages may be currently manifested will disappear over time as other countries discover how best to prepare themselves and determine in which ways they can contribute to the globalized world.

TIES WITH NEOLIBERALISM

Many observers recognize that globalization has two complementary dynamics: economic globalization through a neoliberal development model that emphasizes the market and a technological revolution that has increased the ubiquity and speed of production and information technologies.

Bourdieu (1998) defines neoliberalism (theories and practices) as a program capable of destroying any collective structure attempting to resist the logic of the "pure market." He explains that neoliberalism has acquired a powerful discourse, is extremely difficult to combat, and presents a realism impossible to question because it represents the coordinated actions of all forces that hold prevailing positions. The discourse of neoliberalism calls for a less interventionist state in economic and social arenas and proposes such measures as deregulation (the drastic reduction of rules and guidelines for a number of economic exchanges), decentralization (ostensibly the devolution of governance or administration to local levels but often a delegation of financial responsibility to lower levels), and privatization (the increasing presence of the private sector in all areas of social life). Yet many note that these measures, while tending to weaken the state, in some instances end up making the state more centralized and controlling as it institutes measures to ensure compliance with new procedures and similarity of outcomes; this is especially so in the field of education. Privatization, expected to allow many creative firms to develop new products and services, has led to the dominance of nonnational institutions less interested in satisfying the needs of the developing societies in which they work and much more interested in sending the profits home.

The presence of high-speed communication technologies aided by a deregulated financial world is also enabling individuals and groups to engage in what is considered the "most volatile and unproductive of economic activities," namely, paper exchanges in the financial field or the speculative acquisition of stocks and bonds, particularly in developing countries (Petras 1999).

In examining globalization, therefore, it becomes crucial to recognize that its economic dimension is deeply guided by a development model based on the hegemony of the market and the role of the state as a key supporter of market decisions. While it remains unclear whether neoliberalism is an inherent property of globalization, the current manifestations of what we know as "globalization" are highly linked to the increased power of the market.

ACTORS IN GLOBALIZATION

Analyses of globalization must recognize the new actors it brings in its wake. It is preferable here to talk of "actors" rather than markets or technology because ultimately there are people, that is, active human agents, behind any social process. As Petras (1999) puts it, "The market does not have behavior attributes and does not make political commands"; it is "institutions and decision makers who are market makers and not merely market takers" (14). We must acknowledge, however, that because of the multiple elements operating in decision making as well as the numerous instances of interaction among technologies and between technologies and particular social groups, it is difficult to determine the consequences of any single actor.

Among these actors, all located in institutions, four may be considered as key to the contemporary globalization process: the state, the large economic firms we know as transnational corporations (TNCs), the mass media, and nongovernmental organizations (NGOs). The first three operate to facilitate the expansion of globalization; the fourth has acted to define issues and set political agendas usually overlooked by globalization as well as to question globalization.

Since globalization is a highly interactive phenomenon, it is also appropriate to identify their main carriers at both the macro and the micro level. The media appear as major purveyors of new ideas, values, and mores. But there are also individual-level actors, such as professionals and consultants who travel to many countries, students who go for study abroad and return with new ways of thinking and analyzing the world, and tourists who naturalize high levels of consumption. Petras (1999), for instance, charges that some academics shape the economic programs of developing countries to maximize the global interests of multinationals and receive lucrative consultation fees.

The State

Under globalization, the state (meaning the stable administrative machinery and the institutions that compose the public arena) has become less central to economic development as planning of new industries and services is now left to the whims of demand and supply by market forces. Observing the dominant discourse of the state over the past four decades, Masemann (2000) finds that the state has undergone consecutive and very discrete shifts, from being thought of as a developer in the 1970s, to a mostly debtor party in the 1980s, to a bad manager in the 1990s, and to its current incarnation as an institution in need of much help from the private sector. Wallerstein (1999) attributes the emergence of other macro-level actors to a breakdown in the legitimacy of the state. It could also be argued that for other actors to rise, the legitimacy of the state had to have been contested in the first place.

Today, the state serves different roles in central and developing countries. In the former, the organization of meetings involving the World Bank, the International Monetary Fund (IMF), the Group of Seven (G-7), and the Group of Eight (G-8) summits enables leading states to establish economic policies shaping expansion and competition (Pannu 1996). The increasing presence of multinational global and regional institutions is a strong characteristic of globalization and highlights the importance of the state of central countries because many of these international bodies faithfully reflect interests of the major industrialized countries. Working on high levels of specificity, Petras (1999) contends that it is impossible to understand the expansion of the market in the former Soviet Union, China, eastern Europe, and former "radical" Third World countries without considering policies pursued by the United States.

Also in central countries, the state is able to protect the investment of firms operating abroad, even though it permits great competition among such firms in its own society. Further, such a state is able to influence developing countries to follow its preferences and policies for less restrictive economic rules. Through their special place in multinational and supranational institutions and through their participation in the provision of international assistance, states in the First World are further able to shape events and decisions in developing countries. Tools such as expert knowledge and financial contributions are important to disseminate values and norms favorable to the donor states.

In the developing countries, the state is often much less able to shape its own economic policies. Challenges brought from the production of foreign goods and services that are less expensive and higher in quality render states in developing countries unable to accumulate the wealth necessary to improve their economy and social welfare, resulting in further decline in people's beliefs in the competency of their states. At the same time, however, weak states remain essential to the globalization process because their public machineries are instrumental in the exercise of legal mandates that ensure stability and proper respect for property and profits; in other words, the state facilitates the efficient operation of markets, both capital and labor (P. Jones 2000). States also play important roles in the Third World as important channels by which to introduce ideas about the preferred economic structure, values regarding consumption and competition, and respect for technology over tradition. From these points, we reason that globalization has geography: Although its adherents swear that its intention is to be an even and seamless process, it engages in distinct economic and political practices and produces differential benefits across the world.

It is argued that democracy is needed as the life support of globalization, as a free market requires massive information to circulate and unfettered initiative to materialize. However, the brief analysis of the state presented here suggests that it is possible to create consensual international agreements addressing issues of economic nature without necessarily engaging in either internal or international respect for human rights or equity. The growing recognition of these distinct impacts of globalization on rich and poor nations is facilitating the revival of dependency theory. A basic hypothesis of the dependency framework is that development and underdevelopment are partial and interdependent structures of one single global system of production and distribution (Cardoso and Faletto 1970; dos Santos 1973). Dos Santos (1973) defined dependence as

> a conditioning situation in which the economics of one group of countries are conditioned by the development and expansion of others. A relationship of interdependence between the two or more economies or between such economies and the world trading system becomes a dependent relationship when some countries can expand through self-impulsion while others, being in a dependent condition, can only expand as a reflection of the expansion of the dominant countries, which may have positive or negative effects on their immediate development. (76)

Dependency theory fell into disrepute with the successful developments of some countries in the South, particularly those now known as the "Asian tigers" (South Korea, Singapore, Hong Kong, and Malaysia).[5] Subsequent study of these countries has revealed conditions of exceptionality in terms of international assistance and human capital resources; financial developments in the 1990s demonstrated also the high vulnerability of these economies to central countries. We have learned that the dichotomous division of the world into industrialized and developing countries can be enhanced by considering a set of countries in the middle, called perhaps semiperipheral or newly industrialized, but we know also that in many situations the former distinction between North and South, or central and peripheral, still applies.

Through institutions coordinated by the state, such as schools and universities, much of the new social and cultural order is introduced and sustained. States in both developed and developing countries work to create, for the most part, patterns of convergence in beliefs, values, and practices within their societies and across societies.

In judging the performance of the state, various standards are used. In central countries, the code word is clearly "efficiency." In peripheral states, the criterion seems to be "transparency" and "decreased corruption." In semiperipheral states, which in many respects would include Canada and Australia, the key word seems to lean toward "competitiveness." Issues of equality and social justice are sometimes part of the state discourse but seldom as actual indicators of performance. These various terms in use do not appear at random but rather reflect the relative power position these countries attain under the advancement of globalization.

Transnational Corporations

While much of the globalization discourse refers to the "market," in reality the market takes on concrete forms as business firms on the supply side and diffuse clients on the demand side. And although the discipline of economics makes a stark distinction between who sells and who buys, often those who sell also shape the mentality of those who buy.

Globalization, given its massive scale, has created a market dominated by large firms. Or, rather, large firms have grown to monopolize the market through their steady access to technologies and economies of scale. Production technologies have increased the power of TNCs. Today, a global assembly line is a reality, notwithstanding references in the development literature and popular media to the new forms of production now described as post-Fordist (i.e., no longer predicated on assembly-line forms of industry and manufacture based on a "flexible specialization model," democratic processes of production, and use of high technology).[6]

It remains unclear whether high levels of production and advanced technologies inherently require large firms. The point is that, at present, large firms are indisputable economic actors with dense networks between each other and with significant influence on political and social dimensions of many countries, particularly those in the Third World. It would also seem clear that actions by TNCs, focused as they are on promoting high levels of consumption, promote convergence rather than divergence in the social, cultural, political, and economic dimensions of our lives.

The Mass Media

The communications industry operates through business firms, and many of these are also TNCs. It is useful, however, to treat the mass media as a separate globalizing actor given the frequency, pervasiveness, and importance of the symbols and messages they transmit.

The conjunction of the free-market economy of globalization with the great diffusion of information via satellite-based television programs, Internet-facilitated communications and information dissemination, and availability of movies, music, and video in various forms makes the media highly ubiquitous. One prediction is that economic globalization will increasingly find new and ingenious ways to present messages that promote consumption and to apply pressure on the media to accommodate them. A corollary of this is that the media may attempt to promote entertainment content much more than programs intended to foster critical thought and comprehensive analysis of current trends.

The settings and nexus through which the media transnationally and internationally advance representations (images and texts) that legitimatize the global order must be considered, as Mato (1996a, 66) aptly remarks, not merely as part of the "context" of globalization but, more important, as the "case" itself.

Nongovernmental Organizations

A complex and multidimensional process such as globalization is inherently characterized by tensions and contradictions since dominant forces seldom gain total control over events and outcomes. As time goes by and certain benefits do not accrue to all, a resistance to the prevailing forces begins to develop.

Nongovernmental organizations are social groups that carry out resistance efforts to the status quo. I define NGOs as a subset of civil society.[7] They vary in terms of their altruism and commitment to social justice. A number of opportunistic NGOs have sprung up in eastern European countries seeking to mediate between the transitional society and external donor agencies; in certain African countries, some NGOs function as disguised appendices to existing governments. However, the majority of NGOs seek a public good and struggle to obtain the social inclusion of persons previous marginalized or public and government attention for themes not completely recognized by either the state or the market.

Major adversaries of globalization in the poor countries have been the peasant movements, particularly those in Latin America, parts of Asia, and to a lesser degree Africa. Free-trade policies have produced a situation of considerable disadvantage for many small local producers in both industry and agriculture. Many farmers, for instance, have been simply unable to compete with cheap grain imports. Guided by export-based development notions that are intrinsic to neoliberalism, governments in developing countries have in some cases given subsidies to agro-export producers; this has stimulated the expansion of large-scale land ownership and a concentration of credits and technical assistance at that level at the expense of small producers (Petras

1999). In many countries, the importance attached to export-oriented agriculture has delayed the adoption of land reform policies. Brazil, one of the
prime examples of this trend, has been the site of numerous NGO and
Church-led peasant movements to rectify their situation.

Negative impacts of the globalization project, again felt mostly in the
South, include take-it-or-leave-it small wages for workers, visible pollution
of air and water, reduced and even disappearing forests, and increased levels of poverty within developing countries and between the North and
South. As Petras (1999) notes, "Nowhere has privatization been accompanied by conservation; it always has been and is associated with heightened
pillage, exhaustion and abandonment of people and lands" (19).

Opposition by NGOs to globalization processes is often misunderstood,
particularly by the media, which tends, for instance, to describe the work of
small groups protesting unwanted economic policies as the machination
of anarchists bent on unproductive disorder. Many NGO groups feel that
globalization decisions are dominated by TNCs and core governments, with
little knowledge and even less participation of citizens in developing countries. At present, most opposition by NGOs has been to *defend* existing rights
and interests threatened by the globalist ruling classes (Petras 1999); *proactive* work has not had a substantial opportunity to emerge.

The dynamics of globalization therefore creates a set of determined and
influential agents as well as a set of actors that react to the dominant actors
or are unable to respond with the same degree of power. There is no stark
distinction between the economic power holders in the North and in the
South. Generally, those involved in large-scale production favor the forces of
globalization forces. These include the agribusiness and financial classes, im-
porters, mineral exporters, big manufacturers, and sweatshop owners subcontracted for export markets (Petras 1999). States under the influence of
these groups are also strong advocates of globalization and its neoliberal
economic principles. The powerless states in the South are less enthusiastic
about globalization. Some states have attempted to protect their poor sectors
but generally have been unable to do so; a clear example has been the back-
sliding of the political position of South Africa following what was a major
democratic achievement: the destruction of apartheid.[8]

Nongovernmental organizations occupy the best position from which to
contest globalization policies. They enjoy a certain level of independent action and have developed the knowledge necessary to understand the many
negative consequences of unbridled export-led economic growth. These
groups tend to be small in number and have access to minimal financial resources. Their tools for bringing attention to their concerns are the dissemination of information and knowledge through global networks, public
demonstrations, and the occasional disruption of official meetings.

CONVERGENCE VERSUS DIVERGENCE

In examining consequences of globalization, a debate has emerged on whether the world is now exhibiting more convergence of beliefs, values, and behaviors than in the past. Some of this debate has been framed in terms of the *global* and the *local* responses to globalization. Are we moving toward a homogenized world, or, on the contrary, are we experiencing forms of social organization and cultural manifestation that are rescuing local and even indigenous forms of being?[9] To what extent is international to be equated with global?

We will examine some of these trends, focusing on developments in the area of education, both in schools and at the university level. We will see that both dominant global messages and forms of local expression are in existence. Over time, however, the tendency has been much greater in the direction of uniformity than differentiation. Moreover, it seems that forms of differentiation emerge as ways of surviving and as reactions to exclusion rather than as comprehensive alternative forms to the dominant forces of globalization. Two questions of theoretical importance are as follows: (1) To what extent are differences possible? (2) Under what conditions may diversity emerge, and what areas of social life do they tend to cover?

In the opinion of some, globalization can be seen as a phenomenon "from above" or "from below." The first details how elites function within and across national boundaries, while the latter emphasizes a popular process in which the rank and file in civil society are involved in an effort to respond to the challenges of globalization. In our view, there are indeed many instances of "globalization from below," yet they tend to arise as reactions to "globalization from above" rather than as autonomous initiatives. This proposition is explored in the chapters that follow.

CONCENTRATION VERSUS DECENTRALIZATION OF POWER

Another debate of considerable importance is whether the world is now seeing a diffusion of power or its consolidation. Inherent in the market logic of neoliberalism is that now that the state's monopoly has been broken, multiple agents at all levels are exercising much more influence than before, influence that brings not only increased creativity but also greater productivity, efficiency, and lower costs of goods and services, thus benefiting the entire world through a society of plenitude.

This debate about concentration/decentralization is not mere intellectual curiosity; rather, it constitutes a key issue when we examine the benefits of globalization. As we look into the various manifestations of globalization, it becomes important to determine to what extent actors have gained (or lost), what kinds of influences exist, and how these forms of influence ultimately become used to serve particular interests. Is globalization promoting the democratization of societies, reinforcing existing hierarchies, or creating new divisions? When benefits are produced, how are they distributed among the world's people? In all, what kinds of diversity will be allowed?

Expectations that globalization will produce positive impacts derive from the belief that it will permit people to attain better lives and that over time the existing social inequalities in various arenas of society will shrink. In this book, we examine these expectations by centering on the educational dimension and by considering the impacts of globalization on equality and equity, particularly the degree to which it might transform gender conceptions and practices in society.

IMPACTS ON GENDER

As one of the major social divisions, gender is a construct of considerable importance in assessing positive and negative impacts of globalization. In its pure form, globalization would predict a world so based on knowledge and technological developments that arbitrary markers such as gender give way to more "objective" and "pragmatic" considerations. In a world in which competition enables the best to surface, it would not be important whether a person is male or female. Furthermore, the values of efficiency would privilege the uses of technological advances, which presumably would degenderize any superstitious knowledge and habits we may have accumulated.

If globalization is characterized by new communication technologies, what constructions of masculinity and femininity do the use of these technologies promote as the interaction between economics and culture becomes strengthened? Given the dominant economic dimension of globalization that promotes neoliberal forms of organizing the economy, what are the consequences for women from increasing economic competition based on large firms, from a state each time less engaged in the provision of social services, and from technological advances less demanding of physical strength? Answers to these questions portend conflictual outcomes for women and men.

WINNERS AND LOSERS

Globalization is intimately linked to capitalism. And capitalism is a zero-sum game, defined as any game in which the losses exactly equal the winnings. As Thurow (1980) puts it, "For any winner there is a loser, and winners can only exist if losers exist. What the winning gambler wins, the losing gambler must lose" (11).

Who does not benefit? Under globalization so far, there are losers, and this constitutes a large group. For the most part, they are located in developing countries and comprise workers who must sell their labor at low cost.

A number of observers (Amin 1997; Mollis and Marginson 2001; Petras 1999) find that the relationships between countries in terms of the structure and functioning of their economies have not changed with globalization. Petras (1999) affirms that "globalization is essentially a continuation of the past based on the deepening and extension of exploitative class relations into areas previously outside of capitalist production" (3). Principles that characterized past capitalist relations are still in operation: capital accumulation, high rates of return, greater market shares, and lower labor costs.

Yet there are differences between the situation of the 1970s and the rapid developments beginning in the 1980s. Substantial differences can be seen in the quantitative explosion of material goods and the almost universal acceptance of consumerism. Also noticeable in the 1980s was the beginning of a tendency to mute political critique. The dominant globalized discourse, as expressed by international organizations and national governments, avoids and silences references to power asymmetries and the concomitant criticism of current developments. Discussion of physical and symbolic violence perpetrated on weak groups and nations is seen either as a sign of unreasonable impatience or, at worst, as residuals of negative thinking with no room in the present era. Protest is easily disqualified by asserting that those who engage in it are primarily anarchists, the Luddites of the twenty-first century.

One of the two pillars of globalization is based on the specific and nonnegotiable objectives of its proponents. Such objectives include the liberalization of markets for further expansion of production and sale and a less "interventionist" state. The other pillar of globalization is less amenable to controllable calculation. It refers to technological inventions: the development of communication technologies and advances in production technologies. This conjunction of predictable and unpredictable elements makes globalization an evolving journey into the future.

GLOBAL AND LOCAL CHANGES IN EDUCATION

Globalization gives particular visibility to education. It brings up the notion of the "knowledge society," emphasizing knowledge and skills over natural resources, material endowments, and capital. Globalization takes educational systems out of the state monopoly and into the marketplace. It reorders fields of study according to the needs of the market, increasingly substituting those needs for the traditional search for truth. All this sets up major forces of tension along economic, political, and cultural lines.

Because images and representations are central to the creation of new identities, globalization assigns a special role to education, creating a terrain subject to substantial conflict and contradiction. In primary and secondary education, we see the application of measures that precisely determine the quality of schools and that provide a content greatly in agreement with the economic and cultural policies of globalization. In higher education, privatization is becoming dominant; the principle of diversity will prevail mostly through increasing the growing diversity of institutions (in terms of prestige and competitive niche) rather than through differentiation in the content of similarly labeled programs, diplomas, and degrees. An instrumental philosophy will dominate, seeking to orient new disciplines and degrees toward placement in specific industries; parallel to this, business sectors will seek to gain greater influence in educational decision making.

Especially in Third World countries, the impact of globalization on education will be felt largely through the uncontested adoption of initiatives in developed countries along such lines as decentralization, privatization, the assessment of student performance, and the development of tighter connections between education and the business sector. In this process of adoption, the influence of international lending and development institutions, as carriers of globalizations, is clearly discernable.

SUMMARIZING THE BASIC GLOBALIZATION STRUCTURE

A complete theory of globalization must (1) show the interconnection between economics, politics, technology, and culture and (2) identify the key sets of agents promoting it. Because globalization in its technological form is predicated on advancements in science and technology, globalization theories must also be attentive to the interconnection between power and knowledge.

The exercise of power influences what we consider worth learning, what remains unexamined, and what we know. The dictum of Foucault on the connection between power and knowledge is quite evident in globalization. Ultimately, the driving force behind globalization is economic, and thus, given the crucial role of powerful economic actors, a solid theory of globalization must also introduce the examination of elites and their institutions.

The special role of education under globalization will be subject to contradictory expectations. On the one hand, it must serve to provide both basic and advanced skills. On the other hand, it must do so at minimum cost to the state. Arguments about decentralization of state power will generate a profusion of forms of educational institutions, yet the preference for the development of identities friendly to market economies will press educational systems and programs toward greater uniformity. In consequence, substantial tensions may be expected between local and global expressions in the educational field.

We have identified some key actors and the interests they bring to bear in the globalization processes, highlighting some of the major tendencies in this very complex and multidimensional phenomenon.

NOTES

1. Dobuzinskis (2000) establishes a stark dichotomy between analysts who see globalization as an important, exogenous and uncontrollable process of economic change that creates opportunities for social and political reforms and analysts who perceive globalization as a politically driven process, symptomatic of everything wrong with existing economic and political institutions. In his view, those holding positive views about globalization are primarily economists in developed countries; those who hold negative views constitute a more heterogeneous group and can be found in both developed and developing countries.

2. By the same token, the study of globalization requires a multidisciplinary grasp of fields such as economics, political science, sociology, communications, international relations, and cultural studies, to name but a few.

3. Wallerstein (1999), in fact, proposes the adoption of a new kind of social science, one not merely interdisciplinary but instead a combination of all and thus *unidisciplinary*.

4. In this book, I use the term "Third World" to refer to developing countries. Many scholars assert that now that the Second World (the former Soviet bloc) no longer exists, it makes little sense to continue referring to a Third World. I disagree. I believe that the term still carries the political connotation of living at the margins; furthermore, the conditions of poverty and social exclusion affecting vast regions of Latin America, Asian, and Africa have not disappeared with the demise of socialism/communism. The new term for these areas promoted by several international agencies, "emerging countries," tends to minimize forms of oppression that still prevail. Other scholars (e.g., Marginson and Mollis 2001) recognize the existence of an in-between layer of countries: those who are advantaged though still subordinate. This is true, but it could be contended that their forms of advantage are increasingly reduced or extremely vulnerable to decisions in the North. Throughout this book, I refer to the Third World also as the South and to developed countries as the North and core, or central, countries.

5. Additional reasons for the weakening of support for dependency theory was its limited analysis of within-country economics and the production of more complete economic accounts, such as that produced by Immanuel Wallerstein.

6. Assembly-line work not only continues but also is taking new forms, such as the "massive conversion" of plants into the 24/7 plan, according to which plants operate twenty-four hours a day, 7 days a week, with the consequent deterioration in the family life, health, and safety of workers, who typically work in twelve-hour shifts with a three-day weekend every other week (Ivis 2001).

7. Building on Gramscian thought, I define "civil society" as a set of voluntary institutions outside the state and the market; they include civic organizations, NGOs, labor organizations, peasant organizations, and women's organizations, which through their work advance the well-being of the entire society and make demands on the state for consideration of fundamental social and economic problems. Not included in my definition would be business firms, which are an expression of the market.

8. South Africa initiated its democratic life in 1994 with an ambitious Reconstruction and Development Program (RDP), which, following negotiations with lending institutions, became the Growth Employment and Redistribution (GEAR) policy in 1996, which assigned a much smaller role to the state in the formation of public policy.

9. It has been argued by some observers that globalization has also contributed to negative forms of expression, such as the great resurgence of ethnic strife in Europe and Africa. In my view, this assertion is erroneous. In several European countries, ethnic strife is due much less to globalization than to the demise of the Soviet Union, which was able to impose a check on nationalism. In the case of African countries, loss of Western support made dictatorships more vulnerable to domestic contestation in which various tribal and ethnic groups have vied for dominance.

2

The Twinning of Ideas and Material Conditions: Globalization, Neoliberalism, and Postmodernism

This chapter discusses conceptual and theoretical aspects of globalization, neoliberalism, and postmodernity, seeking to show the close interconnection between globalization and neoliberalism and how postmodernity contributes to neoliberal ideas that seek to eradicate discussions of power asymmetries. In my view, these three concepts are the most important in today's intellectual debate.

Perspectives on these three concepts, including acceptance of the terms, vary, especially on the basis of the geographic location of the person holding the view; thus, it is important to present and compare the views of Northern and Southern scholars as well as those belonging to various positions in the political spectrum. In the North, globalization is felt mostly in positive terms through the large supply of goods and services available to the average buyer. Occasionally, one will find protests by labor and youth movements on issues dealing with the ecology or job loss. For those in the South, especially within disadvantaged sectors of the developing world, the picture tends to be more negative. Globalization is often seen as "strong Americanization which threatens to overwhelm all forms of identity that are not minor variations of global themes" (Marginson and Mollis 2001). Others go as far as to claim that globalization is a new form of imperialism, as in Quesada Monge's (1998) strong indictment that "globalization and dehumanization are two faces of today's capitalism, which is more productive than ever" (122).

GLOBALIZATION

According to the Organization for Economic Cooperation and Development (OECD), the term "globalization" was first used in 1985 by Theodore Levitt.

At that time, Levitt referred to vast changes in economy and finance affecting production, consumption, and global investment as a result of economic and financial liberalization, structural adjustment programs, and the diminished role of the state in the economy (Malhotra 1997). This definition captured very well the economic side of the changes but did not sufficiently grasp the many social transformations incurred as a result of technological developments in communications and transportation. Nor did it capture—and at that time it could not have—the major consequences of these developments in such areas as popular culture, transnational advocacy, and global manifestations of civil society. The term "globalization" is perhaps deceptive in that it sounds neutral or even positive and makes it appear as a force outside people's ability to choose and control it.

Link to Modernity

It is useful to look at globalization as the current phase of modernization because it provides a more solid assessment of the promise and reality of industrialization, a key element in the expansion and diffusion of what today we know as globalization. According to modernization theories, industrialization was to be the main way to generate the income needed to improve the infrastructure of developing countries and the lives of their people. But longitudinal studies of the performance of countries across time suggest a very different picture. Arrighi and Silver (2000) did find that in late 1970s, the semiperiphery, or developing countries, surpassed core countries in the share of gross domestic product (GDP) generated by industry and in the pace of industrialization. Further, these authors found that during 1960 and 1980, there was a trend toward convergence in levels of industrial production not just between Third and First World countries but also among Third World countries. Yet during that same period, they detected no convergence in income levels; in particular, data between 1980 and 1995 found that while the industrialization gap continued to narrow, the income gap "remained remarkable stable" (Arrighi and Silver 2000, 23). So now we have an industrializing South that was nonetheless as poor as ever.

Why is it that the developing countries have not been able to eliminate poverty despite greater industrialization? The reason, essentially, is that the price of industrial goods—no less than that of agricultural products—is set in international financial markets "dominated by a small number of industrialized countries in Europe, North America and Japan" on which developing countries have little influence (Inter-American Development Bank 2000, 137). Industrial goods have not delivered the promise of wealth because many of these new industrial jobs have been set at very low wages. Arrighi and Silver (2000) remind us (1) that the drive for profit-oriented innovations sought by capitalism transforms healthy rivalry into "a cutthroat competition that inflicts widespread losses by making preexisting productive combinations obsolete" and (2) that the innovations associated with industrialization (as predicted by Schumpeter) need not only capital and technological power but also the resilience to withstand losses. Industrialization in developing countries has indeed occurred, and at levels greater than anticipated, but these countries could not compete with the central countries either in price determination or in the constant renewal of production methods. Arrighi and Silver see conditions in the Third World as reflecting a "low-level equilibrium trap" that needs to be overcome with the help of government intervention. They observe also, however, that the current discourse precludes such action by insisting that "there is one and only one general equilibrium" that can be achieved through macrostability, liberalization, and privatization; in other words, the market is seen as the primary, if not exclusive, mechanism.

Relations between industrialized and developing countries have seldom been fair. This has been recognized in previous historical accounts of economic and political events and conditions in the Third World that fell under the heading "dependency theory." But those who see the existence of this manifestation today assert that globalization has brought new forms of economic and political articulation between center and periphery, noting that the penetration of the peripheral states occurs through the transnational corporation (TNCs) and the transnational elites directly by means of commercial and political-diplomatic ties and indirectly through the imposition of transnational capital via its institutional agents: the International Monetary Fund (IMF) and the World Bank (Davies and Guppy 1997; Robinson 1997). In this process, structural adjustment programs (SAPs), debt servicing, and World Trade Organization (WTO) agreements are powerful devices to create and maintain an order in which the countries in the North ensure their advantage. Developing countries have had to restructure their economies toward the production of exports ("tradable goods") according to demands of a world "market," which in reality is the market of developing countries.

A constantly invoked principle of globalization is accountability. Yet it does not apply to the key actors in the process: the TNCs. It is clear today that there are nonelected actors determining significant economic—and indirectly social and cultural—policies: the TNCs and multilateral trade and financial institutions, which some critics call the "unelected technocrats."

The WTO is making decisions that affect others. Through the Agreement on Trade-Related Investment Measures (TRIMs), for instance, developing countries renounced their rights to use trade policy as a means of industrialization.

A key feature of globalization has been the liberalization of the world's economies. Its many advocates argue that international trade expands the opportunities for the acquisition of new knowledge and skills. By engaging in the competitive marketplace of international trade, local companies learn to use state-of-the-art techniques and to produce goods that local consumers are willing to pay for. And when local consumers start buying modern high-quality imported foreign goods, they start to demand the same quality from local firms, who are then pressured into modernizing. In other words, international trade fosters innovations by increasing product market competition. Finally, international trade allows a country to produce a specialized range of goods on a larger scale to meet a global demand while relying on imports to satisfy the local demand for other goods. Liberalization is said also to permit another dynamic: foreign direct investment, which is held to facilitate technology transfers across countries. This investment enables local workers to benefit from the know-how of foreign companies and to learn though practical experience how to become efficient managers and entrepreneurs; it enables local companies to learn by observing at close range how a successful company competes in the global economy (Aghion et al. 2000).

As will be seen in subsequent chapters, globalization has rearranged space and compressed time. This reorganization of space becomes obvious as we see the growing mobility of goods, services, and people across countries. Countries with the highest economic production are becoming magnets for increasingly large and diverse population groups. These countries are also the focus of many exports—good and bad. As both a central and a neighboring country, the United States deeply affects Mexico through migration, agro-exports, and drug traffic (Pérez-Prado 1996). Large numbers of Indian and Chinese engineers coming to work in Silicon Valley in California bring with them cultural forms that are both maintained and recombined in the new settings. As a result, central countries are creating new combinations of peoples and cultures despite the fact that they still possess dominant power.

An Intentional Process

Globalization seems to many to be an unstoppable force. Some of its aspects, such as the speedy adoption of information and transportation technologies, may be such a force, although governments may control them by means of taxation or protectionism. But other areas, including those related to its economic forms, are clearly the result of transactions between institutions and people and hence can be modified according to people's wishes. The economic globalization we know today is reflected in treaties comprising more than 3,000 pages; this represents the conscious efforts of particular groups and countries. The conditions that have emerged under globalization have been shaped by numerous rules regarding specific investments in capital, managerial resources, and scientific know-how.[1] Further expanding this argument, Santos (1995) asserts that the contemporary world faces much fragmentation because "our global irrationality was created by multiple mini-rationalities" (110).

Economically, all countries are required to find their best comparative advantage, or "niche," to succeed in the globalization era. Since a major source of economic activity is that generated by TNCs, countries now must sell themselves in the global market economy.[2] The search for economic niches also occurs internally, that is, within countries. Kenway and Kelly (2000) describe the search for new identities for communities in Australia. The City of Greater Geelong, for example, whose main employer is a transnational involved in car manufacturing (Ford), now describes itself as a "great place to live" in order to attract more investment; and the City of Maribynong, a suburb of Melbourne whose manufacturing has suffered under globalization, depicts itself as "Australia's premier industrial zone" with great access to road, rail, and sea transport despite the fact that its industrial land (reflecting its economic deterioration) is ten times less expensive than that in Sydney (Kenway and Kelly 2000, 188, 189). In the case of the United States, an attempt to widen its tourist niche is evident in Monterey Bay, California. "Whale watching" in this part of the Pacific Ocean used to be possible only three months a year. The "season" now has been extended to cover December to May. Since tourists on the whale-watching boats do not see many whales, a whole series of "watching" techniques has been developed: "blow," "tail flukes," and "footprints," and "advanced whale watching," or the actual sighting of a whale (*Monterey Peninsula Review*, 2001, 1, 10). Like Monterey, in the case of many poor countries, with few possibilities of substantial industrial growth, tourism is emerging as the most likely revenue-generating means in the global economy.

A common belief about globalization is that it is "blurring national boundaries." This is partly correct. Governments in industrialized countries, except in the case of the European Union, do not allow the free migration of labor. Workers in greater demand and thus with greater mobility are those with high levels of education and skills (e.g., engineers and technicians in the microelectronic industry). At the same time, economies in the North also attract persons with low levels of education. This generates illegal migration, a situation that leads to the further exploitation of those with limited skills.[3]

Balancing the Effects

The increasingly international movement of goods, jobs, and capital carries economic, environmental, political, and cultural consequences: some positive, others ambiguous, and yet others definitely negative. Positive impacts of globalization include the spread of a culture of human rights. In many countries and communities, the notions of democracy have become more recognized and respected. There are calls for better standards of law and more transparent judicial systems. These principles have been used in the struggle by disadvantaged groups, such as women and ethnic minorities, in several countries to develop a discourse that is legitimate.

Linked to the growth of human rights, there has been a virtual explosion of nongovernmental organizations (NGOs), a phenomenon that is changing the nature of civil society in many countries. Even China, a previously communist country that remains officially associated with socialism, is being reconfigured. From 100 NGOs in the 1950s, China has moved to 200,000 today (Mazarr 1996, 10). These groups work on such issues as family planning, AIDS, environment, and small business. It is not clear how many of these NGOs can or do engage in transformative work, but the presence of citizen groups outside the tutelage of the state is a welcome development in China. Similar patterns of NGO growth are visible in many developing countries.

Drastically increased migration, also associated with mobilization, has positive and negative features. On the positive side, it has fostered the cultural enrichment of the recipient societies, enhancing such features as cuisine, music, and ways of seeing and feeling the world. But the mobility of people has also created uncertainty and cultural dislocation; many newcomers have not been integrated into the society of destination, and immigrants sense the erection of barriers to jobs and education.

Globalization has brought with it the consumption of new goods and services and in the process is modifying cultures throughout the world. Culture is the product of many political, economic, and social forces. It is affected by and, in turn, affects existing institutions and creates new ones. In particular, education—through formal schooling, the media, and informal networks—is affected by the forces of globalization and creates products (educated citizens) that in turn contribute to what globalization becomes.

A number of problematic aspects of globalization persist. First, despite the all-encompassing label, globalization (in terms of technological and economic networks) is not effectively reaching some of the world's poorest countries, particularly those in Africa. Globalization has manifested strong exclusionary tendencies, as it seeks out those groups and countries with the potential to become clients. Those perceived as weak are discarded. This tendency has been further abetted by the coincidence of the rise of globalization with the demise of the Soviet bloc. Thus, some benefits of the Cold War (using a loose definition of the term "benefit") have disappeared for some regions. The competition to attract countries to either the capitalist or the socialist camp no longer exists. Again, Africa has been a losing party in this new situation.

Two additional negative consequences of globalization are the growing roles of crime and prostitution. The Internet gives organized crime an extraordinary facility to launder earnings through the immediate investment in stocks. It also provides a means for the rapid communication of activities and strategies. Cosa Nuova is a new type of Mafia with worldwide dimensions, from the Atlantic to southern China. It is engaged in arms, drugs, and prostitution, producing an annual business of some U.S.$30 billion. It has used knowledge of computers to modernize its operations (at some point, it attempted to use the University of Messina, Italy, to hack into the system of Banco di Sicilia) (Viviano 2001).

Both communication technologies (the use of the Internet and the cell phone) and the increased mobility of people via tourism have increased the activity of sexual workers.[4] Not only has prostitution been expanded to cover women and men, but children are also involved (Hall 2001). Further, tourism has greatly fostered the expansion of AIDS/HIV in developing countries; Brazil, Mexico, and Thailand are prime examples of the vulnerability of countries to the increase in tourists as customers of sexual services.

NEOLIBERALISM

As an economic model, neoliberalism is a major point of contention in discussions about globalization. From the perspectives of scholars in disciplines such as sociology and political science (some in the North but primarily in the developing world), neoliberalism is fundamental to any understanding of globalization. Other scholars, primarily economists in the North, refuse to acknowledge neoliberalism as a legitimate construct and even to see it as a key component of unfolding globalization events. Several large multinational institutions (e.g., the World Bank and OECD) have adopted a similar position.

The world today has three major economic powers: the G-3, which comprises the United States, Japan, and Germany; the G-7, which comprises the United Kingdom, the United States, Germany, Japan, France, Canada, and Italy, an extended set of countries with considerable economic strength engaging in constant coordination and controlling the most important supranational institutions of the world (the United Nations, the IMF, the World Bank, OECD, and the WTO) (Sana, n.d.); and the G-8, when Russia participates. Specifically in the case of the IMF and the World Bank, G-7 countries control approximately 65 percent of the total voting power in each institution. The IMF, the World Bank, and the various regional banks influence the relationship between domestic economic growth, indebtedness, and debt relief through rescheduling and new lending. They do so on a country-by-country basis, not according to estimates of global needs of economic well-being.

Neoliberalism, simply defined, is an economic doctrine that sees the market as the most effective way of determining production and satisfying people's needs. This perspective, which builds on the theoretical contributions of such classical economists as Adam Smith and David Ricardo, took its twenty-first-century form in 1979 with Prime Minister Margaret Thatcher in

the United Kingdom. Her policies were followed in 1980 by President
Ronald Reagan in the United States and by Prime Minister Brian Mulroney in
1984 in Canada. As Cooper (2000) concisely puts it, "The market model asserts that only individual choices are rational, that the public interest cannot
be determined by a group but only by the dynamics of the marketplace in
which individual preferences are revealed and out of which broad social
trends emerge" (26).
  Neoliberalism emphasizes three policy prescriptions:

1. Deregulation: Favors a general withdrawal of the state from control or
   oversight over economic and financial transactions and removal of all
   government/public interventions that might affect the free functioning
   of the markets (removal of price controls on goods and services, elimination of public subsidies, and so on)
2. Privatization: Requires an increased role of the private sector in providing goods and services, prioritizing full cost recovery and efficiency
3. Liberalization: Relinquishes domestic protection over most sectors of
   the economy (including trade and finance), eases control of foreign investment and capital, reduces trade tariffs and duties, and permits foreign companies to own key enterprises such as national banks (Guttal
   2000). According to the liberalization principle, the cost of products
   and services is no longer set by public or social criteria. Since liberalization applies to all sectors (with the exception of national defense), it
   affects traditional social sectors, such as education, health, transportation, and basic services, such as electricity, water, or access to staple
   foods (Quebec Network on Continental Integration 2001)

What the economist Lester Thurow (1980) described more than twenty years
ago as a hard-core conservative solution is now the standard: "liberate free enterprise, reduce social expenditures, restructure taxes to encourage saving and
investment, and eliminate government rules and regulations that do not help
business" (7). The compound effects of the three neoliberalist principles—
deregulation, privatization, and liberalization—reduce the power of the state
to intervene in the economy and related facets of collective life.

The Philosophy of Neoliberalism

  The essential tenet of neoliberalism is the extraordinary importance attributed to market mechanisms. One of the key exponents of neoliberalism is
Friedrich Hayek (1899–1999), winner of the Nobel Prize in Economics for
1974.[5] In Hayek's view, prices in a market economy provide the best possible information regarding the relative efficiency of many possible combinations of physical and human resources affecting the link between supply and

demand. Private property, crucial for a market in a capitalist economy, offers the major incentive to innovate, adapt, and develop new products. Hayek also felt that the market permitted a coordination not possible under socialism because the market, in decentralizing production, enabled every producer to identify consumer needs in many contexts and locations and every buyer to manifest his or her preferences. He considered individualism to be superior to any form of collectivism, which he saw as fostering group thinking and eventually dogmatic beliefs. Further, he opposed the state's monopoly of the provision of social, medical, and educational services since that preempted the competitive processes through which new and better means could be invented (Muller 2001).

Resistant flaws in this posture are neoliberalism's assumptions that (1) the market affords equal opportunities for competition among small-scale firms, incipient industries, and TNCs; (2) different actors have similar degrees of access to information regarding supply and demand on which to base decisions; (3) historical and political factors are only incidental to the functioning of the market; and (4) the possibility of social consensus is seen as both impossible and undesirable.

An intrinsic element of the free-market paradigm is competition. In that framework, Thurow (1980) argues that inequalities today between individuals and groups are justified in terms of their contribution to economic growth and the achievement of economic justice tomorrow. Neoliberalism, as an expression of capitalism, is a zero-sum game. It is an inarguable principle that market efficiency produces winners and losers, as less productive firms and people will lose. The quest for efficiency has created and intensified the polarization between and within countries. As Malhotra (1997) and others have noticed, there is a growing North in the traditional South, especially in large parts of eastern and Southeast Asia, and a rapidly growing South in the traditional North (the United States and the United Kingdom) as evinced by the absolute number of people living below the poverty line and current inequities in access to basic services, particularly health (Malhotra 1997).

The biggest state intervention that is allowed in the competitive process under neoliberalism is in the formation of "safety nets," as a transitional process for individuals but not firms (Thurow 1980). The philosophy of safety nets assumes that assistance in the form of social services can be provided, but only in very limited circumstances, mostly for individuals under extreme economic duress.

An example of how the ideology of neoliberalism works is reflected in the power attributed to the liberalization of growth in certain economies. Discussing the rapid industrialization of South Korea, the World Bank insists that liberalization contributed significantly to this improvement. In its explanation, the role of government in providing subsidized credit to *chaebols*, the large business and industrial conglomerates that account for much of

Republic of Korea's GDP, was muted, as was the government's role in pursuing a heavily subsidized export strategy.

At the discursive level—which so affects the creation and maintenance of symbolic reality—neoliberalism has not abandoned the principle of equity, but it has transformed it. In the field of education, the argument for equity is now being directed toward "ending the injustice of social promotion," "holding all students to the same high standards," making students "work hard," and creating "world-class schools." But since principles of equity now operate in parallel with reductions in government support of public education, the drive for student success ends up placing responsibility (and thus blame) on parents, students, schools, and teachers. An argument embedding considerable paradox is that used by the World Bank in favor of equity. Asserting that public universities in developing countries tend to support middle and upper social classes since most students indeed come from those strata, the World Bank proposes the privatization of universities or the charging of tuition fees at public universities in order to achieve greater "equity."

Within the framework of neoliberalism, education—and especially formal schooling—is given a key role for the attainment of social mobility under the assumption that the market does not discriminate and that the merit of individuals will naturally come to the surface, enabling the best and brightest to be recognized. Against this optimistic scenario and expanding on Bourdieu's notion of the reproduction of cultural capital, Arrighi and Silver (2000) contend that groups who occupy the upper tiers of wealth do not sit passively waiting for challenges by others but rather act to reproduce "relative scarcities" (29). This maneuver is directed at both access to technological advances and admission to the most prestigious universities. To achieve the desirable effect, the wealthy groups engage in symbolic struggles and make investment in higher levels of education imperative. One of the most important symbolic struggles today centers on access to advanced levels of education and to fields connected to science and technology. Instead of pressing the state to improve their condition, people are taught to believe that betterment depends on individual effort and attainment. One of the specific scarcities today is "access to computer technology." The new myth argues that having this access will enable individuals (and indirectly nations) to succeed, an argument that reduces the role and influence of other factors on one's life chances and that denies that "computer access" is unequally distributed throughout the world. The neoliberal process tends to hide the political and social choices that shape organizational culture and prevents others from considering alternative ways of being (Currie et al. 2000). As a means to neutralize explanations concerning the existence of inequality in wealth between and within countries, neoliberal policies put exaggerated weight on the role of knowledge and thus of education.

Structural Adjustment Programs as Neoliberal Tools

In effect since 1981, when they were first tried in sub-Saharan Africa
(Green 1998), SAPs are credited with being the most effective means by
which neoliberal policies, greatly beneficial to the North, have been extended to developing countries (Mato 1996b; Mittleman and Tambe 2000).
SAPs have been promoted by institutions such as the IMF and the World
Bank as means to stabilize economies and improve their performance. Far
from being mere economic prescriptions by international financial institutions, SAPs are the reflection of social and political relations in which capitalist countries in the North dominate and decide in their favor. Further, they
are part of a system of social representation in which the ideals of "progress"
and "development" play a crucial role (Mato 1996b).

Following the oil crises of 1973 and 1979 in the Western countries that dra-
matically increased the price of gasoline, Arab oil producers generated large
amounts of revenue that they subsequently brought for investment into
Western banks. Relying heavily on this capital, the Western lending institutions (multinational and private) negotiated many loans with developing
countries on the basis of mostly flexible interest rates and the assumption
that the high prices for the raw materials that the developing countries would
export would make such loans easily repayable. When this scenario did not
materialize, many of the lending countries in the South produced national
economies incapable of paying either the interest or the principal of the
loans they had obtained.

The Bretton Woods institutions (i.e., the IMF and the World Bank) then
initiated a series of interventions that were later known collectively as SAPs.
Such programs were less along the lines of correcting structural economic
and social inequalities and more centered on finding institutional mechanisms capable of paying back the debt efficiently. Ostensibly designed to
address the specific economic problems of debtor countries, SAPs have
been remarkably uniform in their proposed solutions: liberalization of the
economy, reduced government budgets, privatization of state enterprises
and services such as education and health, free exchange rates, elimination
of subsidies for agriculture, and an export orientation to production—all neoliberal principles. In this process, the IMF negotiated the SAP agreements;
the World Bank, following the IMF's approval of a country's new economic
plan, then enabled the country to obtain new loans.

Today, the IMF manages SAPs in some seventy countries. The IMF im-
poses conditionality on all its SAPs, threatening to halt credit if conditionality is not met.[6] Conditionalities are typically adjusted to suit the political
needs of the largest debtors, and "monitoring compliance [has become] a
major activity [by the IMF], relying on detailed reporting and involving
shared administration" (Haas 1990, 148).[7] All donor countries currently

condition development assistance to the recipient country's adopting World Bank–coordinated structural or sectoral adjustment programs (Elson and McGee 1995). The constant debt repayment, coupled with the decrease in international assistance and the decrease in the price of commodities produced in the Third World, has generated a flow of capital from the South to the North, something unforeseen at the time of the creation of the IMF and the World Bank. According to the United Nations Development Program (1999b, 32), the net outflow from the developing countries is increasing, moving from almost U.S.$15 billion in 1988 to about U.S.$60 billion in 1998. The key impact of SAPs on the educational systems of developing countries is the constant reduction of educational budgets, with the concomitant low raises of teacher salaries and the lack of attention to illiteracy.

A study commissioned by the U.S. Congress on the role of the IMF and the World Bank concluded that the IMF became "a source of long-term conditional loans that has made poorer nations increasingly dependent on the IMF and given the IMF a degree of influence over member countries' policymaking that is unprecedented for a multilateral institution" (Meltzer et al. 2000, 18). In part because of this strong U.S. critique, the World Bank has been producing strategy papers seeking to work toward poverty reduction; yet these measures—also known as safety nets—are limited to the creation of very few low-paid and unstable jobs, reintroducing the populist nature of governments in poor countries and not generating the capital needed to move large groups of people out of poverty.

The consequences of SAPs for the educational systems of developing countries have been amply documented. SAPs tended to curtail educational budgets in the 1980s and 1990s, primarily by not increasing the number of teachers to match rising enrollments, by providing reduced salary increases that in effect amounted to a decrease in the living standards of teachers, and by promoting measures such as decentralization of the public school system and the privatization of schools and universities. As will be seen in chapter 4, decentralization is more accurately described as a financial-driven reform (Carnoy 2000) in which the main objective has been the reduction of costs rather than community participation or improvement of student performance, even though these two reasons frequently accompany official discourse.

Neoliberalism has also affected education in central countries, particularly English-speaking ones. There is a vast array of new measures affecting public schools, including the adoption of state and national testing, the emergence of national standards for science and other subjects, increasing partnerships between schools and corporations, a reduction of investment in public education, and a shift toward private schooling. One important observation regarding educational changes in central countries is that these have fostered centralization of decision making and hence greater control by the state and the groups that exert substantial influence on it.[8]

Data from New Zealand, where a "radical" experiment in free-market economics took place from 1984 to 1999 (Boshier 2000), offers additional glimpses of neoliberalism's impact on education. In a single year, adult education was cut by 78 percent.[9] A peculiar characteristic of the policy changes was their occurrence in "quantum leaps" or large "policy packages," which Boshier interpreted as a strategy to preempt the mobilization (i.e., their ability to present a collective response) of opposing interests. The New Zealand experience witnessed the disappearance of adult education personnel in its Ministry of Education, the abolition of the Trade Union Educational Authority and "any hope for paid educational leave for workers," the withdrawal of government funding for the Worker's Educational Association, reduced funding for other adult education providers, and decreased interest in fostering community approaches in adult education. According to Boshier (2000), the reduction in financial resources created lower levels of cooperation among adult education providers and hence reduced solidarity among adult education activists.

Beyond the creation of SAPs and the impacts on education in both the North and the South, neoliberal thought has had impacts on culture as a whole. As Deem (2001) observes, culture has become a commodity to be sold in the form of handicrafts, music, books, films, and tourism. Studies by the United Nations Development Program (1999a) corroborate that culture has been commodified and that protection applies primarily to things that can be bought and sold, neglecting many aspects of community and tradition.

One basic feature of neoliberal thought is that it has proceeded in ways that have avoided political argumentation and, even more, considered politics remnants of old Marxist thought that at this moment are unnecessary, divisive, and paranoid. González Casanova (1996), Sen (2001), and many others deplore the direction that the primary ideological debate has taken from "capitalist versus socialist" to "state versus market" and the lack of any meaningful debate about an alternative paradigm to the market.

POSTMODERNITY

In developed countries, the academic world has been introduced to the approach of postmodernity, or postmodernism. Hailed by many as a new form of analysis that liberates the mind from rigid paradigms, postmodernism has had a greater impact in the North than in the South. To a considerable extent, this differential impact has happened because the stark realities of social inequality, exclusion, and poverty in the South make it imperative to consider discrete populations and their concrete problems of survival, for which the recognition of cause and effect—not appreciated in postmodernity texts—is of critical importance.

Contributions from postmodernity to analytical thought include the technique of deconstruction of discourse (determining what specific arguments say and do not say), the avoidance of polar opposites in describing reality (e.g., men vs. women, whites vs. African Americans, capitalist vs. socialist, rational vs. irrational, and objective vs. subjective), the recognition of identities as phenomena that are constantly negotiated, the acceptance of the validity of subjectivity, and the importance of culture and the discourse it generates in shaping reality.[10] In an endorsement of postmodernity, for instance, Viesca (2000) notes that postmodernism wants to move away from binaries, including discussion of global-local because they erase the existence of the myriad forms of "multiple globalities" and "local identities." He argues that Chicano identity in the United States is influenced by a variety of alternative social formations, from the Chicano, black power, and hip-hop movements of the United States to the Zapatista struggle in Mexico. He notes also that non-Chicanos appropriate Chicanismo across the city, such as Filipinos in Hollywood, South Asians in El Monte, African Americans in Compton, and even whites on the West Side in Los Angeles. Postmodernity takes much pride in "decentering" analysis, noting the many manifestations of a phenomenon and the diversity of actors that influence it. This analytical approach introduces complexity to the study of social phenomena but also makes it so ambiguous that every factor seems to have equal importance and to be sui generis.

The critiques of postmodernity are many. It is charged with avoiding with focusing on discourse, to the detriment of the recognition and analysis of actual experience, so that it produces a perspective that is "disembodied from experience" (Chaudhuri, n.d.). Along the same lines, Molloy (1999) deplores postmodernity's tendency to reduce the value of experience by its assertion that experience cannot be taken either as self-evident or as a validating mechanism; further expanding on this criticism, Probyn (1993) firmly maintains that there are gendered, sexual, and racial *facts* that shape the social experience. A critique raised by Cole (2000) is that postmodernism fails to analyze society as a whole and focuses instead on a myriad of discrete situations. Despite postmodernity's abhorrence of presumed simplifications such as binary categories, the fact is that we still need to be alert to powerful dichotomies affecting everyday life, variables that include macro/micro forces, structure/agency, society/individual, and social order/social change (Shain and Ozga 2001). Additional critiques of postmodernity are that it assigns a secondary role to history and that it questions the possibility of human progress. Especially the latter argument seems to dissuade political action since it implies that human beings are too weak or unstable to set up goals that envision better collective life.

Intellectuals from the left of the political continuum, such as the Spaniard Heleno Sana (n.d.), are not convinced that postmodernity brings substantial improvement to alternative conceptual and analytical paradigms. In this view, the attack by postmodernity of comprehensive theories as arrogant and totalitarian is misplaced and rather abets the "consolidation of irrational differences, including social and economic inequalities"; moreover, postmodernity is critiqued for avoiding accounts of how power actually works and diminishing the importance of history as a means of understanding the past. Sana calls postmodernity the "deregulation of thought," thus establishing an intriguing parallel between intellectual and economic deregulation. As with several other critics of this paradigm, he finds postmodernity highly congruent with ongoing changes in the economy, seeing postmodernists as similar to the monetarists (a variant of capitalism) in that both evince a "poverty of sentiments" and the absence of altruism and solidarity.

Other views critical of postmodernity highlight the priority it gives to cultural matters and to how discourses continuously shape our understanding of the world and thus reality. In a direct confrontation with these ideas, Mazarr (1996) declares that "the leading challenge for the world community over the next decades is not culture at all, but socioeconomic issues such as inequality—the vast social disparities inherent in the information age—and the energy requirements of growing Asian economies" (14). Scholars such as Bamyeh (2000) find it ironic that poststructuralism (a form of postmodernity) would talk of fragmentation, multiculturalism, and difference precisely at a time when global economic norms have become so prevalent. He argues that the IMF and the World Bank have been issuing structural adjustment plans and economic blueprints that are uniform, regardless of religion, culture, and ethnicity and even regardless of the consequences of such plans for political stability. On the basis of their economic and longitudinal analysis comparing industrialized and developing countries, Arrighi and Silver (2000) conclude that western European and other OECD countries are becoming "convergence clubs"—groups of countries that are experiencing income convergence in relation only to one another but not to other countries. A researcher whose fine qualitative research methods and interpretive analysis have had a major impact on educational research, Paul Willis (2002) recognizes the crucial importance of culture and asserts that culture cannot be reduced to merely a reflection of something else. Yet he also observes that culture is not infinitely plastic but strongly articulated with specific forms of production. In his view, for example, capitalism must be seen as a complex system of exploitation, not limitless opportunities.

In noting the arguments that circulate in our contemporary world at both the popular and the academic level, Arrighi and Silver (2000) raise a very challenging point. They argue that the ideas that dominate today, particularly in the economic terrain, are the effect of a "neo-liberal *counterrevolution* in development thinking," which they interpret as the "U.S. response to the decline of U.S. global power in the 1970s (following the defeat of the U.S. in

Vietnam and the collapse of the Bretton Woods systems) through which the U.S. had governed world monetary relations since the end of WWII" (20; emphasis added).

SOME CONCLUDING REFLECTIONS

Globalization, neoliberalism, and postmodernity present some interesting similarities in their analytical distance from power, their avoidance of the examination of social and economic differences, their resistance to the notion of national projects, their acceptance and endorsement of cultural fragmentation, and the minimization of collective action by citizens to counter what is perceived—by either objective or subjective standards—an undesirable set of conditions. Globalization, particularly economic globalization, has clear actors with definite intentions whose work produces undeniable consequences. Neoliberalism works as the economic model behind contemporary globalization, although it remains to be seen whether this is the only possible model under globalization. It is possible that as opposing forces to the notion of the market as the ultimate arbiter of social relations interact and organize at various levels and in many countries, this model may be substantially altered.

Despite the increased trade among countries and the labor mobility it has generated, there are still vast differences in income and standards of living between the North and the South and in a growing polarization of economic conditions both within the North and within the South. In looking at these stark contrasts, we must ask the following questions: (1) What mechanisms reproduce the North–South divide in income and wealth despite the decolonization and industrialization of the South? (2) What connections between globalization and neoliberalism may contribute to change the way these mechanisms currently operate? (3) What kinds of macroeconomic coordination to achieve greater equality between societies may be possible under globalization?

Many scholars in developing countries see neoliberalism as a major force in our contemporary world. The sociologist Pablo González Casanova (1996), known by many as the grandfather of critical social science in Mexico, considers neoliberalism "the most important intellectual problem confronting the social sciences of our time" (47) and argues for solutions requiring moral, political, and social elements.

Postmodernity has introduced greater complexity in our thought. At the same time, it avoids dealing with the concrete problems brought about by globalization and neoliberalism, preferring instead to assume limitless individual agency and choice. It might be that critical theory, which is alert to power differences, conflict, and collective action as sources of social transformation, rather than postmodernity holds more potential to revise and question current development and educational theories.

NOTES

1. In the United States, specific regulations have been made through gas taxes to provide subsidies for a nationwide automobile-based transportation system, fixed-rate mortgages for single-family dwellings that ended up encouraging urban sprawl, oil depletion allowances to reduce the price of oil, investment tax credits for business to decrease prices of equipment, and higher taxes on labor to increase the price of workers. In this context, the state through legislation has been a major mover in creating conditions favorable to globalization.

2. This was recently exemplified by visits by President Ricardo Lagos of Chile with Bill Gates and other technology industry leaders in the United States during which Lagos presented a seventy-four-page book depicting Chile's "sound economy, stable political system, developed telecommunications, and educated workforce" (Langman 2000).

3. Those who come to the North are exploited but are able to improve their economic situation vis-à-vis that in their country of origin. Further, they hold the hope that their children will occupy better positions than they do.

4. International travel, including tourism, grew from one million persons daily in 1980 to three million persons daily in 1999.

5. It is interesting to observe that the economics prize for that year was shared with Gunnar Myrdal, a profound advocate of collective principles and ethics.

6. The IMF frequently demands removal of all limitations on foreign ownership of financial firms, particularly the abolishment of the common 49 percent limit on shares of publicly listed companies owned by foreigners. Ownership, however, has repercussions for further use of capital and profits. Each year, about U.S.$20 billion leave developing countries to be invested in Northern banks. There are also instances in which business firms sell to their own conglomerate at low prices to avoid taxes.

7. The power of the IMF was likely to increase further in 2001, pending a change in its Articles of Agreement, if the Board of Governors permits the IMF to use capital account liberalization as a conditionality for its seal of approval and hence future loans.

8. For a detailed account of educational changes in the province of Alberta, Canada, where processes similar to those in the United States are taking place, see Kachur and Harrison (1999).

9. The Ministry of Education who presided over this (Maris O'Rourke) was later made head of education at the World Bank.

10. Some postmodernists would like to claim that another contribution is that of discovering the connection between knowledge and power, but this has been detected much earlier. In the twentieth century, Gramsci and Paulo Freire are two well-known exponents of this argument. Postmodernism would also claim the ability to see the operation of power at all levels of social life; this is a contribution clearly made by Michel Foucault, for whom the term "postmodern" is not entirely accurate.

3

Educational Impacts of Economic and Cultural Globalization

Our consumption of material and expressive goods is influenced by social and cultural factors and simultaneously contributes to shaping them. Choices of such goods are cultural because individuals respond to "particularized meanings instilled in them" and social because "these meanings emerge in social interaction" (DiMaggio 2000, 39). This chapter introduces a number of impacts on education, nearly all traceable to changes in the economy. The evidence presented herein regards mostly changes in the United States, yet their reach on other countries can be increasingly felt.

These changes are affecting the objectives, quality, and composition of educational organizations. Here we focus on changes in educational systems at primary and secondary school levels, noting how new values, procedures, and actors are permeating these systems. Without question, the dynamics emerging in industrialized countries are different from those in the developing world, with the first positioning themselves as sellers of technology and procedures and the latter framed mainly as clients. The educational systems across nations are changing, becoming less a public good and more the manifestation of an economic sector that happens to be concerned with knowledge. This altered view reflects the desires of individuals who favor an increased private entrepreneurial presence in education; one such view defines educational institutions as "essentially a web of relationships among individuals, each of whom is pursuing what he or she more values," that is, "maximizing his or her utility" (Hentschke and Krinsky 2000, 1). The assumption therefore is that the common good is unproblematically the sum of individual preferences rather than a hard-won compromise on many issues.

THE INSTRUMENTAL ROLE OF EDUCATION

Today, at the beginning of the twenty-first century, we find educational systems much more attuned with business values and needs than in previous decades. This has not been a natural evolution but rather the result of explicit pressure by the business sectors on educational systems, a phenomenon most conspicuous in the United States, the leading force behind the process of globalization.

Since 1985, business groups have been charging that the public education system fails to respond to their interests in developing a well-trained, efficient labor force that will increase economic productivity and thus the status of the United States in the world. According to Cuban (2001), "U.S. presidents, corporate leaders and critics have blasted public schools for somehow contributing to a globally less competitive economy, for helping sink productivity, and for helping lose jobs to other nations" (1C). These complaints have led to what educators term a false connection between test scores and economic growth. They have been followed by calls for privatization and for measures to improve the public school through the adoption of stricter graduation requirements, a longer school year, new curricula, and more student testing (Cuban 2001). Such demands emphasize the importance of technical skills and competencies for the production of goods. They do not seek (and probably wish to avoid) the development of any critical thinking—the reflection and interrogation that might end up challenging the new values.

Attached to the notion that public schools are essentially deficient because they operate under monopolistic conditions (i.e., since the state owns the schools, there are no incentives to perform well) are strident voices calling for the privatization of education. There is a prevailing belief among market sponsors that competition is necessary to increase educational standards, improve efficiency, and reduce costs. So the market solution to educational problems must necessarily pass through privatization. It is expected that the emergence of multiple schools under the influence of the marketplace will increase parental choice and thus cause high quality to emerge over shoddy schooling.

Actions favoring the role of the market in education have gone beyond the utilization of constant discourse attacking public schools. Economic groups investing in high technologies have demonstrated a strong interest in educational programs by pushing legislation to respond to their educational concerns. This has been sought not via legislation but through popular approval in the form of ballot propositions, a method that appeared more likely than a congressional debate to give them what they wanted. In California, the state with the largest number of jobs in the high-tech industries, measures were advanced by business interests during 2000: Proposition 38, which focused on school vouchers and would have permitted parents to send their children to private or religious schools by granting them vouchers for U.S.$4,000 per child per year; and Proposition 39, which sought to lower the threshold for school bond passage from two-thirds to 55 percent. Proposition 38 raised U.S.$31 million from supporters, but it generated U.S.$32 from oppositional forces and did not pass. Proposition 39 gathered U.S.$28 million from supporters, gathered U.S.$4 million from opponents, and was approved (Bazeley and Folmar 2000). Passage of school bonds, funded through property taxes, is influenced by the proportion of families with school-age children; the reduction for passage from two-thirds to 55 percent therefore becomes very significant because it facilitates the shifting of school expenditures (new construction, quality improvements, and so on) from the state to citizens. Two years earlier, in 1998, California voters passed Proposition 227, which eliminated bilingual education. In all three initiatives, the participation of business leaders was salient. Proposition 227, indeed, was originated and strongly promoted by venture capitalist Timothy Draper, who contributed U.S.$5.2 million in stock.

The intensified participation of economic interests in education is not accidental. First, economic globalization places emphasis on the creation of a skilled labor force, and, even if the connection between education and economic productivity is far from strong, educational policymakers consider themselves to be responsive to business needs by increasing pressure on educational systems. Second, as the economic area of life acquires increasing importance and, simultaneously, the public school system is found deficient, it makes sense to open the educational system to market forces and thus the market-preferred system, which is privatization. In other words, the attribution of failure to schools is also convenient to educational entrepreneurs who see schools as the new business arena.

Contrary to the official and prevailing rhetoric, the introduction of market forces to education is being accompanied by decreased concerns with equality and equity. Lipman (2000) finds "a striking relationship between the evolving educational differentiation and the requirements for simultaneously upgraded, downgraded, and excluded labor" (31). Other educators observe that the pervasive market ideologies support structural inequalities and foster cultural politics to ensure the eligibility and competitiveness of children through merit criteria; they argue, however, that both mechanisms in essence ensure that currently privilege groups preserve their competitive advantage (Oakes 2000). Still other educators deplore the artificial link between education and economic productivity. Cuban (2001), for instance, holds that decreases in economic productivity are due mostly to shifting technologies, restructured industries, and poor managerial judgments.

BUSINESS NORMS IN EDUCATION

Schools today present an array of features that reflect business influences. Notable among them are regulatory systems emphasizing accountability, uniform standards with very instrumental ends, and performance-based rewards (Cuban 2001; Lipman 2000; Oakes 2000).

Describing developments in the United States, Lipman (2000) finds that educational reforms are based on high-stakes accountability; the centralized regulation of students, teachers, and schools; the production of a semi-scripted curriculum for all subjects at all grade levels; standards and "supports" for learning, including after-school programs and special transition classes for failed students; and new and expanded special programs, academic offerings, and schools.

Linked to accountability is the notion of managerialism, which assumes that workers and managers are on the same side and which emphasizes compliance over questioning for various proposed solutions. Managerialism is said to push a perspective that considers restructuring, accountability, performance or "performativity," and measurement of educational activities as solutions to both social and educational problems (Boshier 2000). This perspective, which dominates educational systems today, is not strictly an attribute of globalization. Rather, it is a manifestation at the educational level of economic tendencies promoted by neoliberalism. In the same vein, decentralization—which is being promoted as a way to increase efficiency in schools—is also linked to economic neoliberalism because this practice has served to deunionize workers, in this case teachers.[1]

The influence of the business sector on education is also noticeable in the persons being appointed as leaders. A number of school districts in the United States are beginning to appoint people with business or leadership skills but limited educational knowledge to lead districts in crisis. This has been the case in large school districts, such as those in Chicago and Detroit. In both cases, the position of the superintendent was renamed "chief education officer," giving the title holder the same acronym (CEO) as the chief executive officer of the firm. The image of discipline and drilling is also fashionable. In 1996, a retired army general became superintendent of District of Columbia School District. School administrators are reported to be creating highly punitive climates in low-income schools by making teachers and site administrators almost solely accountable for student performance. From one angle, therefore, management and the notion of managerialism are serving as instruments of internal control instead of being tools to facilitate the educational process.

The increased importance of business in the educational arena is introducing new values. These include individual responsibility, parental choice, efficiency, accountability, quality control, and the student as consumer;

these values, as we will see in this chapter, become easily interlinked. They include also reference to partnerships and empowerment, concepts that they have borrowed from civil society but that acquire different meanings in the context of an educational system influenced by economic interests. And some of these values can be mutually contradictory. For instance, while some forms of assessment can foster autonomy, the types of testing and evaluation at work often promote the convergence of norms and thus the standardization of institutions. In the case of efficiency, it has been observed that having economic and bureaucratic efficiency in schools does not mean serving a national public interest; it might mean merely that each school has a strong financial incentive to attract customers or be disciplined by its failure to educate students (Kachur and Harrison 1999).

Accountability and Testing

Perhaps one of the strongest business norms applied to education—accountability—is being fostered on the basis of two principles: first, efficiency in the transmission of knowledge, defined as providing the greatest coverage and impact at the lowest possible cost or with the minimum degree of wastage, and, second, equity in the provision of knowledge. In the United States, equity is invoked in assertions about "ending the injustice of social promotion," "holding all students to the same high standards," and creating "world-class schools." Unfortunately, the translation of this principle into the specific mechanisms of school and student accountability ends up placing blame for failure on students, parents, teachers, and schools, while the real causation is much more complex (depending on an interaction among sociological, cultural, economic, and pedagogical factors).

Following the practice of relying on the least cumbersome indicator, accountability of institutions and teachers is being operationalized in terms of student success, and student success, in turn, is measured primarily through standardized testing, the results of which are being used to determine whether a student can be promoted to the next grade or receive a diploma for successful completion of high school (and increasingly of junior high school).[2]

Testing in the form of standardized national assessments is being argued on multiple reasons: to provide the schools with up-to-date information, to support better management and thus greater school autonomy, to foster a more efficient allocation of resources, to select students, to evaluate the productivity of teachers, to assess the impact of educational policies and innovations, to develop a more productive labor force, and so on (Benveniste 2002; Ravela 2000). These multiple functions of student tests have been questioned by prestigious institutions, such as the U.S. National Research Council, which observes that "it is inappropriate to use the same tests for different decisions, since the validity of a test is developed "when used for specific purposes" (Heubert and Hauser 1999).

High-stakes testing (those used for major decisions regarding students, such as whether the student can graduate from high school) constitutes the most fundamental reform since 1983, when *A Nation at Risk* was published, and represents the victory of corporate forces in shaping education. Despite the strong advocacy by business groups of high-stakes testing and the use of economic arguments to justify this testing, the evidence for testing as a predictor of productivity is meager. According to the economist Henry Levin (2000), workers' skills are important, but current achievement tests are not strong predictors of economic success. It is very difficult to measure economic productivity, as it varies with the type of activity being considered. So, studies use essentially two proxies to assess it: earnings and supervisory assessment of workers. In terms of earnings, Levin found that all tests are poor predictors, as 96 percent of the variance is not explained. In the case of supervisory ratings, about 6 percent is correlated with test scores—a very low figure (see also Benson 1978; Sweetland 1996; Bowles and Gintis 2002).

Certain avowed functions of testing, such as giving the schools more autonomy or assessing teacher effectiveness, cannot be empirically validated. The extent to which a system will decentralize, for instance, does not depend on student performance. The imputation of student performance solely to teacher effectiveness is easily rejected by available research showing the complexity of factors that affect learning. A large body of empirical research shows that cognitive development is also linked to social conditions in the community and at home. Schools and teachers can make a difference, but the difference is not linear and is much less immediately noticeable than is assumed in yearly measurements.

To some extent, student testing can be used constructively to assess the quality of schools, particularly in cases where teachers may have little training and where teacher attendance is poor, as happens in many large cities in the industrialized countries and in many rural areas in developing countries. But then the test must be designed in such a way that it matches what should be taught in the classroom. In developing countries, the reliance on testing to improve the educational system, in the absence of the consideration of improvements in teacher training and remuneration, seems misplaced. The use of testing as the main mechanism by which to judge a school's performance is also held to be untenable on the basis of existing research on individual cognitive growth, which suggests a more complex sets of inputs on student learning motivation and study capabilities than those provided by the school. There are many educators, strongly convinced of the need to have schools that offer environments that are conducive to both high-level teaching and learning. Many of these educators also agree that accountability is one side of the equation (the results schools should produce) but that quite often the other side of the equation (the provision of needed capacities to the schools, especially those serving underprivileged children) is not sufficiently considered.[3]

In many schools in the United States, particularly those serving minority students, a substantial amount of time is devoted today to preparation for test taking. There are reports that in some schools whose academic year goes from August to June, teachers prepare students for test taking from January on. An unintended effect of accountability policies, therefore, has been the incorporation of testing as a regular classroom practice; this promotes pedagogies and curricula heavily focused on testing success. In preparing students for test taking, teachers become managers of students and technology rather than facilitators of wider knowledge and social values. Since student testing is used to evaluate schools, testing introduces not only competition among students but also competition among schools, among districts, among regions and states, and among countries, establishing an interlocking chain of competition—all predicated on the ability to do well in multiple-choice tests, many of which bear little resemblance to the regular curriculum.

In light of the fact that ethnic minorities tend to perform poorly in standardized testing, critics of this form of assessment argue that testing functions as a symbolic form of regulation of minorities, leading low-performing individuals into believing that they are incapable of attaining the life chances to which they may rightfully aspire; thus, testing is said to function as a socially engineered device to promote individual acceptance of failure. A number of educators (Darling-Hammond 2001; Heubert and Hauser 1999; Luke 2000; Orfield and Kornhaber 2001) consider that testing is leading to a narrowing of the curriculum and that policies such as retention (the cost of failing a test) are being enacted and implemented without evidence that grade repetition helps students learn. In looking at the prevailing practice of high-stakes testing in public schools today, some consider it a result of responses by education authorities to public concerns regarding the quality of schools. But researchers who have been following the role of "public" pressures on education note the tremendous growth of specialized interest groups (lobbyists) in recent years. In the particular case of the United States, from 4,000 groups operating in 1977, these groups have increased to 17,000 in 1999. Among them, business interests are the most numerous (Opfer 2001).

In the developing world, testing has also become a major practice. Before 1991, only four countries in Latin America (Chile, Colombia, Mexico, and Costa Rica) practiced nationwide evaluations of basic education. By 2000, almost every country in the region was attempting to test student performance. In the adoption of the testing policy, UNESCO has played a role, but so have international lending and development institutions, such as the Inter-American Development Bank (IDB), the World Bank, the Organization of Iberoamerican States (Spain), and USAID, which "have made critical

investments in the design and implementation of education assessments"
(Benveniste 2002, 91).

The Marketing of Educational Programs

A marketing of educational products has clearly accompanied globalization. The literature on educational marketing first appeared in the United
States and the United Kingdom at the beginning of the 1990s. Today, marketing has become a pervasive practice of school administrators. Henry
(2001) notes that in the United Kingdom there has been a visible shift from
a bureaucratized to a quasi-market-based form of governance based on the
principles of competition and consumer choice. In the new climate, it is
common to rely on the publication of "consumer guides" in the forms of annual prospectuses, reports, and related forms of self-promotion to sell one's
educational program.

It must be noted that public schools are still quasi markets in the sense
that money does not change hands in the educational negotiation and that
"clients" (unlike clients in the marketplace) are forced to "purchase" the service of schooling. Schooling still has what might be termed "core components" (teachers, courses, and exams), and its purpose remains regulated by
government agencies. How marketing processes affect the everyday life of
public schools are just beginning to be documented. Oplatka's (2000)
account of educational marketing in comprehensive high schools in Israel
offers important insights. Oplatka found that high school principals did not
advertise their programs in the feeding junior high schools or in the local
newspapers, but they did invite parents and prospective students to visit the
schools or to participate in an open day/evening and interact with staff and
students. The transaction with potential clients emphasized the competitive
advantage of the schools, what they offer, the facilities they have, the
schools' academic tracts and extracurricular activities, and the schools' relationship with the local community (Oplatka 2000). School principals asserted
that they did not like to engage in marketing but that in practice that is what
they did: They sought to convince parents that selecting schools would result in "a high level of satisfaction and well-being" among students. Principals also mobilized parents and students into marketing activities by asking
parents to participate in telemarketing and open evenings and even to organize meetings in their own houses for prospective parents (Oplatka 2000).
An important feature of successful marketing was finding a niche to distinguish their school from others, applying such phrases as "we have an academic library," "we have small classes," or "this is an integrative school."
Marketing also called for setting up special offerings, such as curriculum or
academic tracks in the sciences and the arts, courses for gifted students,
courses in biotechnology, and programs with the cooperation of high-tech

companies. Oplatka (2000) notes that principals have become very aware of the need to segment the market and attract specific students. He contrasts this behavior with Israel's core objective of promoting the "national socialization of the younger generation." Reich's (2000) response to this growing marketization of education is that "instead of liberating us, the new world of choice is making us more dependent on people who specialize in persuading us to choose this or that" (66).

In addition to the marketing of educational programs, in which public educational authorities "sell" their schools to parents, there is an actual selling of educational programs and schools to firms so that their logos may be used in schools in return for financial contributions. Educational institutions (both schools and universities) generate income from contracts for exclusive sale of foods or drinks (e.g., selling Pepsi Cola but not Coca-Cola on the school's premises), displaying sponsors' logos on athletes' uniforms, and advertising such sponsors via television programs used by schools and in the "free" Internet access they offer. While the association with a particular set of business firms is not inherently negative, it is evident that boundaries between material production and knowledge are being increasingly crossed.

The Issue of Parental Choice

The argument in favor of parental choice asserts that enabling parents to select schools promotes competition among schools and that, through this process, such choice will improve school performance and give all children access to a good education. Parental choice is therefore being closely linked to the principle of equality of opportunity. But a number of critics have countered that "equality of opportunity" now means that parents are free to move their children to whichever school they so desire *and can afford* either financially or logistically (Kachur and Harrison 1999; Lipman 2000).

At the present, there are two primary forms of school choice: a system of vouchers to help parents pay for private schools and charters to allow parents and others to use public funds for schools they themselves design (Minow 2000). Both cases raise the possibility that the school as a commonly shared public institution will disappear. While presently charter schools, magnet schools, public/private voucher programs, interdistrict transfers, and open enrollment policies coexist with the fixed attendance boundaries of neighborhood public schools (Hentschke and Krinsky 2000), it may well be a matter of time until the school linked to its proximate community becomes a thing of the past. Although these two innovations dominate in the United States, they are establishing models that could lead to significant adoption in other countries, a possibility that is facilitated by their popularity among international development organizations that are advocating their use at the moment they provide loans or grants to countries in the Third World.

Charter Schools

Charter schools are set up through an agreement between charter school founders (private, nonprofit, and for-profit groups) and charter school authorizers (public education agencies, which can be either state departments of education or school districts). Two major types of charter schools are emerging: those created at the requests of parents to establish a school according to their educational preferences and those created generally by the school district to reconfigure schools with poor student performance. Founders apply for a charter to run a school according to the terms and conditions of the charter application, which often exempt them from many of the legal regulations that guide public schools. Authorizers, in granting the charter, release public funding to run the charter school after stipulating various forms of monitoring to ensure that the school functions according to the specified conditions. Often, however, charter schools do not require credentialed teachers, and such teachers need not be union members. The use of nonunion teachers is perceived by critics of school charters as weakening the collective bargaining of teachers (and thus diminishing their rights); proponents, in contrast, hold this a virtue inasmuch as it allows schools to become less bureaucratized. Proponents of charter schools argue also that they increase the efficiency of schools since they are liable to be closed if they do not produce satisfactory results (Finn et al. 2000). "Efficiencies" introduced by charter schools are said to be the use of parental "sweat equity" (e.g., contributions in kind) and leverage to create other nonmonetary resources to supplement the school's budget, the reduction of administrative personnel to a bare minimum, the use of teachers to do double duty as counselors and sports coaches, and the ability to avoid extracurricular activities that regular schools normally offer (e.g., sports and drama).

Charter schools exist today in the United States, Australia, Canada, and New Zealand. They present different features in different countries. For instance, in New Zealand they enjoy various freedoms but must follow a nationwide curriculum and teacher contract. In the United States, the state of Arizona, called the "Wild West" of the charter movement, grants charters for fifteen years, compared with the three to five years typical in other settings. Many for-profit firms are operating charter schools in the United States, and often there is no cap on the number that can be sponsored by local school boards. These schools operate in converted public and private schools and in new buildings.

Finn et al. (2000) assert that charter schools are not an example of "privatization" because the "public retains an interest in the successful delivery of education services paid for by public funds" (71). But at the same time, proponents of voucher systems, such as economist Milton Friedman, contend that the charter movement "steals the thunder" from vouchers: "When Edison [a private firm operating in the provision of education] sets up a private school, its customers are parents and children; when it competes to run a charter school, its customer is the board of the charter school, not individual parents and children" (Friedman 1962, cited in Finn et al. 2000, 182).

At the heart of the charter school budget is per pupil base funding, determined on the basis of state average per pupil expenditures (as is the case in Minnesota) or district average revenue or expenditures (as in Massachusetts) or negotiated between the charter school and the chartering agency (as in Colorado) (Nelson et al. 2000). By the end of 2000, charter schools educated less than 1 percent of U.S. schoolchildren housed in 1,700 such schools, but the concept is expanding.

Evidence about the effectiveness of charter schools in terms of student performance is mixed, leading its advocates to argue that "it is so difficult to generalize about charter performance" (Finn et al. 2000, 77). The prevailing empirical evidence (cited in Finn et al. 2000, strong supporters of the charter school) indicates that these schools do not perform very differently from regular public schools but that everyone who participates in them is "happier."

Vouchers

Essentially, vouchers function by giving parents a certain amount of money to be used to pay for educational services in either a private or a religious school. Friedman, a proponent of voucher schemes since the early 1950s, justifies this mechanism when he complains that "the educational system is failing kids in low-income schools and high-income schools" (cited in Bazeley 2000, 12A). Friedman and other supporters see vouchers as a way to introduce competition into the educational system and thus provide quality control as (presumably) exercised by the market. Consumers, in this case parents, can, according to their desire, choose and create a more efficient system of public schooling in which financial and human resources can concentrate on maximizing pupil performance. In the view of voucher proponents, this initiative would give parents tremendous freedom while making public schools face the challenge of having to improve if they are going to retain any students. Some sociologists, notably Christopher Jencks, point out that with tuition grants poor families could opt out of failing public schools, thus helping to equalize opportunity for their children (cited in Finn et al. 2000).

Often, however, the payment is not sufficient to cover the full costs. And this is a major weakness of voucher plans. Moreover, the concept of parental choice assumes parental information levels that in some documented cases are very low; it also assumes parental ability to provide their children with transportation to the new school, something that is often very difficult and occasionally impossible, particularly among low-income families, which are the ones supposed to benefit the most from voucher mechanisms.

McEwan (2000), reporting on studies based on both experimental and nonexperimental designs in the United States, found that private schools produced modest gains in mathematics but no reading gains, that competition among public schools has not yet resulted in benefits in terms of reduction in expenditures or school quality, and that parents who take advantage of choice allowed by the voucher programs are those with higher levels of education and schooling.

Vouchers are the most widely known form that allows parental choice for nonpublic forms of education, but there are also several types of public–private partnerships emerging. These include leasing or renting by public authorities plants designed and built privately to house public services, assumption of control of failing public schools ("takeovers") by private firms in order to improve them, and tax credits to families choosing to send children to private, fee-paying schools.

There is a close affinity between vouchers and charter schools. Both allow for parental choice, the latter being within the confines of public schools and thus more palatable to constituencies across the country. The most recent educational policy in the United States, enacted in 2001, paves the way for the increase of charter schools by enabling parents from "failing schools" to take their children to alternative schools using public funds and by granting funds for start-up costs to groups that may wish to establish charter schools.

PRIVATIZATION AND EDUCATIONAL ENTREPRENEURS

The French philosopher Lyotard (cited in Burton and Robinson 1999) predicted in 1986 that one aspect of globalization would be the "mercantilization of knowledge." This indeed now seems to be the case.

In the United Kingdom, the origins of profit making from education have been linked to neoliberal policies first voiced in a speech by Prime Minister James Callaghan in 1976 and later followed by Prime Minister Margaret Thatcher; in the United States, the same movement has been attributed to the publication of *A Nation at Risk* in 1983 (Fitz and Beers 2001). Both documents present the same argument: Public education not addressing the needs of industry and the economy; in the case of *A Nation at Risk*, it is further argued that the quality of public education is poor.

With neoliberal economics, in which the market is seen as a key path to efficiency, quality, and innovation, a large number of enterprises are entering the educational arena. For them, while the question of efficiency is important, the main objective in setting up educational institutions is the procurement of profits. With the speed of communications and easy dissemination of information, the life cycles of venture capitalism are becoming shorter. According to Evans et al. (2000), start-up capital for educational investment used to take four years to be gathered; now it can be raised in less than three years.

As noted previously, the arrival of private entrepreneurs to the field of education was preceded by several years of attacks on the public school in which it was charged that students were performing poorly in international comparisons and that the teaching workforce was poorly educated.[4] These attacks were motivated not by a simple desire to improve the public school but rather by the hope to replace it with the private sector. As one of the key publications for educational entrepreneurs stated,

> Education: the last frontier for profit. The World spends two trillion dollars or one-twentieth of global gross domestic product on education. The private sector, which accounts for roughly a fifth of the amount, is determined to capture a larger share of this giant market. The business world is investing in this new field with a managerial mindset and enterprising spirit. (*EdInvest News*, October 2000)

Evaluations of school marketing conditions by private entrepreneurs often conclude with assertions such as, "K–12 education in the U.S. is fueled by U.S.$350 billion in government expenditures annually" (Evans et al. 2000, 16), suggesting that U.S. public education can be a large market. Sandler (2000) ensures potential investors that the private educational market in the United States is already profitable, claiming that K–12 education generated U.S.$4 billion and that higher education resulted in a U.S.$10 billion profit in 2000. A drastically different estimate is offered by *Education Week* (cited in Fitz and Beers 2001), asserting that in 2000, private entrepreneurs in the United States generated about U.S.$100 to U.S.$123 billion. Revenues by private investors in the United Kingdom were estimated to be £5 billion for the same year (about U.S.$7 billion) (Fitz and Beers 2001).

Using tools of marketing, private firms are conducting extremely comprehensive and detailed studies of educational markets in central countries and in developing countries as well, identifying such elements as number of students, types of education, and resources in government hands (Evans et al. 2000). Firms such as EduVentures are currently researching education as an industry for potential investment. MediaMatrix is a corporation tracing Internet activities related to education. Sandler (2000), president of EduVentures, claims to have produced a report that has been read in seventy-six countries and that is the most downloaded document ever produced for the U.S. Department of Education.

With such promise and positive evidence of profit in education, public education emerges as one of the prime business targets in the globalization world. Prospectuses seeking investors in this field state that venture capital in education today is getting a 15 percent return on investment. A 2000 study by EduVentures focusing on the United States notes that the private tutoring industry in this country already generates about U.S.$2 billion. Corroborating the extent of this interest, the U.S. Department of Education reports that 31 percent of elementary school children, or more than ten million children nationwide, are enrolled in after-school programs (Evans et al. 2000). Studies of international arenas remark that while the international market in education and technology is 2.5 times bigger than the U.S. market, only 18 percent of the educational economy is outside the United States; thus, there is a major market that is presently unexplored. In China, for instance, children today are required to learn English (Sandler 2000), creating a clientele of major magnitude. Marketing studies in India, another populous country, indicate that between 1986 and 1993 enrollment in registered private schools grew by 9.6 percent annually, compared to 1.4 percent at government schools (EduVentures study).

The mapping of the educational market by entrepreneurs reveals that there are opportunities for helping to close gaps in both access and performance. It also tells them that the market consists of not only setting up new schools and training institutions but also providing consulting services for testing, evaluation, teacher training, and a wide array of services, ranging from noneducational services such as catering or cleaning the schools to substantial functions such as inspection of schools and the collection and analysis of data on educational expenditures (*EdInvest News*, 2000). Some major firms are, indeed, making their appearance in education. The most important corporations in U.S. education are Advantage Schools, Inc.; Edison Schools, Inc.; Nobel Learning Communities; and the Tesseract Group. In the United Kingdom, the most important are Nord Anglia and the Centre of British Teachers (CfBT), the latter a nonprofit trust with yearly revenues of £65 million (or U.S.$92 million). In addition, "educators are forming new businesses and conducting business with new educational institutions as a means of maximizing their utility" (Hentschke and Krinsky 2000, 1).

A common feature of the private firms now in education is their narrow focus. In the United States, Futurekids provides teacher training in classroom applications of computers, Sylvan Learning Center provides tutoring in reading and math, and Edison comes closest to providing a comprehensive service but markets only its own educational model. Among the commercial incursions into the educational arena, mention must be made of Channel One. By leasing television sets, VCRs, and a satellite dish on inexpensive terms to school districts, Channel One (owned by Primemedia) has access to an estimated eight million students in 12,000 classrooms in the United States. Under the terms of the contract, Channel One must be watched in the classroom for twelve minutes a day. Researchers from Vassar College and Johns

Hopkins University found that only 20 percent of the programs deal with "recent political, economic, social, and cultural stories"; the rest of the time, the content comprises "advertising, sports, weather and natural disasters, features and profiles, and self-promotion of Channel One" (Corporate Watch 1998). Although Channel One has evoked protests from more than fifty professional associations of teachers and administrators and from parents, it has been in operation since 1990. Since Channel One offers equipment that poor schools do not have, it ends up influencing many low-income students.

Telecommunications and Privatization

The emergence of educational enterprises has been helped both by the prevailing norms of privatization and by recent developments in communication technology. Satellite dishes can receive hundreds of television channels, distributing values, beliefs, and norms worldwide. Internet use has been growing exponentially. Because of its potential to facilitate the customization of products and services, it is predicted that the Internet will enable firms to provide individually tailored study programs for high school students, incorporating both school-based and on-line resources. Many predict that the Internet will serve primarily for tutoring and test preparation at that level. Indicative of the growing use of the Internet is the existence of more than a billion Web pages in the world, most of which are presently located in industrialized countries. Consequently, much of the investment by private firms in education is geared to the provision of distance education or telecommuting. Consortia on distance education are multiplying rapidly (Kovel-Jarboe 2000).

EdInvest News (October 20, 2000) announced a partnership launched between Nobel Learning Communities (based in the United States) and the South Ocean Development Corporation (based in China) to connect Nobel and South Ocean schools so that schools, students, and teachers "may share cultures, histories and subjects of mutual interest." Nobel was said to operate in 162 private, charter, and special education schools in the United States and to have the capacity to educate 26,000 students. South Ocean was described as having seven private schools and two colleges, but those alone represented an enrollment of 20,000 students.

Reviewing the privatization process in the United Kingdom, Fitz and Beers (2001) note some characteristics of its trajectory. Although then–Prime Minister Thatcher had been advocating privatization since 1979, it took until the Education Reform Act of 1988 to strengthen the education–business connection. Various means were used to this effect: The national curriculum subject panels were to include lay and business representatives in their membership; the governance and financing of schools were to be modeled on a market system; schools were to compete for students, and poor schools would be forced to close; governing bodies were to include members of the civic and business communities; grant-maintained schools (the equivalent of U.S. charter schools) were to be created, thus allowing parents to move out of district control; and, in what became a very powerful measure, the government was to mandate compulsory competitive tendering as the principle on which to organize local services (subcontracting to reduce costs). Fitz and Beers (2001) accurately noted that through these mechanisms, business was able to not only consolidate its presence in education but also define education itself as a business.

Forms of Privatization in Education

It is informative to review the forms of enterprises that exist in education in the United Kingdom today, in part because of the range of forms they assume and in part because they will likely serve as models of privatization in other parts of the world. Fitz and Beers (2001) identify four such forms:

Compulsory Competitive Tendering

Compulsory bidding among profit firms in the United Kingdom started in 1980 under the Local Government, Planning and Land Act, which required local authorities to put highways and building construction and maintenance up for bidding. The Local Government Act of 1988 extended the requirement to bid work to a larger range of activities, including the provision of education. One significant application of the principle of compulsory competitive tendering has been the privatization of the system of school inspection, now monitored by the Office for Standards in Education (OFSTED). This privatized inspectorate began as a cottage industry but is now in the hands of a few contractors: the Centre for British Teachers, Millwharf, Seven Crossing, Cambridge Education Associates, and Nord Anglia. Soon after its creation, OFSTED was given the power to determine whether a school was failing to provide an adequate standard of education and enabled the education secretary to take over failing schools by enabling a private institution to run them (Fitz and Beers 2001; see also Finkelstein and Grubb 2000).

Private–Public Partnerships

These are forms of collaboration between the public and private sectors to provide new kinds and forms of education. City Technology Colleges have existed in the United Kingdom since 1986 and the Education Action Zones since 1997, both targeted mostly at inner urban communities. The Technology Colleges comprise some twenty secondary schools offering science and technology programs of instruction. Education Action Zones, which are clusters (two secondary schools and surrounding primary schools working to-gether to improve school and student performance) have been established at fifteen sites in England.

Another instance of public–private collaboration is the National Grid for Learning, an effort to link all schools in England and Wales via the Internet. Several corporations are involved (Microsoft, Compaq, Research Machines, and BT) in the provision of expert advice and service for the Grid. Report-edly, there has been some modest success, but more important, the Grid has been shown to be a good way for corporations to introduce their software (Fitz and Beers 2001).

Private Finance Initiatives

In this modality, the private sector designs, builds, and finances facilities for which the public sector subsequently pays a charge to use. By November 2000, there were seventy-one projects planned or running in the United Kingdom, worth £680 million (or about U.S.$963 million) (Fitz and Beers 2001; see also Finkelstein and Grubb 2000).

Takeovers

As noted previously, a school found to be performing poorly can be as-signed a private company to run it. In the United Kingdom today, of the 150 English local educational agencies (the equivalent of the U.S. school district), 120 have been inspected. Twenty of these have been required to hand over some or all of their services to outside organizations. It is not known at this point whether the private organizations perform better than public schools (Fitz and Beers 2001).

In the case of the United States, other forms have emerged. Some twenty corporations provide educational services, and thirteen of these provide *instructional* services. Fits and Beers (2001) note that education-oriented businesses in the United States play essentially two roles: as for-profit firms directly providing education and as financial institutions that provide the funds for firms to enter the education business. Examples of the latter are EduVentures, Lehman Brothers, and Montgomery Services. Advantage Schools has been identified as a new group that plans to buy schools in the future. Other large investors are J. P. Morgan Capital Corporation and In-vestor AB, Vulcan Ventures (owned by Microsoft's Paul Allen), UBS Capital, Leona, and Mosaica. Private entrepreneurs anticipate that charter schools will become more popular, a position that was given strong support in the federal educational policy of 2001, which gives subsidies to parents from fail-ing public schools to take their children to private schools. In fact, by 2001, Prudential Insurance Group had loaned $20 million in support of charter schools. Educational firms are "in an extremely powerful position to shape national and local agendas about the desirability of handing over public education to private providers. . . . [The American Federation of Teachers] suspects there are powerful lobbies operating at national, state, and local levels" (Fitz and Beers 2001, 15).

The performance of private investors has been quite mixed. One group, Educational Alternatives, Inc., started in 1990, had its contracts terminated for multiple reasons: lack of student achievement, failure to reduce costs, denial of special education programs, and misrepresentation of test score results (Fitz and Beers 2001, citing the General Accounting Office 1996). The firm changed its name and reemerged as the Tesseract Group in 1997. At present, it concentrates on charter applications with states with permissive charter school legislation and operates mostly in Arizona (Fitz and Beers 2001).

The trajectory of Edison Schools, Inc., formed in 1991, has followed a similar mixed pattern. Considered the largest school management firm, Edison Schools had by 2001 been able to raise U.S.$232 million from private investors. The firm worked for four years, spending U.S.$40 million in research and development to create a unique model before it started running schools in 1995. It currently operates in twenty-one states through 113 schools, and it typically enters into contracts with school districts to operate failing public schools. In several districts, Edison's schools have not been able to deliver the promised increase in student achievement.

The promise that business firms have been making to educational authorities is that they can produce gains in standardized tests that are the same or higher than in comparable public schools. The profit logic behind business firms in education is that, on receiving funding from the school district based on an average per pupil allotment, they can reduce expenditures within the classroom, generally by hiring less experienced teachers or uncertified staff, thereby decreasing teachers' salaries—often the largest single educational expense. The difference between the funding received and the expenditure is their profit (Fitz and Beers 2001).

Comparing privatization trends in the United Kingdom and the United States, Fitz and Beers (2001) note that privatization in the United Kingdom, which is tied to the central government's control of the educational system, has been moving slowly because of the many regulations, including the teaching of a national curriculum and the requirement that schools be subject to regular full inspection. In the United States, in contrast, the existence of fewer regulations has permitted the introduction of innovations, such as longer school days, centrally designed literacy and curriculum programs, and enforcement of codes of behavior that appeal to certain parents. The more relaxed regulation has also permitted staff reductions, use of nonqualified teachers, and the easing of difficult students with special educational requirements. Fitz and Beers (2001) conclude that because of the different dynamics, the emphasis in the United Kingdom has been for private firms to take over failing schools, while in the United States, where they have enjoyed greater discretion, private firms have been more involved in setting up charter schools. In discussing the influence of globalizing norms on education, the distinct situations in the United Kingdom and the United States indicate, as Fitz and Beers (2001) highlight, that national policy contexts provide different structures of opportunities and constraints for entrepreneurs. However, it must also be remarked that despite variation, the end result is the substantial presence of the private sector in education.

Is the presence of business firms in education a positive or a negative development? Advocates of a greater role for the private sector in education maintain that "educators near the top of educational system will forgo decision rights over procedures in order to gain decision rights over performance or outputs" (Hentschke and Krinsky 2000, 1). But giving up governance in exchange for better outcomes is not a simple trade-off. With market regulation of education, Kachur (1999) notes, "Once power is removed from citizens, monopolized by technical experts, and assessed by the market's 'invisible hand,' an ethical and political debate about educational goals does not—*cannot*—arise" (p. 118). According to Kachur and Harrison (1999), privatization appeals to two constituencies: to business because the privatization of education creates market niches for possible exploitation and to moral conservatives for whom private education represents an "escape from the valueless purgatory of public schools, while enhancing the status qualifications of the wealthy and their offspring" (xxiv). Another major issue, looming in the background and perhaps not evident until a few generations have gone through privatized schooling, is whether citizens who have not had the experience of a common socializing institution can develop values that contribute to a social glue across groups of different social classes and ethnicities.

THE ROLE OF THE STATE IN THE BUSINESS ENVIRONMENT

Faced with decreasing funds allotted to education, a frequent objective of government-led initiatives has become to promote "the participation of profit-seeking enterprises in the production and distribution of goods and services that previously were not 'priced,' but instead were for public provision through a variety of non-market arrangements" (David 2000, 18). Today in the United States, federal planning and implementation grants provide several hundred dollars per pupil during a charter school's first two or three years of operation. Several states provide additional start-up financial support (Nelson et al. 2000).

It could be asked, To what extent are government or public educational agencies losing their power? There is no clear picture, as contradictory sets of forces appear to be in operation. At first sight, it would seem that governments are stepping aside from establishing educational leadership and control, but when the full evidence is considered, the picture is more ambiguous. Even in the United States, where so many regulations in education have apparently been dismissed, the federal and many state governments are exercising solid control of the curriculum and even teacher practices via the use of standardized testing to determine student success and school performance (Lipman 2000).

An analysis of eleven contracts for charter schools—the most common form of private presence in the U.S. school—between for-profit firms and governing school boards showed great variability in wording agreements and thus also in their objectives and governance procedures. A study by Hannaway (1999) found that the objectives of these contracts tended to be either financial (revenue enhancement, cost containment, or cost reduction to attain a certain objective) or educational (improving performance). However, financial objectives appear to dominate. Examples of contracts by two major private providers reflect the variability in provision and objectives. Edison's contracts were established around a well-defined curriculum and education program. The contracts gave considerable information about student-to-teacher ratios, the curriculum, professional development, technology, and relationships with families. They also stipulated that enrollment below a set minimum would be grounds for termination. Sylvan Learning Center offered a narrow model that concentrated on remedial instruction in mathematics and reading. Sylvan's contracts stipulated that the firm employ its own personnel, many of whom were not certified (Hannaway 1999). Sylvan's contracts also promised at least two normal curve equivalents (NCEs) of growth, an increase that is quite modest and may not necessarily be higher than that attainable through comparable public schools.[5]

A contentious issue in the increased use of the private sector in education concerns special education. Public schools must serve all children without reservation, whether they are normal children or have some kind of disability. Private providers, however, guided by profit motives, consider first whether the state will fund these children on the basis of average school district special education spending or on the basis of the specific needs of the students enrolled (Nelson et al. 2000). If the former, private providers are reluctant to participate.

MANIFESTATIONS IN REGIONAL BLOCS
AND IN DEVELOPING COUNTRIES

Examining the influence of three economic blocs (the North American Free Trade Agreement [NAFTA], the European Union, and the Asian Pacific Economic Conference [APEC]), Dale and Robertson (2002) find that these bodies approach education with different levels of coordination and influence. NAFTA was found to leave explicit references to education but to enable its being defined as "any other tradable good or service (24). The European Union sought the creation of a European identity and to this effect is operating through "benchmarks and performance indicators as a means of bringing together different national goals and aspirations for education in a more coherent way at the European level" (28). APEC showed little interested in formal coordination of educational activities but has created the Education Network, whose first task is to promote information technology "as a core competency in education, through physical or virtual exchanges, networks, and programs," and has enacted declarations on the need to foster stronger ties between the educational system and work and is encouraging governments to facilitate links with business.

Through these regional bodies, therefore, educational systems around the world are being asked to recognize the importance of information technology, testing, and a closer interaction with business. Another regional group, de facto an educational bloc, in Latin America is PREAL (Partnership for Educational Revitalization in the Americas). This body is promoting the participation of business leaders in Latin American education and promotes discussion on educational reform, student performance, accountability, and decentralization. Interestingly, PREAL has two main offices, one in Washington, D.C. (at the Inter-American Dialogue) and the other in Santiago, Chile (at the Corporación de Investigaciones para el Desarrollo).

Unquestionably, the calls to follow certain policies and practices have not been responded to in identical manner. As Buenfiel's (2000) case study of the "modernization policies" promoted by the World Bank in Mexico shows, actual implementation is characterized by local interpretations and particular political and technical conditions. We argue, however, that although singular manifestations may emerge, core practices are being implanted in many educational systems, and it is likely that these practices will acquire more convergent features over time.

The economic impact of globalization has been felt in developing countries primarily through calls by international agencies to privatize schooling (particularly the tertiary level), through introducing greater accountability via testing mechanisms, and through decentralization. Decentralization has been known in educational circles in the Third World since the 1960s, when significant policy shifts took place in countries such as Colombia (1968) and Venezuela (1969). Originally, decentralization was characterized as means to improve the efficiency of public administration and to devolve some decision-making power to lower levels of government organization, generally moving from the capital to regions (Hanson 1986). With the influence of neoliberalism in the last decade, decentralization has acquired a new objective: the diminution of state funding of public education and, concomitantly, the participation of parents and communities in the funding of schools. Decentralization under globalization has also moved from the regional level to the municipal, community, and school levels. The "World Declaration on Education for All" (United Nations Development Program et al. 1990) paved the way for decentralization at lower levels when it called for "national, regional, and local authorities" to provide basic education and "revitalized partnerships at all levels" (161).[6] In the case of Latin America, most efforts toward school level decentralization occurred between 1992 and 1998 (Winkler and Gershberg 2000, 3). One of the few studies attempting to evaluate the impact of this type of decentralization on school effectiveness found such assessment difficult because of a lack of data, incomplete implementation of the reforms, and the varying times between implementation and changes in behaviors and the allocation of resources. This evaluation, which covered three countries and a Brazilian state, concluded that school-based decentralization was associated with greater student and teacher attendance. El Salvador showed no increased student achievement, Nicaragua and Chile did, and the evidence was mixed in the case of Minas Gerais. Student performance in Chile was not easily attributable to decentralization because there had been other reforms, such as teacher training, efforts to provide remedial education in low-income regions, and an increased educational budget (Winkler and Gershberg 2000).

LESSONS FROM WORLD CITIES

The emerging literature shows a very interesting and powerful intersection between public schools and what is increasingly known as "world cities," a development we explore in greater detail in chapter 5. Changes in the space and institutions of the city are affecting the composition of public schools, and the power of TNCs now residing in world cities is further influencing the decisions adopted by school systems based in large urban settings.

World cities, to a greater extent than other large cities, show an increasing segregation of minorities—primarily African American and Latino communities in the United States. These groups are also frequently displaced by gentrification processes in urban centers as the construction of better housing forces poor people to move. In all, these minority groups end up with reduced access and poor services in many areas, including education (Wilson et al. 1998).

Lipman (2000), who has produced a very rich case study of the education in a major world city, Chicago, shows that these cities (her term is "global cities") are characterized by high growth and wealth for some groups and segregated low-income neighborhoods for others. Often, the loss of manufacturing jobs has shifted the latter groups into low-paying service jobs. She demonstrates that dual economic systems produce dual educational systems with distinct types of students.

Cities in the United States have experienced "white flight" since the 1970s, a phenomenon motivated much more by avoidance of civil rights laws than by globalization. However, with selected reinvestment by TNCs and the emergence of dual economies, global cities are finding their minority populations earning about 60 percent of the average for all workers and a large number of them below poverty lines. In Chicago, 33 percent of African Americans and 24 percent of Latinos (compared to 11 percent of whites) live in poverty; thus, public schools are their only option. Not surprisingly, about 90 percent of the students in Chicago public schools are students of color. Lipman documents that world cities undergo substantial changes in space to accommodate the gentrification of neighborhoods and to provide students from wealthier families with a more appealing type of school offering. In the case of Chicago, Lipman found a reorganization of the city and its schools along lines of race, ethnicity, and class. Similar racial profiles can be observed in other large cities, such as Los Angeles and New York.

Public schools in world cities become prime targets of external sources of pressure (primarily the business sectors) to improving student performance and school accountability. In the new climate, schools become bombarded with achievement tests and serious penalties for poor performance by students, forcing teachers and administrators to create learning environments in which test taking dominates. At the same time, world cities also emphasize "standards of excellence" because such cities must attract professionals. Lipman (2000) found that Chicago created strong distinctions simultaneously between high- and low-status schools, the former comprising college preparatory and math/science academic work, the latter concentrating on vocational education, school-to-work experiences, and military academic work.

In looking at the new array of educational programs offered in Chicago, Lipman (2000, 26) categorizes them into plus and minus: "plus" she defines as those that prepare for college or offer intellectually challenging curriculum, whereas "minus" are those that offer vocational education and restricted curricula, with rigid instruction and control of students. Mapping the physical area in which courses are offered, Lipman found that "minus" schools and programs were located in the African American South Side and African American and Latino West/Southwest side of Chicago. "Plus" programs, such as the Elite International Baccalaureate program, were found distributed equitably (two in each region of the city), but they served only thirty students at each high school grade, so they involved only 1.89 percent of all Chicago high school students. Lipman found also that while the supportive services allowed by these innovative programs were minimal, their existence was exploited to legitimate a highly unequal educational program.

The generally negative transformations in the world city of Chicago were accompanied by a discourse that denied them. References to features in the economy, using the concepts of "flexibility" and "opportunity," were frequently juxtaposed to concepts prevalent in the social sciences under postmodernism, such as "diversity" and "fluidity," and concepts in education, such as "equity" and "quality"—all this while providing a very limited set of educational programs to help minority students.

It has been found in several U.S. studies that repeating grades does not help students learn and that, on the contrary, the stigma of repetition seems to foster dropping out (Darling-Hammond 2001). In the case study of Chicago, Lipman (2000) found evidence that some retention policies were negatively affecting "capable students with strong grades and attendance, including some top students who had won prestigious academic awards" (20) by mandating repetition following poor performance in standardized tests. Global cities enforce educational standards but also attempt to provide student support. Yet in the case of Chicago, support tends to be provided in name only: summer school, transition high schools, and after-school programs. Regardless of name, most of these schools offer a very homogeneous curriculum for the low-income student, characterized by basic skills and not bilingual education, despite the fact that many are immigrants who speak other languages. Further, many of the anticipated remedial programs were not in effect or functioned in particular ways. For instance, "summer bridge programs" for failing students were strongly aligned with testing programs and were conducted by teachers who were not experts in the content area of the courses (Lipman 2000, 22).

While one might expect some of these problems to be found elsewhere, no solid generalizations can be made on the basis of Chicago alone. More qualitative studies of other world cities and their impact on public education remain to be made.

SUMMARIZING

Economic forces and agreements are influencing countries directly and indirectly. We have seen concrete manifestations of policies that change the nature and objectives of educational systems. We have also seen the decided presence of the private sector in terrains that used to be defined as the "common good" and the reframing of schooling as a site for financial investment.

The presence of the private sector both as a major influence on educational policy and as a direct provider of educational services is increasing. These trends are greatly facilitated by the juxtaposition of neoliberal ideologies, technological developments, and the quick dissemination of economic values in education. At the same time, the influence has a physical location, as the development of global cities and the decisions by regional blocs show.

Under the influence of globalization, there is a great amount of discussion about educational reform, and the new emphasis on economic competition promises radical changes in what is learned and how it is learned, even though there is little evidence that this change is or will be accompanied by positive social transformation, as many private forms of schooling may be weakening the already fragile bonds across social classes. In several cases, noticeably in the United States, it is becoming possible for communities to select schools that minimize integration along class, race, gender lines, and physical disability. The logic of "parental choice" might lead to smaller class-rooms and more responsive teachers, but it does not build on helping the weaker student. In the name of "excellence" and "accountability" high-stakes testing ends up hurting low-income children, demoralizing teachers, and turning schools into drilling exercises. Less effort is now being assigned to the development of personal autonomy, social criticism, solidarity, and social justice.

Today, empowerment through education is presented as the strongest axiom of globalization, yet the reality around us attests to a different scenario. There has indeed been an increase in the proportion of high-level professionals and technicians in the economy who require higher levels of education and earn increasingly larger salaries than those with lower levels of education. But most workers function in low-paid service jobs calling for low skills, and thus education as a means of social mobility faces clear ceilings in the current economy. Castells (1997) observes that almost 30 percent of U.S. workers earn poverty-level wages. Can privatization of schools and related business norms prevent this ever growing gap? Minow (2000) warns us that "privatization can subvert the very idea of a collective civic obligation to provide reasonably equitable services to all members of the community. And with that subversion, the vision of community itself is eroded" (69).

NOTES

1. Decentralization, by often not requiring certified teachers or by hiring teachers at the local level, has been known to weaken considerably and even destroy nationwide teacher unions. Only in the case of Chile is there evidence that teacher organizations were able to survive after substantial municipalization measures.

2. Performance in a new high school test in Chicago, known as CASE, will represent 25 percent of the grade in each academic year. This will most likely cause the test to dictate a significant portion of the curriculum (Lipman 2000).

3. A key capacity ingredient for poor-performing schools is the provision of trained and experienced teachers. Unfortunately, for a variety of reasons that go from

safety fears to racism, most recently credentialed teachers fail to apply to the largest 120 school districts in the country, with the result that emergency and noncredential teachers constitute the staff of the most vulnerable schools. Social policies to help poor families in inner cities, who move during the school year from apartment to apartment in search of affordable housing, would represent another major capacity input.

4. One of the most important cross-national comparisons used to gauge U.S. student performance is the Third International Mathematics and Science Study (TIMSS). Conducted in 1999, TIMSS is the largest international study of student achievement ever undertaken. It found that Singapore, the Republic of Korea, China, Taiwan, and Hong Kong had the highest average math and science achievement at the eighth-grade level, while the United States showed the 19th and 18th position, respectively, in the ranking of the 38 participating countries. Attracting the greatest attention were results showing U.S. twelfth graders in the nineteenth rank in math achievement and in the sixteenth rank in science achievement among twenty-one industrialized countries.

5. A normal curve equivalent is a measure of standardized test scores with a mean of 50 and a standard deviation of about 21. Over the school year, students are supposed to increase their scores, and many do. Whether an aggregate gain of 2 points out of 100 signifies good performance by a school is subject to debate. Normal curve equivalents are used to permit the comparison of student performance even when different tests have been used. However, like most of the commercially developed tests, they are based on the notion that cognitive abilities and knowledge exist in society in such a way that only very few know a lot, very few know very little, and most of us know about an average amount. While this principle may not be incorrect, tests are designed to produce such a "normal" distribution; in other words, by statistical manipulation, tests identify geniuses and losers—a way of making reality fit one's preconceptions.(See Wainer 2000 for a related discussion.)

6. Other parts of the document made reference to "increased efficiency through local and private support" (87) and to "empowering the education manager" at all levels: "the central or minister level, at the regional or district level and, most importantly, at the school level" (85).

4

Consequences of Communication Technologies on Culture and Education

There appears to be a consensus that the twenty-first century will continue to devote unabated attention to science and technology, carrying on the accelerated pace of development begun in the 1970s. Significant among the consequences of this development is the increasing use of the mass media throughout the world and the growing popularity of the Internet. These two advances, along with many related developments, are creating major repercussions in cultural patterns worldwide as well as in the definition and practice of educational offerings.

It has been asserted that the culture of globalization will be a mass culture in which media dominates. As the media become progressively ubiquitous, they also become powerful.[1] Much of the so-called compression of time and space that characterizes globalization is a function of the news media and the communication technologies. The mass media are determinant in the emerging forms of individual and collective identities. Repeated and pervasive messages create uniform symbols that affect the way we see and think. Our mental structures are not impervious to the form and content of messages and images. Our symbolic world today is rich but also tends toward substantial convergence. In contemporary society, media-based communication is a primary means of social integration. Yet this integration can take place in defense of values and practices that are not always in the best social interest.

Some argue that as borders between countries become easier to cross, new transnational identities are being shaped and created. Others hold that there exist some complex and unavoidable relations between global capitalism and local identity formation, as national identities depend on and usually reflect adaptations to political and economic circumstances; in their view, the local reacts to the global by creating specific, if not unique, responses.

Many more commodities and services are becoming globalized (i.e., being distributed in many places of the world) than in the past. Text and images are also becoming commodities—goods for sale much like any other product. The commodification of messages brings many consequences for the type of culture that emerges, as the dominance of certain messages has major repercussions on what individuals consider information and knowledge worth having.[2]

This chapter explores the nature of the expansion of the role of communications in contemporary society and the simultaneous concentration of knowledge and information in a few institutions. It discusses the implications of this concentration for the knowledge we seek to learn and consider important and for the knowledge we discard or fail to learn. This is discussed in the context of the weakening of nation-states in their ability to control external influences.

FORMS OF DIFFUSION

Communications in the global era utilize a variety of means, from the immediacy of massively broadcast television and radio to products of greater individual-level consumption, such as cassettes, video, and the Internet. In the case of the Internet, new communication modalities, such as chat rooms, teleshopping, and distance education, are opening people's homes to the world.

Additional technologies enabling visual exchanges, "streaming" audio and video, and "live cams" make global communication more "real." Unquestionably, these modalities are also redefining time and space, creating settings in which one's presence "there" is no longer necessary and the "when" can be controlled to mean any time.

MEDIA CONCENTRATION

The increasingly sophisticated technology of communications has been accompanied by the frequent mergers and growing size of firms in the communications field. Concentration is so intense that it has been asserted that "nine companies dominate the world" (McChesney 2000, 3): General Electric, which owns NBC; Time Warner, which is part owner of AOL Time Warner (both merged in January 2001); Viacom, which owns MTV, CBS, UPN, and Paramount Studios; the Disney Company, which owns ABC, ESPN, The Disney Channel, and SoapNet; the Fox Family networks; the News Corporation (owned by Rupert Murdoch), the largest conglomerate of newspapers in the world; German Bertelsmann; AT&T (the largest cable company in the United States); Sony; and Seagram (McChesney 2000). In 1996, the media industry in the United States generated $287 billion (Compaine and Gomery 2000), an amount that clearly competes with the combined educational budgets of all fifty states (estimated to be $350 per year in 1999; see Evans et al. 2000).

A characteristic of these media conglomerates is the diversity of communication means they own and thus control. McChesney (2000) notes that Time Warner owns a large film studio, publishes leading magazines, produces major television shows, publishes books, and owns the largest cable television company in the world and numerous movie theater companies. Through the 2001 acquisition of the Fox Family, Disney gained immediate access to eighty-one million cable subscribers throughout the world. Sony represents major film, musical, and electronics interests. Seagram, a beverage manufacture, has film studios and massive music and tourist interests.

MEDIA IMPACT ON CULTURE

We define culture as the complex set of beliefs, values, and practices that unify a given social group. Following Prosser (1999), we consider that culture comprises several subsystems, notably those of organization, communication, resource allocation, social interaction, reproduction, and ideology. It also includes such factors as statuses, roles, rituals and traditions, and the nature of time and space.

It is crucial to recognize that cultures and the identities they foster constitute social constructions—and not passively inherited legacies. Hence, the production of symbolic representations is constant and includes cases ranging from fully unconscious constructions to fully and consciously intended constructions (Mato 1996a). Kachur (2001) argues that under current globalization trends, there is a new form of cultural regulation brought about by the revolution in new communication technologies and the application of the science of consumer management. As a result, cultural regulations are said to have become more anonymous and less focused on developing people's intelligence than on exploiting and mobilizing their desires.

This is occurring through the advertising and polling industries and through positioning consumerism as the basis for social service provision. Kachur (2001) asserts that from the many related textual presentations, by avoiding the "political-me," a form of collective mythmaking enterprise is emerging in which authorship is attributed not to any one individual but to a neutral corporate entity, such as the Government of Canada, the Hudson Institution, or the Business Roundtable on Education, and thus presumably made less political or subjective.

Culture is a highly disputed terrain within globalization, and there are many different opinions about the impact of globalization on cultural forms. In the view of some, there is an increasing homogenization of ideas and practices, and this is considered both positive and unavoidable. In the view of others, cultural globalization is being utilized to disguise the uneven nature of economic globalization; thus, it has been noted that the media display very selective attention to topics. For instance, while the reality of workers in sweatshops is often not reported in the news, consumers frequenting designer shops are highly visible in advertisements and television programs (Taylor et al. 2001b). In the United States today, about 80 percent of the media are syndicated rather than independently owned—a reversal of the pattern existing twenty years ago. A key implication of this is that similar messages circulate in what consumers believe to be different television channels and newspapers.

It would be beyond the scope of this book to present a detailed account of the accomplishments of all media in our globalized world. The discussion in this chapter is extremely selective and serves to highlight the key influences promoting change in our cultural and educational understandings.

Film

The easy acceptance of film as a form of artistic expression has been replaced among culture critics by a realization that it is a cultural commodity produced by multinational corporations. Today, the U.S. film industry, itself largely multinational, dominates the world. Indeed, the largest U.S. export is entertainment. It is estimated that 50 percent of Hollywood revenues come from overseas markets (United Nations Development Program 1999a, 33). Market shares of U.S. films shown in the European Union increased from 56 percent in 1985 to 76 percent in 1995 (Meckel, cited in Dahl 1998). Competition with U.S. films has been extremely difficult. Mexico once produced 100 films per year; today it manages to produce ten films per year (Deen 1999).

Few countries have had the power to protect their own cultural values in the face of the foreign media onslaught. Among the developing countries, only in India and Thailand do its citizens watch more local than imported films. In its free-trade negotiations with the United States and Mexico, Canada has maintained that film, television and radio broadcasting, periodical and book publishing, and video and sound recording are not to be part of economic liberalization. Canada holds that cultural industries are vehicles of cultural expression through which national identity is created and preserved (Goff 2000). France has adopted the same position. These two countries bring a new dimension to globalization in which economic motivations are resisted by a concern for a country's collective identity.[3]

Television

Television operates as a key terrain for the creation of shared thoughts, feelings, values, tastes, and desires to match the needs of the institutions who send the images. Central countries, in producing these programs, become also their main users. Presently in the United States, 98 percent of the homes have television, and at least 88 percent have at least two sets. The average American home keeps the television going for seven and a half hours per day, and children ages eight to thirteen, on average, watch about four hours daily. Schools also use televisions, sometimes as a condition for accepting free equipment. Channel One, mentioned in chapter 3, gives schools free monitors on the condition that at least 90 percent of the students watch its news and advertisements, even if for a few minutes each day (Power and Whitty 1999).

The transnational flow of visual cultural forms has been facilitated by a combination of technological developments (especially satellite and fiberoptic transmission) as well as by neoliberal policies that have widened existing markets and created new ones.

There are several very positive impacts that derive from the expansive presence of television. Through cable and satellite channels such as Discovery, History, and Biography, useful knowledge and information is reaching places and homes that may have no other access to high-quality formal education. The Sundance Channel enables access to alternative films. Although mostly available to the upper and middle classes, cable television is being increasingly subscribed to by poorer families, who recognize the cost-benefit of such an investment. On the other hand, many programs that go under the name of "entertainment" present stories or circumstances with little redeeming social value. It is common knowledge that the most popular television series in the world is the girls-in-swimsuits series *Baywatch*. Another series that has been highly popular in developing countries is the soap opera *Dynasty*.

More than 50 percent of the children in the United States have television in their bedrooms. Television seems to have been the original virtual reality and, perhaps, the strongest socially *unifying* reality. It is capable of homogenizing not only thoughts and feelings but also the way we communicate. The paralingual rhetorical devices (clothing, facial expression, body posturing, gestures, the smile, the look, and so on) depicted in "living color" establish models that are cutting across cultures. Many languages now say "Wow!" to express surprise or amazement.

Referring to the diaspora of Indians throughout the world, Mazumdar (2000) notes that "the new global space of the song and dance sequence of Hindi film songs—and all others—creates a utopian world where people feel their own presence, gliding across different landscapes and nations in a virtual form of travel. TV enables songs to function like electronic catalogues."

Indeed, by watching these and other television programs, viewers get a sense of how to behave, what to wear, and what to aspire to, although several cultural critics indicate that it is very difficult to compare impacts of television programs across cultures because what some groups may see in, for instance, *Dynasty* is not what other groups may be reacting to. In any case, there is acceptance that it is through television that many indigenous[4] groups are becoming "modernized" and learning to behave in the world of the "white" persons.

MTV

Especially among young people, music conveys strong messages about acceptable feelings and concerns. But music, more than other forms of expression, may call for combining globalizing messages and local adaptations.

Started in 1981, MTV reaches a billion viewers in 140 countries, making it the largest television service in the world. Surveys conducted by media specialists indicate that the average U.S. teenager watches six hours of MTV per week compared to two hours of all other television networks combined. A particular feature of MTV is the constant repetition of its music videos. During 2000, these videos were played a total of 29,920 times, making it a major source of informal learning. Some messages contain violence, racism, homophobia, and sexist attitudes toward women; others bring up issues of domestic violence, drug use, safe sex, and political engagement. While no formal studies could be found, MTV reportedly has effects on race relations, popular culture, fashions, and even politics (McCollum 2001).[5]

Observers of the indisputable influence that MTV carries believe that its success in becoming the world's most recognizable global media brand is due to the strategy of localizing regional programming while maintaining a consistency to the MTV global brand. For example, MTV Europe (launched in 1987) originated in London but has since split into four separate "feeds" or programming for the United Kingdom and central, southern, and northern Europe. In Latin America, MTV Latino broadcasts different Spanish-language programs for the northern and southern regions and a Portuguese-language program for Brazil. MTV Asia, the fastest-growing MTV regional market, has three programs: Southeast Asia, Mandarin, and India (McMurria 2000). A key conclusion reached by McMurria is that we need to give greater attention to the spatial logics of global media branding use. In his view, branding is a central cultural technology that blends global media delivery and local specificity (McMurria 2000). It would seem that it is in the area of music that some local differentiation is emerging and that this diversity is utilized by transnational capital to reach others and thus increase their potential clients.

Internet Communications

It is undeniable that the Internet has become an instrument of massive global communication, increasing from nine million users in 1995, to 350 million users in 2000, to 700 million projected in 2001 and two billion for 2007, or one-third of the world's population (Castells 2000). The popularity of the World Wide Web is also growing extremely fast, from fifty pages in 1993 to more than 50 million in 2000 (Annan 2000, 32); one of the key search engines, Google, conducts about 100 million searches each day (Heron 2001). Yet the Internet and the Web remain highly concentrated in industrialized countries, particularly the United States.[6] It is particularly with regard to the Internet that claims are made that communication technologies are democratizing the world. Although men dominate the Internet, youths prevail over older groups (United Nations Development Program 1999a). Thus, it is a technology in hands of new generations.

For analytical purposes, it is useful to distinguish between e-mail and Web sites. The number of e-mail users is rapidly increasing, and there is talk of the Evernet, an Internet that is on twenty-four hours a day and is wireless. In contrast, the Web has somewhat more limited accessibility since it requires computers with a certain minimum processing capacity as well as financial resources to pay for any meaningful service and telephone connection time, requirements that restrict its use in developing countries. "Internet cafes" are filling the gap to some extent.

Policymakers throughout the world consider that Web-based education has great potential, and some are concerned with using the Web to create better educational materials and provide more technology training for teachers and administrators. A few developing countries have made investments to incorporate the Web in schools; two-thirds of all schools in Chile, for instance, now have Web access (Longman 2000). Those less inclined to endorse this form of educational technology argue that there is no evidence that computer use enhances learning. Along similar lines, it has been noted that the current pressures on schools to develop "new computer-literate, multi-skilled, infinitely adaptable, flexible workers" may be a camouflage for the consequences of flexibility, such as "underemployment, poor working conditions, little protection from exploitation, and low wages" (Roberts 2000, 241). In other words, there is skepticism that the computer in the schools will reach the full promise it has been attributed.

Examples of the power of Internet communications to democratize information (by enabling easier access and inexpensive diffusion) include the ease with which individuals and groups in civil society, through stable and wide-reaching networks, can circulate information about actions by dominant groups and conduct studies about them. Perhaps one of the most important examples occurred when groups critical of the negative effects of globalization realized that large transnational corporations (TNCs) and some governments had been meeting for thirty years in the World Economic Forum (in Davos, a small village in Switzerland). Oppositional forces organized a countervailing World Social Forum to discuss issues that were cast aside by more economic concerns. The first World Social Forum took place in Porto Alegre, Brazil, in 2001 and was expected to be held subsequently on an annual basis.

THE DOMINANCE OF ENGLISH

English is by far the main language of the global economy. It is used not only in market transactions but also in science, international politics, and even sports. It dominates international exchanges of knowledge, which are central to technological development. Today, about 1.5 billion persons speak English, and about three billion others (one-third of the world) are exposed to it. It is the language of 80 percent of all Web sites (United Nations Development Program 1999a). Key international bodies, such as the World Bank, the European Union, and the United Nations, use English.

Some consider the use of English beneficial: "The use of English as the lingua franca for scientific communication and for teaching, especially when combined with the Internet, makes communication easier and quicker" (Altbach 2001, 2), thus facilitating access to curriculum innovations for countries with modest higher-education systems. Others see the domination of English as carrying with it the hegemony of particular ideas and ways of looking at the world. They see the international use of English not as the simple adoption of a lingua franca but as another way to diffuse Western, primarily U.S. ideas.

INDIVIDUALISTIC AND COMPETITIVE VALUES

The values transmitted by the mass media today, especially through entertainment programs, tend to support a society oriented toward consumption and competition. Extremely popular television programs, which have spawned similar programs across the world, such as *Survivor,* emphasize competition and blind obedience to orders in order to succeed. In *Survivor,* the "tribal council" had meetings to make decisions not about how to spend time or develop collective strategies but to eliminate members on the basis of producers' demands. Although this program was presented as "unscripted," in fact participants closely followed a top-down script. Similar effects, this time in favor of consumerism, could be observed in the program *The 1900 House,* ostensibly an experiment that followed a family as it attempted to adjust to life as it was 100 years ago. It showed that the participants expressed so much stress and disgust with life in past times that their behavior ended up being a disguised endorsement of the consumerism of today.

And while people today have much more *technological* connectivity than ever before (the Internet, cellular phones, portable radios, and CD players), they also evince a lack of *social* connectivity. This can be seen particularly among young people as they pass through crowds oblivious of others, totally absorbed in their portable CD player or cell phone. The slogan "speak freely" is defined in certain advertising as what you do from a cellular phone that allows unlimited "mobile to mobile" calling. It does, in fact, appear easier for some people to communicate in this fashion than face to face.

CRITICAL THOUGHT

Many media developments demand or foster little reflexivity (or critical thought) on the part of the mass media audience. A number of sociologists have expressed great concern about this trend. In an extensive treatise on the media, the French sociologist Pierre Bourdieu (1996) noticed that in the United States control of entertainment and news was exercised at the time by three channels that in turn were linked to large TNCs (i.e., NBC, owned by General Electric; CBS, owned by Westinghouse; and ABC, owned by Disney) and utilized to disseminate the features of a culture necessary to accomplish the neoliberal model. In Bourdieu's opinion, real information, analysis, in-depth interviews, expert discussions, and serious documentaries are pushed away by shallow entertainment and, in particular, by "mindless talk show chatter between approved and interchangeable speakers," and, because the world is ruled "by the fear of being boring and anxiety about being amusing at all costs, politics is bound to be unappealing, better kept out of prime time as much as possible" (2). Bourdieu is particularly critical of the time-limit formats of many of the shows that preclude serious discussion of events and issues and creates "demagogic simplification," for it is not possible for most people to think as fast or argue as briefly as television "conversations" require. He also asserts that journalists today censor themselves toward political conformity because competition among them creates little job security. Other observers are also critical of the privileged status of technology in contemporary Western society and argue that it now functions not only "as a weapon in the conquest of nature, but also as a means of social regulation" (Leed 1980, 41).

Since the late eighteenth century, philosophers have recognized the tremendous importance of language and communication. Ideas advanced by Johann Gottfried von Herder as earlier as 1772 recognized that languages were not only signs for the transmission of ideas but also a primary means through which the self is objectified and realized (cited in Leed 1980). Herder believed that the essential nature of language was best revealed in poetry and song and that the national language was a vehicle for the real-ization of the national self. Later, in 1944, Max Horkheimer and Theodor Adorno were observing the linkages among business, media, and culture when they asserted that the cultural industry uses technology to extend the domination of capitalism. Later observers, such as Zipes (1980), present a stronger indictment of the media, holding that in the twenty-first century, both the media and many cultural forms have become simple commodities and that this development has affected people's ability to distinguish the real from the unreal, the rational from the irrational. The same author maintains that the autonomy of the mind is seriously challenged both at work and in the home by the demand for standardization.

Bourdieu (1996) reminds us that, according to free-market economics, monopoly creates uniformity and competition produces diversity. But he ar-gues that competition in fact fosters homogenization, a phenomenon that oc-curs as newspapers, for instance, become subject to identical pressures and opinion polls and respond with the same basic cast of commentators. Pro-duction of news and programming becomes a collective enterprise in a neg-ative sense. Bourdieu remarks that in the case of France, it is easy to see that *Le Monde, Le Figaro,* and *Liberation,* supposedly very different newspapers, are now saying the same thing. Competitive pressures are so strong that jour-nalists are forced to do things that they would not say if the competition did not exist: "To know what to say you have to know what everyone else has said" (Bourdieu 1996, 24).

The German theorist Jürgen Habermas considers communication to be cen-tral to a process of social transformation. His theory of communications re-quires opportunities in which people can have "public, unrestricted discussion, free from domination, of the suitability and desirability of action-oriented prin-ciples following purposive-rational action" (cited in Zipes 1980). In this regard, it is evident that the mass media today, guided as it is by neoliberal forms of competition, heavy advertising, and time fragmentation, are not enabling com-munications to play a more transformative role in social relations.

The use of e-mail and Web pages disseminates information in seconds. Such use is contributing to the creation of multiple, nonterritorial communi-ties but is also fomenting fragmented and nonnational identities (Louw 2001). Will the consumers of Internet communications develop loyalties to their nation-state and seek to improve it, or will these consumers develop ideas that the successful world for them is elsewhere?

THE LOCAL VERSUS THE GLOBAL IN MEDIA PRODUCTION

In looking at media production, some observers believe that it is an over-simplification to see it only as unidirectional and coming mostly from central countries. Appadurai (1996), who introduces the concept of the "technoscape," sees at work a process of border crossing that "reconfigures cultural symbols and turns them into signifiers for a whole new set of meanings."

Those who argue that there is substantial production going on at the local level tend to be scholars in the field of cultural studies, which blends literature, media, and analysis. Such scholars hold that there are forms of regionalization that should not be minimized. For instance, there has been a strong influence of Japanese popular music in Hong Kong's popular arts scene since the 1970s. Also in Hong Kong, it has been observed that magazines there reflect the dominant global beauty feminine notion (exemplified by tall, slim, and white models), but there are also magazines that sensitize local readers toward their unique positions as members of an Asian, nonwhite, pluralistic community. A similar process of regional influence is said to be taking place in Vietnam, which is adopting multiple forms of eastern Asian popular culture, including Taiwanese soap operas, videos from Hong Kong, popular music from China (Cantopop), and Japanese animation. The variety of responses in Vietnam is presented through multiple media expressions and reflects the emergence of a complex Asian-based cultural profile in that country.[7] In the Silicon Valley of the United States (San Jose, California)—unquestionably the heart of the technological revolution so inherent to globalization—seven of ten new jobs earned less than U.S.$10,000 in 2000. The majority of these jobs are filled by African American and Hispanic minorities. As a country, the United States has seen the emergence of the "working poor"—people whose salaries do not allow them to live comfortably. Many menial workers earn an hourly wage of U.S.$7, or U.S.$13,000 per year. Assuming a family of three (one adult and two children), an income of U.S.$30,000 would be needed for decent living (Ehrenreich 2001).

Continuing the argument that there is neither blind absorption of Western messages nor overt resistance to them, several critical studies experts remark that parallel cultural forms are emerging. Thus, in three Russian cities it has been observed that while there is a consumption of Western cultural forms, there is also a distinct consumption of local programs that have remained impervious to global intrusions (Volkova 2000). Similar forms of local production have been observed in Portugal. Globalization is said also to have accentuated local differences in music. For instance, there are some local expressions of hip-hop in the German cultural scene.

In the case of television, it has been found that in Russia the channels are presenting inexpensive programming imported from Europe and the United States, soap operas from Latin America, and "Bollywood" Indian films. Russian television programs have incorporated new formats, such as the game show, the talk show, crime docudramas, and the situation comedy, redefining the structure of Russian television programs. However, it is also noted that the content of these forms—the linguistic and cultural materials that fill them out—"refer to a Soviet past and a turbulent, transitional present moment that are far from Western" (Heller 2000).

Examining the media in Japan, Martinez (1998) concludes that all their productions have home-grown roots, whether or not the technology or some of the formats came originally from external sources. Thus, Samurai dramas, Kabuki theater, medieval novels, modern fantasy fiction, Buddhist cartoons, and the comics industry are very interrelated. Martinez holds that most of the depiction of international cultures in Japan is actually elite culture, including the arts, opera, and ballet.

Other manifestation of the local in the view of some cultural critics is what they call the emergence of the Third World in the First World, noting the growing production of hybrid forms of music, culture, education, and popular culture in world cities such as New York, London, Los Angeles, and Chicago (Leonard 2001).

There are indeed local takes on global cultural symbols that are different from those intended. One example is the role that McDonald's restaurants played in South Africa before the end of apartheid, when they provided the only place where different races could share public space on an equal basis. Yet, despite some locally distinct manifestations, the majority of people in developing countries, both scholars and observers of their own society, maintain that the movement toward the creation of a *global* culture is stronger. This cultural globalization is being attained largely through the relentless export of U.S. production. In fact, it is now asserted that the dissemination of cultural values through the media has become more important than that through schooling (Fritzberg 2001).

The dissemination of cultural values through the media occurs through both explicit and underlying messages that make local cultures appear backward. Locally produced television in many countries is minimal, limited generally to news programs and comedy hours. Some programming, such as Latin American soap operas, are exchanged regionally. The rest originates mostly in First World countries, primarily the United States. *Who Wants to Be a Millionaire,* a television game show that is broadcast in the United States, the United Kingdom, Spain, and Italy, though seemingly adapted to national circumstances (in the questions asked), retains in great detail the original format, down to the way participants respond to equally banal questions and effect the same intense look when searching for answers.

Lull (2000) is certain that the rapid and massive development of communications technology and the simultaneous opening of borders through globalization cannot but affect the nature and meaning of culture. He sees a fusion of the near with the far, the traditional with the new, and the relatively unmediated with the multimediated communication, all of which create material and discursive worlds that transform life experience and reconfigure the meaning of cultural space. He sees also an undeniable link among what he calls the "global middle class," the product of a process that is creating superculures promoting new meanings of self-understanding, belonging, and identity.

In addition to those who prefer to emphasize the substantial local production and those who see the world as succumbing rapidly to dominant (usually American) norms, there are others who argue that there is no such thing as an American culture: "The American culture is an amalgam of influences and approaches from around the world. It is melded—consciously in many cases—into a social medium that allows individual freedoms and cultures to thrive" (Rothkopf 1997, 4). Such a position incorrectly denies what many other observers perceive as a distinct influence on those cultures.

KNOWLEDGE MANAGEMENT SYSTEMS

With the constant improvements and widespread use of computer-mediated technologies such as e-mail and the Web has come the expectation that information and its more complex articulation—knowledge—will become increasingly accessible, designed to meet the needs of specific social sectors and decisions makers and thus become a major enabling force to improve public policies in most social and scientific fields. An increasingly common strategy to facilitate access to reliable and timely information is the deployment of knowledge management systems, commonly known as KMS.[8] Typically, a KMS seeks to select existing knowledge and information on a given subject, reduce and synthesize its content into manageable text, attach to it key descriptive categories for future location and cross-reference, and then make it available through the Internet to KMS subscribers.

Knowledge management systems are being developed in all types of organizations, ranging from business firms to international bureaucracies. Among the development assistance organizations, the World Bank is playing a leading role since KMS is considered a main pillar in its "Strategic Compact," initiated in 1997, which will make the World Bank a "knowledge bank," the main product of which will be advice to developing countries. This is intended to make the Bank become "the world's premier resource of all development knowledge by the year 2000, whether it be the Bank's advice or expertise from another organization" (World Bank, cited in Stromquist and Samoff 2000, 325). Other international agencies, such as the Organization for Economic Cooperation and Development (OECD), USAID, the Department for International Development (DFID; United Kingdom), and the Norwegian Development Agency (NORAD), are engaging in the development of similar systems.

Those who see great potential to Internet communication believe that a knowledge-based economy will give birth to a world without experts or leaders by promoting instead the creation of working groups without hierarchies in which everyone contributes more or less equally to the solution of complex problems. That prospect, which presents a strategy for rapidly closing the development gap, is especially attractive to the world's poorest countries. Echoing the sentiments of several African scholars, Adesida maintains that the current "information and knowledge revolutions offer Africa a real chance to achieve its own vision of the future" (cited in Stromquist and Samoff 2000, 325). A major promise is that knowledge will reach marginal groups who cannot afford to conduct their own research and that these groups themselves can become more active in the participation of knowledge generation via less expensive forms of collaboration. Another important promise is that as clients become more heterogeneous, there will arise a need to develop collective ways of producing knowledge. This collaboration is expected to bring together actors from both the South and the North. Within countries, the new knowledge is expected to promote greater cooperation among TNCs, universities, communities, and marginalized groups. The scenario anticipated by those who endorse KMS is that these alliances will cut across social classes, cultures, and disciplines.

Large international assistance agencies already engage in significant dissemination of hard-copy (i.e., paper-based) documentation of their products addressing issues of national development across many disciplines. A case in point is the World Bank, whose documents have worldwide distribution. Its annual *World Development Report* alone is printed in about 150,000 copies and widely distributed; moreover, it is free of charge for governments in developing countries.

While relying on computer assistance for the development and dissemination of existing research and "best practices" lessons of a variety of organizations, KMS are no more neutral or objective than the authors who produced the studies in the first place. In fact, KMS may end up reflecting particular biases about the area in which they work because they imply a selection and data reduction process of enormous scope. Knowledge management systems depend on a manager to administer the input and output of knowledge and information. On this person or small team fall the tasks of selecting the knowledge deemed valuable, synthesizing it to "weed out material that has become obsolete," and creating the most relevant "knowledge classification schemes," according to the American Productivity and Quality Center (APQC), one of the major firms engaged in the development of KMS.

As one might expect, the KMS innovation is predicated on the utilization of what is deemed to be "quality research." Unfortunately, what constitutes quality research is determined by those who organize the system. If in the North, it is likely that the studies that so qualify will be those published in refereed journals in industrialized countries. These outlets disadvantage scholars for whom refereed journals are expensive and mostly inaccessible. It is likely also that KMS will privilege standards of science particular to the North and topics considered of importance to the North. Large, controlled sample surveys will be considered more reliable sources of knowledge than individually conducted cases studies, which in turn will be considered more reliable sources of knowledge than local folkways and customs. Parker (2000) observes that the World Bank's recommendations expressed in its *Knowledge for Development* report consider mostly the development of Western knowledge, and although it calls on developing countries to "explore all the means available of acquiring knowledge from abroad and creating it locally" (World Bank 1999c, 145), in fact the definition of "local knowledge" refers to the "local creation of centers of Western expertise, not the development of strategies for the fostering or recovering of 'other' knowledge" (5). Ironically, the collection of "indigenous knowledge" may end up marginalizing indigenous researchers.

A feature of KMS is its tendency to reduce large amounts of text to short summaries. This approach is based on the argument that policymakers have neither the time nor the inclination to read long studies. But the abbreviation of detailed research on a complex issue reduces the phenomenon to inadequacy, rendering it too abstract and fragmented to understand its real features or applicability to other settings. Although the new synthesis may be cross-indexed in ways that allow fast retrieval of sources through the use of key words, the text that is accessed may be too brief and decontextualized to qualify as "knowledge." The APQC and other consulting firms promoting KMS argue that there exist such things as "just-in-time knowledge" and "just-enough knowledge."

This point brings to mind the difference between information and knowledge. It has been remarked that some agencies, such the OECD and the World Bank, tend to conflate the two (Roberts 2000). Information can be construed as pieces of data about a given phenomenon. Knowledge is a more complex ordering of that information into a dense network that must include the contextual factors in which the phenomenon arise plus an understanding of how and when any or all of the constituent information may apply to different situations. Knowledge thus implies an understanding of how certain factors characterizing the phenomenon interact with other factors/variables and an awareness of the possible consequences of applying (or not) the information to action. A useful elaboration of the distinction between knowledge and information is provided by Roberts (2000):

> Knowledge implies depth and breadth in understanding, rather than a mere acknowledgment of the presence of information or the ability to make information circulate. Information "moves about"—in flows and relays—in the

contemporary world in a myriad of contexts: as part of global systems of trade, within political circles, in school classrooms, among government departments, between chat groups on the Internet, and so on. Moving into the realm of knowledge involves asking questions of information, disrupting its flows (from time to time, where possible) and trying to historicise it and place it in its appropriate social and political and cultural contexts. (447)

Will the availability of information on the Internet create the knowledge KMS predicts? It is highly probable that it will not. It is also likely, however, that it will produce the illusion not only that its information constitutes knowledge but also that it is precise, complete, and unbiased. Moreover, it is not certain that all information and knowledge conveyed by KMS setups will be accessible to important actors. Privatization in education, as we have seen in earlier sections of this book, is growing rapidly and is based on profits and competition. It is thus to be expected that some information and knowledge will become secret in order to protect the competitive advantage of the companies that produce it and that some will become for-sale commodities. By 1997, the private sector owned 78 percent of all databases, greatly up from a share of 22 percent in 1977 (David 2000, 32).

In addition to the problem that the content of the knowledge and information is dependent on Northern perspectives, its distribution is likely to foster a centralized rather than decentralized system of information. While KMS promises rapid and nearly unlimited access to knowledge, in practice it will favor those wired to the Internet and with Web access. Since the World Bank's KMS already has a head start over other institutions, especially national institutions in the developing world, users will increasingly rely on the World Bank system, and some will discard, or not learn about, alternative sources of educational knowledge.

The most recent knowledge-related World Bank initiative, the Global Development Gateway (GDG), is a very ambitious, broad-reaching, and well-funded effort (U.S.$69.5 million during three years) to improve and expand its current KMS. It is expected to become fully operational in 2003; according to World Bank sources, the GDG will provide "development knowledge and development solutions worldwide." The centralized determination of what constitutes knowledge entrenches the role of elite education and research institutions, nearly all located in the most affluent countries. A token number of scholars and institutions in poor countries will be integrated into official knowledge generation and management, primarily through studies and research at or associated with those elite institutions. But, with few exceptions, they will remain junior partners in this effort or serve as commentators and interpreters.

The technology on which the storage, manipulation, and dissemination of KMS relies will also remain a limiting factor for the developing countries.

While the current technology may become increasingly available to poor countries, that technology (hardware and software) will continue to be developed and refined under the control of the more affluent countries. In 1993, ten countries accounted for 84 percent of global research and development and controlled 95 percent of the U.S. patents of the past two decades (United Nations Development Program 1999a). Each new increment of communications or database development requires ever faster processors, more memory, larger data storage capacities, more rapid access to distant computers, and more complex operating systems and applications software, further distancing developing countries from access.

The KMS innovation assumes that it is possible to develop knowledge that is exclusively technical (as opposed to political). A key document by the World Bank (1999b) distinguishes between knowledge about technology (which it calls technical knowledge, or "know-how") from knowledge about attributes (which is said to refer to evaluation about things, such as the quality of a product or the credit worthiness of a firm). The World Bank document calls the uneven distribution of know-how "knowledge gaps" but calls the difficulties from inadequate knowledge about attributes "information problems." But ongoing experiences with information and knowledge exchanges, particularly in the field of education, show the political nature of the dialogues. Several virtual seminars sponsored by agencies such as the World Bank reflect how the organizing agency has the power to filter the information and decide what is circulated as part of the dialogue and what is not. Comments made by participants in these virtual seminars are not automatically disseminated but go first to the central coordinator, who may then abbreviate them as needed and post them (or not). This coordinator can eliminate unwanted comments simply by declaring them "beyond the scope" of the seminar.

In a larger context, KMS may end up driving away any knowledge that is considered humanistic or critical. Some institutions that have and aspire to have a greater hegemonic role in the control of knowledge tend to play down the politics of knowledge. Parker (2000) observes that in addressing social or political conflicts of interests regarding dams and forestry projects, the World Bank reinterprets them as resulting from "lack of complete knowledge" (4). Parker further notes that the World Bank's recommendations expressed in its *Knowledge for Development* report (World Bank 1999c) consider mostly the development of Western knowledge, and although the Bank calls on developing countries to "explore all the means available of acquiring knowledge from abroad and creating it locally" (145), in fact the definition of "local knowledge" refers to the "local creation of centers of Western expertise, not the development of strategies for the fostering or recovering of 'other' knowledge" (Parker 2000, 5).

The politics of knowledge is concerned with the relationship between knowledge and power. This requires understanding the social, political, and cultural contexts under which knowledge is produced. Any politics of knowledge addresses such questions as, Whose knowledge? For what purpose? In what contexts? (Parker 2000).

Research in contemporary culture makes sense only when it is rooted in a social theory or historical perspective that treats the present as a historical problem (Woodward 1980, xxvi). Yet several large organizations engage in simplistic productions of knowledge, often to present evidence justifying their own beliefs. Such dubious contentions have been offered in explanations for the failure of Argentina and the success of several eastern Asian countries in their economic performance. One version places all the blame for Argentina's problems on its failure to follow neoliberal policies: While being among the most prosperous in the world at the beginning of the twentieth century, Argentina has now fallen behind as a result of tariff protection, state regulations, domestic ownership requirements, and paternalistic labor laws, all of which contributed to isolate this country from the world economy (Aghion et al. 2000, 18).

In contrast, it can be argued that the Argentine reality is more complex: It includes the role of the military in forcing a repressive rule, an exploitative oligarchy that failed to see the need to develop industrial resources, a state bureaucracy that preyed on business through corruption, the decay of the Atlantic trade, and the world position of Argentina away from the centers of power.

The KMS style of knowledge production includes also that which attributes enormous and autonomous powers to formal education. This tendency has prevailed in many accounts by the World Bank and others to explain the economic growth of Hong Kong, Taiwan, Singapore, South Korea, and China. Relying on the Schumpeterian approach to global growth, which is based on the diffusion of technological knowledge from richer to poorer countries, it is often concluded that the eastern Asian economies had in common their willingness and ability to absorb and adopt new technologies. In these accounts, cast aside are the role of the state in protecting incipient industries and subsidizing them through various periods in their development and the role of historical and political forces in helping countries in proximity to previous communist China succeed through the use of the capitalist model.

IN BALANCE

A main source of technological progress in communications resides in innovation in the creation of new products, new management approaches, and a new organization of production. But these innovations are never devoid of content or free of intentionality. Media are not neutral, and ownership of media influences the nature of the messages (Chomsky, cited in Wilson et al. 1998).

The power of the media as a shaper of cultural norms has grown substantially under current globalization processes. Between 1987 and 1996, the information industry in the United States (which sells its products abroad) grew at almost twice the rate of the overall economy as measured by gross domestic product. Most of this growth has occurred in advertising, movies, cable television, and music (Compaine and Gomery 2000). This media production is also known to be immediate and emotional, characteristics that do not foster critical thought.

The impact of mass media technologies on cultural norms and representations reaches so deeply that educational systems can no longer ignore this parallel form of "education." Some of it is positive, yet negative formulations are also present. Through the increasing presence of new communication technologies, we are experiencing a moment of great creativity in which new forms of conveying ideas and images are in constant effervescence but also a time of contradictions and tensions. Globalization is promoting the homogenization of cultural values and forms of expressions. It also creates instances of specific local and regional responses with change occurring at every level. Several observers fear that globalization has been successful in introducing uniformity of thought inclined toward consumerism and individualism, a process greatly assisted by the use of global media and the increasing concentration of decisions on programming by a few media firms.

The increased concentration of the ability to shape cultural programs in a few corporations could be taken simply as a sign of the times in which the most efficient firms will impose themselves. From another perspective, this concentration raises concerns when we realize that the content of these programs may be guided more by the notion of quick and shallow entertainment than by the development of solidaristic and thinking spirits.

With the enormous potential of communication technologies in terms of speed and access, some undue connections are being made between technology application and knowledge production. In the elaboration of these linkages, the views and power of the North in defining what is worth knowing seems at present to prevail. It remains to be seen how forms of local expression or local appropriation of global messages may lead to forms of communication and knowledge that in the end may produce more egalitarian norms and practices throughout the world.

NOTES

1. It is estimated that the average American watches 3,000 discrete television advertisements per day. Ads are an effective way of distributing information about new products, but they are also powerful shapers of needs and wants.

2. In all these transformations, it is apparent that there is still little importance given to the media reporting of education, an area so central to the production of cultural identities and representations. A survey in 1986 of U.S. daily newspapers found that 250 of the 1,730 such newspapers had an educational reporter or editor; some of these reporters were not trained in education, and two-thirds have not even taken a single course in education (Wells, cited in Lieberman 1993). This indicates that important educational phenomena may not be adequately captured and that what is captured may not be adequately examined.

3. To enforce policies of cultural protection, the instrument of choice is not tariff but rather subsidies, taxes, and quotas.

4. "Indigenous" is not a unified category. They can belong to one or more of the following political types: those who are distinct along racial and ethnic lines from the ruling majority of the country (e.g., peoples in certain parts of the United States, the former Soviet Union, Asia, and South America), a majority that is ruled by a colonial minority (e.g., South Africa under apartheid), or those residing in countries whose population and government are largely indigenous (e.g., Africa and Papua New Guinea) (Barkan 2000, 164).

5. Another major influence on young people, and decidedly a negative one given the dominance of violence embedded in the scripts, are interactive video games. These games, targeted at teenagers, are said to be influencing movies and fashions (*San Jose Mercury News,* 2001).

6. It must be remembered that the Internet is far from universally available, even in U.S. schools. In 1999, 95 percent of all public schools had Internet access, but in 37 percent of schools it existed as only a single installation (U.S. Department of Education 2000).

7. Critical studies scholars also remark that the relation between the global and the local is far from easy to pin down or analyze, as many international products and messages tend to be "domesticated," that is, fit to the local. Martinez (1998) states, for instance, that horse racing and horses have meanings that are different for the Japanese and the British. On a personal note, I remember watching a group of women in rural South Africa follow an episode of the television show *Dynasty*. They were clearly more intent on discussing the nature of the clothing and jewelry the characters were exhibiting than the plot.

8. This section relies on portions of two articles previously published by Samoff and Stromquist (2001) and Stromquist and Samoff (2000).

5

Transnational Corporations and the Creation of New Values and Citizenship

Globalization has brought with it an undeniable new actor, the transnational corporation (TNC).[1] Large and complex because of their economic success and influence, TNCs bring considerable change not only to the particular economic spheres in which they operate but also to other global milieus and down to their surrounding local environments. In examining TNCs, we see the connection between economic power and political influence and, in turn, the ability of this new power to shape education and culture. These connections create multiple consequences in their wake, some positive and some negative, for developing countries.

High levels of interdependence among nations have always existed, but today the intensity is far greater than one hundred or even ten years ago. Now that communications are so easy and inexpensive, financial transactions are so frequent that the global stock market never closes. The lower costs and increased capacity of telecommunications networks make it possible for accounting, engineering, research, software development, conferencing, and other services to be performed at distant locations. At the same time, the form that globalization has taken (crystalized in TNCs) and its speed of proliferation exceed the ability of national governments to create the necessary macroeconomic framework conditions for stabilizing world economic interrelationships (Messner 1999).

THE ECONOMIC POWER OF TNCS

Transnational corporations can be defined as firms (whether service, manufacture, or industry) with at least one production unit abroad (Mucchielli

1998). Some, such as Hirst and Thompson (cited in Harvey, ca. 2000), contend that the volume and openness of the world economy and the international movement of labor are not much greater than in the late nineteenth century. But most people can readily see that TNCs are significantly different actors. They have been growing rapidly: from 7,000 in 1970 to 37,000 at the beginning of the 1990s and to 44,000 with 280,000 foreign affiliates by 1996 (Malhotra 1997). Of the 100 largest economies in the world today, fifty-one are corporations and forty-nine nation-states.[2] Transnational corporations can be categorized in terms of foreign assets—value of investment abroad in financial terms—and in terms of the portion of production that is globalized, particularly in industry.

In 1990, each of 135 TNCs had sales in excess of U.S.$10 billion, while each of sixty countries had a gross national product (GNP) of less than U.S.$10 million. Today, 70 percent of all foreign direct investment is made by the top 300 TNCs, and 25 percent of all capital is held by them. The global reach of these firms is pervasive. IBM and ICI rely on foreign sales for over half their revenue. Nestlé, the most extreme example, has 98 percent of its sales outside its Switzerland headquarters (Harvey, ca. 2000). Eighty-two percent of TNCs are in industrialized countries, and one-fifth of their employees (totaling fifteen million in 1990) were in developing countries (Malhotra 1997). Table 5.1 shows the top ten TNCs in terms of foreign assets by industry. (See appendix A for a list of the 100 largest economies in the world and the profit trends among the top 200 TNCs.)

In reaction to complaints about the economic power wielded by TNCs, some argue that these corporations create jobs and wealth and have provided consumers with a much wider array of goods and services. Undeniably, economies are more active with the presence of TNCs than without

Table 5.1.   Top Ten Transnational Corporations by Foreign Assets, 1996

Ranking	Corporation	Country	Industry
1	General Electric	United States	Electronics
2	Shell Royal Dutch	United States/Netherlands	Petroleum
3	Ford Motor Company	United States	Automotive
4	Exxon Corp.	United States	Petroleum
5	General Motors	United States	Automotive
6	IBM	United States	Computers
7	Toyota	Japan	Automotive
8	Volkswagen	Germany	Automotive
9	Mitsubishi Corp.	Japan	Diversified
10	Mobil Corp.	United States	Petroleum

Note: Data from the UNCTAD.
Source: Van Reisen 1999, 241.

them. Yet as profit-seeking businesses, TNCs are imbued with an overriding concern for growth and the bottom line, leaving little room for sensitivity to social justice. Multinational capitalism has become dominant and has brought with it the logic of capitalist economics in its neoliberal form and the consequent ascendancy of markets, free initiative, a minimal state, and strengthening of lifestyles predicated on individualism and consumerism, with little sense of compassion and solidarity among nations (Santos 1995). At the most basic level, TNCs contribute to the maintenance of poverty via very low wages (Townsend 1993).

More than half the sales of the top 200 TNCs are in four economic sectors: financial services (14.5 percent), motor vehicles and parts (12.7 percent), insurance (12.4 percent), and retailing/wholesaling (11.3 percent) (Anderson and Cavanagh 2000). Industries in which TNCs are involved are primarily food and beverages, chemicals, electronics, oil, and telecommunications (Harvey, ca. 2000).

Transnational corporations function in the global economy in two main ways: They either invest domestically and export the goods (typical of Japanese firms until recently) or produce and distribute abroad directly (a practice typical of U.S. business) (Salt et al. 2000). The latter practice tends to create unemployment at lower levels of education in core countries and thus generates some resistance by affected groups in those countries.[3]

Rauch (2001) maintains that there is now a "New Old Economy" characterized by a positive feedback process. Unlike the negative feedback economy, which reportedly was bounded by short-term constraints of supply and demand, the positive feedback economy relies on information and new technologies that have generated an "avalanche" in productivity. Rauch's key point is that there have been a series of "interlocking technologies that have improved incrementally, but [have nonetheless produced a] revolutionary effect" (44).

This "revolutionary effect" can be seen in the extraordinary concentration of wealth. Statistics capture important conditions of distribution: The top 200 companies have twice the assets of 80 percent of the world's people, and 70 percent of global trade is estimated to be controlled by 500 TNCs (Malhotra 1998). According to the United Nations, the top 200 TNCs have wealth equivalent to 28.3 percent of the world's GNP, while 150 developing countries constitute 24.5 percent of the same GNP. A fundamental fact associated with this concentration of wealth is that five core countries alone[4] (the United States, Germany, Japan, France, and the United Kingdom) represent about 90 percent of the ownership of those 200 companies.[5] Sales by TNCs exceed world exports by a growing margin, and 85 percent of trade is within TNCs (Annan 2000), giving these firms enormous economic decision-making power.

INVESTMENT IN DEVELOPING COUNTRIES

Because of concern that international investors may have little interest in the Third World, the World Bank was created in 1945 to provide developing countries with access to foreign capital. Now this situation has changed, but in a perverse way. Today, private direct investment, or foreign direct investment (FDI), is unquestionably the major source of foreign capital. As a percentage of the world's gross fixed capital formation, FDI has nearly doubled since the beginning of the 1980s, with FDI contracts providing most of the capital and skills in technology and management.

Those in favor of economic globalization see FDI as a way to enable local workers to benefit from the know-how of foreign companies and learn though practical experience how to become efficient managers and entrepreneurs; they also see FDI as enabling local companies to learn by observing at close range how a successful company competes in the global economy (Aghion et al. 2000). But there are more critical views of FDI. Since FDI follows the potential for profit, it is far from evenly distributed. The United States is the greatest recipient of foreign investments, at U.S.$230 billion in 1999. In the developing world, Chile receives about U.S.$333 per capita, but a country such as South Africa, which is by far one of the most industrialized African countries, receives only U.S.$31 per capita (*The Economist,* 2001). Most of the FDI investment comes from the European Union, Japan, and the United States, and 60 percent of it goes to five countries: China, Brazil, Singapore, Mexico, and Indonesia (Van Reisen 1999). A region undergoing economic and social crisis such as sub-Saharan Africa, in which the average annual per capita income is about U.S.$500, attracts a very limited share of global flows. In 1996, thirty-three sub-Saharan countries received only 3 percent of the world total of U.S.$244 billion in direct loans. Unable to generate substantial income, several countries in this region have outstanding external debts often in excess of their entire GNP. Further, some countries in the region are experiencing huge capital flights. In contrast, Asia receives almost twenty times more FDI than sub-Saharan Africa (Annan 2000, 39).

Sen (2001) identifies two major revolutions in the globalized world of today: the information revolution and the biotechnology revolution. Expanding on the importance of information, Sassen (1999) asserts that with the greater speed of communications, the temporality of global finance has shrunk to one minute.[6] Indeed, cross-border sales of equities and bonds in the United States, according to several accounts, have exploded from being the equivalent of 3 percent of the U.S. gross domestic product (GDP) in 1970 to 136 percent in 1995.

There is almost no national economy that is not part of the global market, a condition that enables people to speak of the economy as "integrated."

However, this linkage is occurring primarily through unregulated global finance markets that do not show much coherence of purpose and that leave certain population groups outside the potential benefits. Foreign exchange transactions involved more than U.S.$1.5 trillion a day in 1999, 100 times more than the U.S.$15 billion a day in 1973, the year when the regime of fixed exchange rates collapsed (Annan 2000).

A further, crucial development is in the nature of the financial flows. In the early 1900s, 10 percent of the circulating capital in the world was of a speculative nature; today, it is more than 95 percent (Quebec Network on Continental Integration 2001). The interlinking of several service sectors behind some financial flows has major implications for the ability of the states to manage what is going on (Sen 2001). The emergence of giant firms has transformed the rules of the economic game. Not only have new players appeared with substantial unchecked power—TNC executives, bankers, financiers, speculators, and investors—but there has developed a great volatility within international capital markets since 70 percent of cross-border capital investments last less than one week (Messner 1999).

TNCS AND THE STATE

Navigating through the relations between TNCs and the state on our way to examining the connections between TNCs and education, it can be seen that TNCs behave in an ambivalent way toward the state.

Often, TNCs, through the various information and lobbying mechanisms at their disposal, question the performance of the state. The state is accused of tight controls and inefficient management, resulting in restrictive trade barriers and poor delivery of public services. It is accused also of widespread corruption (Annan 2000). Such criticisms pave the way for the TNCs to argue later that the state should not engage in any activity affecting production and that such activity should be entirely in private hands. This attack is extended to various institutions supported by the state, such as the public schools and universities. Researchers closely following the work of TNCs note that

> unimaginable billions of tax-deductible corporate dollars still gurgle through corporate public relations, advertising and law firms. Radio, television, magazine, and movie corporations keep selling their relentless message: Corporations: efficient, good. Government: wasteful, bad. Giant corporations bully and browbeat. They denounce people like you and us as Luddites, Commies, tree huggers and 1960s leftovers. They homogenize people into consumers. They turn life into corporate parks. (Corporate Watch, ca. 2000, 2)

In addition, TNCs often play states against each other in order to gain financial advantage. Large transnational firms obviously have advantages over

single-nation rivals, such as the ability to have access to reduced labor costs
in different parts of the world and to engage in transfer pricing practices that
benefit TNCs greatly. In 1999, Brazil's President Fernando Henrique Cardoso, under pressure to attract U.S.$50 million in foreign investment,
declared a ten-year moratorium on penalty fees for environmental crimes
(International Forum on Globalization 1999). Observers note that malprac-
tice by TNCs is protected by their remarkable invisibility (Salt et al. 2000).

But most often, the TNCs have need of the state, be it at home or abroad
(Ball 1998; Pannu 1996). Japanese companies, for instance, are protected
by their own government, which frees them of many of the legal, consumer, media, shareholder, and regulatory threats faced by their counter-
parts overseas (Magnier 2000). In developing countries, TNCs (and thus
globalization dynamics) require a strong nation-state to provide the stability required to attract economic investment; they need also a state with a
national political leadership willing to privatize ownership. Further, they
need the state to create inducements, such as labor laws (cheap wages)
and financial agreements (primarily low taxation), that are favorable to the
TNCs. Corporate entitlements are granted by Third World states, usually in
the form of low-interest loans, export incentives, land grants, and subsidies
for plant construction, infrastructure development, and research and development. As Thurow (1980) summarizes, "Multinationals need low
wages, stable governments, and educated labor forces to establish facilities
that can compete with those in the U.S." (92). All this is often accompanied
by sharp reductions in transfers in the form of social services to wage and
salaried people (Petras 1999).

Some countries have attempted, generally without success, to impose restrictions on foreign ownerships of certain key national resources, such as
the media, defense industries, or certain financial institutions, as well as regulatory standard-setting in matters such as accounting, safety, and environmental impacts (Holton 1997). A strong sign of the TNCs' continued reliance
on the state is the location of ninety-four of the top 200 TNC "government relations" offices within a few blocks of the lobbying target of the world: the
U.S. Congress in Washington, D.C. (Anderson and Cavanagh 2000).

Capitalism is operating at a higher degree of global coordination, centralization, and systematization than in the 1920s, when Keynesian paradigms
were at work (Bamyeh 2000). In the current process, states from central
countries play a major role. The main beneficiaries of the market-opening
policies of the major multilateral development institutions (which tend to be
dominated by the large core countries) over the past fifteen years have been
large corporations, especially the top 200 (Anderson and Cavanagh 2000). In
fact, lending policies of the World Bank and the International Monetary Fund
(IMF) have established the regulatory groundwork for TNCs to enter the
economy of many developing countries, thereby securing TNC access to re-

sources and the capability to export them back home with minimal restrictions (Menotti 2000). According to Shiva (2001), the support of the World Bank and the IMF was instrumental in opening the agricultural market in India to TNCs; as a condition for getting loans, her country had to agree to open its seed market.

In some cases, there are visible examples of collusion between TNCs and states, particularly when it comes to the exploitation of natural resources. A case in point is offered by Colombia, a country in which Occidental Petroleum Company and the Colombian government have allied against the U'wa people—a small community in northern Colombia where half the nation's proven oil resources lie. In exchange for rights to these resources, Occidental lobbied in the United States for military aid to Colombia, assistance that was granted in 2000 in the amount of U.S.$1.3 billion (Wirpsa 2001).

Although TNCs unquestionably need the state to create stable conditions for the market, it is also the case that much of the international trade occurs outside the "free" market. The classical theory of comparative advantage based on differences in relative prices and its neoclassical version based on particular endowments enjoyed by nations assume the existence of free-market prices. But TNCs, through their dense network of relations, facilitated by their numerous branches in many countries, determine transfer prices as well as prices negotiated in contractual arrangements that are not free-market prices but rather the product of oligopolistic arrangements between large firms.[7]

At present, 1 percent of TNCs accounts for 50 percent of world FDI (Malhotra 1998). Therefore, trade that is embedded within FDI does not reflect free-market dynamics, either. Today, trade is an integral part of a firm's investment decisions, marketing strategies, and research-and-development goals. In consequence, "individual countries achieve competitive advantage not from their natural resource endowments, but based on how well their institutional structure fits into the goals of transnational firms" (Champlin and Olson 1999, 4).

From this discussion, it can be seen that the state is not disappearing as speculated by some but rather is taking on new forms in the context of rapid international transfers of capital and to a lesser extent of labor. The most rapidly mobile of corporations depend on the apparatus of the nation-state to guarantee their property and contracts. As Tsing (2000) observes, national deregulation—one of the key tenets of current globalization—creates new regulations in the economic terrain in the interest of global capital.

Research and statistics have illuminated many of the activities conducted by TNCs. However, much also remains to be known about how economic elites and their transnational agencies in the First World interact and make decisions affecting the Third World. The need to focus on dominant social subjects for the complete understanding of social dynamics is not new, but it continues to be very difficult to study, mostly because of the reluctance of such subjects to become available for examination.

DISREGARD FOR SOCIAL ISSUES

Transnational corporations can have an enormous impact on human rights through their employment practices, environmental practices, support of corrupt regimes, and direct advocacy for policy changes. Again, however, under conditions of economic competitiveness and search for profits, there is little evidence of positive impact among these areas.

While the available data are far from exhaustive, there are strong indications of "misbehavior" by TNCs. Civic groups constituted to protect the environment point to the rapid spread of environmental damage, particularly deforestation and pollution, a direct consequence of export-oriented policies imposed by the World Bank and the IMF, affirms Victor Menotti, director of the Environmental Program at the International Forum on Globalization, a nongovernmental organization (NGO) monitoring various developments under globalization (International Forum on Globalization 1999).

Other critics of TNCs propose the use of global public agencies to oversee their actions. But these requests are contested. Nike, a well-known corporation that manufactures sports shoes and clothes, opposed the work of the Worker Rights Consortium (WRC), which conducts an independent monitoring activity endorsed by union and human rights groups of TNC production practices. It cut their support of funds to the University of Oregon, Brown University, and the University of Michigan after they joined the WRC. Nike changed its position only after becoming the object of considerable public pressure. At one time, the United Nations had its Center on Transnational Corporations (UNCTC), which carried out research on corporations. Not surprisingly, the TNCs were hostile to it. In 1993, the UNCTC was dismantled as part of a "reorganization," and the UN Commission on Trade and Development (UNCTAD) became the new UN focal point for work on TNCs. UNCTAD does not, however, address the regulation of TNC activities; it works primarily to stimulate foreign investment flows to the Third World. The drafting of a code of conduct on TNCs that was being conducted by UNCTC ceased with its demise.

Since TNCs see no need for a social pact between workers and employers or, rather, actively avoid such a pact, there is a widening rift between groups who have the skills and mobility to flourish in global markets and those who do not. As the provision of social insurance diminishes in developing countries, the disparities between professional and unskilled members of the labor force have increased.

CHANGING THE NATURE OF THE STATE

In the past, states drew much of their financial resources from taxation. The contemporary tax systems that we know developed following World War II, when cross-border movement in goods, capital, and labor was small. But now that firms and people are more mobile, they can exploit the tax differences between countries and in some cases avoid taxation altogether.

Multinational firms typically design their products in one country, manufacture in another, and sell in a third. This gives them broad opportunities to reduce tax bills by shifting operations internationally or by ingenious transfer pricing. By paying inflated prices for components imported from a subsidiary in a low-tax country, a firm can move its taxable profits to that country and so reduce its tax bill. Not surprisingly, the contributions by TNCs to the national treasury of the countries in which they operate have reduced considerably, even in the core country that serves as TNC headquarters.[8] Thus, prior to World War II, U.S. corporate taxes accounted for one-third of total federal tax revenues and represented a proportion greater than the personal income tax. Now they account for only 12 percent, or about a quarter as much as personal tax. A similar pattern obtains in other industrialized countries. In the European Union, the average rate of taxation on income from capital (which includes TNCs) and self-employed labor fell from almost 50 percent in 1981 to 35 percent in 1994. Personal income taxes have become by far the most important source of government revenue in all rich economies. No doubt, the globalized nature of TNCs limits the ability of any nation to check the accuracy of the profits they report. In 1970, a typical large U.S. firm earned 10 to 20 percent of its income abroad; now this proportion is about 50 percent.

Three supranational institutions give evidence of the growing power of TNCs. The first is the World Economic Forum, which brings together the world's leading politicians, chief executives (only those occupying the first or second position in companies with a minimum turnover of 620 million euros), scientific experts, and other major figures of the economic and political world. The World Economic Forum has been meeting in Davos, Switzerland, since 1971. It discusses issues such a high technology, micro- and macroeconomics, and various crises; thus, it is widely considered to set economic policy informally (Quebec Network on Continental Integration 2001).

The second body is the International Chamber of Commerce (ICC), an organization that represents primarily the interests of the largest transnational corporations. In the past, it lobbied in favor of global economic deregulation with the World Trade Organization (WTO), the G-7, and the Organization for Economic Cooperation and Development (OECD); at present, it is lobbying with the United Nations. The ICC president is said to have stated that "business is not just another pressure group but a resource that will help governments set the right rules."

The third organization, and certainly the most powerful of the set, is the WTO. Its critics maintain that it is emerging as the world's first global government despite the fact that it was elected by no one, it operates in secrecy, and its agenda tends to alter the constitutional rights of sovereign states. The WTO has been seeking approval of the Multilateral Agreement on Investment (MAI), a proposal that will introduce a new set of rules for international capital flows, giving TNCs the right to overturn national laws and even sue national governments under some circumstances (Sen 2001).

The WTO in several ways already allows countries to challenge on behalf of their corporations other countries' national or local laws. In short, corporations are being endowed with the rights of persons and will emerge as new global citizens. If a law impedes trade, the offending nation must eliminate the law or face severe economic penalties. So far, in every case in which corporations have challenged environmental or public safety laws, the WTO has ruled in favor of the corporation. In view of the simultaneous developments affecting the community of TNCs, their record of success in dealing with obstacles, and the enormous impact of their actions, it is correct to conclude that "the organization of the transnational economy creates differences of class, power, and value that forge subaltern and dominant social niches of identity and agency" (Tsing 2000, 12). The WTO's next agenda item is privatization of public services, including education, health, welfare, social housing, and transport. An important WTO priority is also trade-related aspects of intellectual property rights (TRIPS). This mechanism would oblige countries to enforce patents on food and drugs, including those for AIDS, which would have the effect of making such products very expensive.[9]

TNCS AND WORLD CITIES

While the common discourse of TNCs invokes the virtues of decentralization and deterritorialization of management operations, this appeal obscures the material requirements for global communication—telephone and computer connections and the specialized labor of advertising, finance, and other services—all of which are demonstrably concentrated in particular cities. The mobility of information, capital, products, and production facilities depends on these coordinating centers, which have become known in social science literature as "global cities" and, more recently, "world cities." World cities have developed through the presence of TNCs in their physical environment and are defined as the "control and command centers through which multinational corporations organize their global production" (Taylor 2001b: 2). They comprise multiple office networks of corporate service firms and are characterized by a network of corporate boards linked together through overlapping directorships (Taylor 2001a). In particular, these cities have become "centers for the production and consumption of the advanced services in the organization of global capital" (Taylor 2001a: 3; see also Castells 1996).

Research being conducted by the Globalization and World Cities Study Group and Network (a real and virtual organization established at Lough-borough University in the United Kingdom) is of particular relevance. These scholars maintain that global firms select world cities for their location. A study based on sixty-nine firms (five in accountancy, fourteen in advertising, eleven in banking/financing, and thirty-nine in law) found substantial degrees of concentration in some cities (although this concentration varied by field, with accountancy being the largest) and a great degree of articulation among them. Many such cities do extend their economies to the world economy, while in others a more regional strategy is at work (Taylor et al. 2001a). An implication of regional networking is that the needs of TNCs may call for intense homogenization of the educational system at that level.

World city networks stand in stark contrast to previous social networks co-ordinated by states. While governments operate as key agents in their network production and reproduction, world cities are characterized by the behavior of firms within and across cities. This crucial distinction means that the "world city network formation is more an outcome of global corporate decisions than the collective works of urban policy makers" (Taylor 2001a, 2). Under globalized economic situations, then, TNCs are emerging as somewhat autonomous and unquestioned political actors, greatly impacting many aspects of city governance, including schools.

All eight prime world cities are located in the most dynamic globalization arenas (Beaverstock et al. 2000). Under globalization, to a significant extent, instead of a set of sovereign states, a network of information flows with world cities dominates. Castells (1996) maintains that through this process, a global future of humanity is being actively constructed beyond the recall of "politicians," but, revealing a strong optimism, he affirms that this network of world cities is not beyond the control of "citizens."

A practice of TNCs with direct consequences for the educational system and for culture in general is the use of transient professional migrants to bring human capital and advanced technical knowledge to their operations either in the home country or in developing countries (Beaverstock and Boardwell 2001). In the United Kingdom, professional and managerial international immigration has become an important characteristic of its economy. Several geographers note that transient professional migration remains an invisible fact of globalization processes despite the fact that it is through this mechanism that world cities attain significant social and cultural influence in the world economy (Beaverstock and Boardwell 2001). Migration is often discussed as the collective product of individual mobility, but this movement, in turn, requires the creation of institutional ties linking sending and receiving areas. The process of migration is key to understanding the micro and macro linkages that emerge from globalization. These "flows" are movements made possible through political and economic channels (Tsing 2000).

Typically, TNCs have international officers who continually move on cross-border assignments to many countries. Through this migration, knowledge and expertise is transferred over space and time (Beaverstock and Boardwell 2001). As professionals come from other countries, they make demands on the public school system to accommodate the desired form and quality of their children's schooling. Furthermore, and crucial for the support of the professional elite in global cities, is the low-waged immigrant sector (Taylor 2001a). Thus, TNCs' decisions to attract highly trained professionals generates at the same time what might be a form of "globalization from below." This occurs through the migration of low-skilled workers as people with minimal income and job opportunities in their country of origin search for a better life in more developed economies. The presence of children of highly trained professionals, combined with the increased presence of children of low-skilled families, generates substantial challenges for the educational systems of world cities.

As TNCs plan for production, trade, financial transactions, and technological transfers and use strategies such as commercial agreements, economic blocs, and regional integration, they create a new territorial division of labor on a global scale (De Oliveira 1996). The restructuring of the economy thus leads not only to a reallocation of power among different geographic scales but also to new structures of power. Cities are becoming major sites for global governance. Their mayors and other significant political actors, with an eye to this potential, are carefully and constantly trying to ally themselves with network capital, offering possible investors many financial, infrastructural, and education incentives.

It is crucial to observe that no matter how far a global economic system seeks to disperse, it will still contain within it the enormously powerful and shaping dynamics of centralized control, centralized management, centralized property, and centralized appropriation, not only of profits but also of a wide array of externalities (Sassen 1999). Corporations cannot be placeless; on the contrary, they maintain the national characteristics of their base despite global expansion (Beaverstock et al. 2000; Sassen 1999). The new global spatiality also has temporal dimensions, given the access that firms have to instantaneous communications. In some respects, the space of the global networks of cities overrides the older constitutions of territory, that is, the nation-states. The North–South divide between countries is still an important duality, but TNCs create multiple centers. This leads Fossaert (2001) to conclude that the world can no longer be represented by a center and a periphery but rather by regional systems in which world cities play a major role.

As world cities become "disembedded" from their old nation-state, they have been noted to produce with other such cities a new "network governance regime" (Fossaert 2001; Taylor 2001a). They have been noted as well to create internal differentiation within the cities as power, based on hierarchy and regionality, is drawn from different subsections of the world city network (De Oliveira 1996; Taylor 2001b).

Tracing the pattern of business operations reveals that there are key services for which TNCs need cities to adapt knowledge to legal, fiscal, and various cultural contexts (Fossaert 2001). At present, these services include retail trade, finance, and telecommunications along with civil aviation, accounting, law, engineering, advertising, insurance, and health care. New targets in the future will be utilities (gas, water, and waste disposal), transportation (road, port, and airport operations), and education (Hufbauer and Warren 1999). Cities are at the vanguard of the globalization of services. Urban conglomerates such as London, Frankfurt, Hong Kong, and New York excel as providers of financial services because of a tradition of innovation among top firms (Hufbauer and Warren 1999). In law, there is the dominance of London, which accounts for 17 percent of all offices of U.S. law firms abroad; second is Hong Kong, outscoring both Tokyo and Singapore. New York is home for one-third of U.S. law firms having foreign offices. Other U.S. cities after New York are Washington, D.C., Chicago, and Los Angeles (Beaverstock et al. 2000). Interestingly, these locations have also operated as major terrains for the contestation and subsequent reform of public educational systems.

EMERGING CONNECTIONS BETWEEN TNCS AND THE EDUCATIONAL SYSTEM

As noted earlier, Thurow (1980) holds that "multinationals need low wages, stable governments, and *educated labor forces* to establish facilities that can compete with those in the U.S." (92; emphasis added). Thus, education becomes a concern to develop labor force competitiveness. Education acquires importance through the prevailing rhetoric that makes education the primary means to achieve social mobility.

The presence of professional elites in world cities leaves an imprint on the society they join, even if temporarily. Their influence on education, via demands on the public education system, is highly noticeable. World cities create in their wake a new host of social actors: In addition to the transnational class comprising TNC executives, there are globalizing state bureaucrats, politicians, professionals, and consumerist elites in merchandising and the media whose interests are global and who exert major influence on the world economy (Sklair 1996).

In the field of education, TNCs are playing an ambiguous but fundamental role: extolling the importance of education and supporting improved public schools while attacking the low quality of public education and calling for its replacement by private schools. The values of economic competitiveness and efficiency have permeated the schools since the industrial revolution, but what is new today is the strong intervention by business in public schools and their direct intervention as providers of educational services. Through their presence in world cities, TNCs make demands of large urban schools on issues of accountability, testing, parental participation, and community involvement that are then imitated by smaller districts. Given their access to policymakers, it is easy today for large corporations to exercise their influence.

Standards-based education (the provision of a selected content) has been promoted by a coalition of groups, including teachers' unions, but the most demanding and persistent groups have been the National Governors' Association, The Business Roundtable, and the U.S. Chamber of Commerce. However, extensions of this concern to have high-stakes testing to measure student attainment have been made mostly by business sectors. Sometimes this influence is exerted in obvious disregard of existing educational research. For example, part of the accountability position advocated by these groups calls for an end to automatic student promotion and its replacement instead by tests to move from grade to grade. But in moving to this new policy, proponents and implementers alike are ignoring a large body of research that shows that test-based accountability systems are flawed and that they promote instead dropping-out behaviors, particularly among minority students (Darling-Hammond 2001).

That decision makers listen to the voices of business firms and the conservative think tanks they often fund is evident: High-stakes tests—those used to determine who gets promoted or receives a diploma or what schools receive adequate funding—have been the key elements of educational reforms enacted in thirty-nine states by 2001. Further, thirty-six states today produce school-level report cards.

Transnational corporations have also become active in the shaping of higher education, as the WTO began in 2001 to consider a series of proposals to import and export higher education. In the United States, groups that influence the WTO through the National Committee for International Trade in Education include major for-profit providers: Sylvan Learning Center, Jones International University, and the University of Phoenix. Multinational institutions of higher education will disseminate curricular and other innovations and meet the needs of students who lack adequate colleges and universities in their respective countries. However, turning knowledge into a global commodity will create severe problems both because the knowledge to be disseminated originates in center countries and because the relevance of this knowledge will be decided entirely by a combination of world-class universities and TNCs operating in information technology, biotechnology, and publishing fields. A well-established authority in higher education predicts that "the norms and values of those countries [will] crowd out other ideas and practices" (Altbach 2001, 2).

There are concerns that as academic institutions and other providers of education located in the North set up branches and award degrees and certification using mostly distance technologies, they will be able to function with minimal restriction (Altbach 2000, 2001). This triggers questions regarding the accreditation and quality control for higher education that is being imported. And two serious questions looming in the distance are (1) whether profit-driven multinational enterprises, having the advantages they do, may eventually force nonprofit institutions, both public and private, out of business and (2) whether universities in developing countries will be able to conduct research adequate to their national development needs and to enable them to strengthen their civil society (Altbach 2001). Like many other scholars, Altbach (2001) argues that every country needs to control its own academic institutions and that individual universities need an adequate degree of autonomy and academic freedom to pursue their own objectives.

THE ROLE OF TNCS IN CULTURE

Many observers of the functioning of power in society realize that consent is essential to the maintenance of cohesive and stable societies (Fossaert 2001; Gramsci 1971). In the development of this consent, ideological means are crucial, and culture thus is an indispensable venue for the creation and sustainability of such consent.

As corporations become increasingly important in the determination of cultural norms and values, forms of privatized norm making are emerging. In other words, the function of shaping norms, previously held by the state or institutions imbued with public legitimacy and authority, has now shifted to the private sector—and a private sector that is becoming increasingly denationalized (Sassen 1999).

A major form of promoting globalized forms of culture occurs through "branding," that is, the promotion of commercial logos in nearly every area of social life, from stadiums to schools. In addition, there are chains of stores and restaurants, such as McDonald's, Burger King, KFC, Office Depot, Ace Hardware, and Blockbuster Video, operating from Israel to Peru, in which tastes and products are creating a homogenized way of life. As some cultural analysts have remarked, McDonald's brings not only a certain type of hamburger but also the value of "McDonaldization," representing efficiency, standardization, prediction, and control (Rebhun and Waxman 2000). The same authors maintain that in Israel—a religious state by design—exposure to American styles of dress, sexual mores, music, and values of materialism and individualism is creating U.S clones. Similar patterns could be documented in numerous other parts of the world, from Peru to China.

Important cultural changes are being propelled also by what appears at first sight to be beneficial or at least innocuous forms of intellectual protection. According to Shiva (2000), TRIPS agreements, strongly advocated by the WTO, will introduce agricultural patents and seed industry monopolies. In her view, "Planet Earth is being replaced by Life, Inc., in a world of free trade and deregulated commerce" (118). Indeed, the industrialization of the food system is creating a reduction of biodiversity, a phenomenon already evident in the new variations of rice, corn, and potatoes.[10]

The transmission of new cultural values by powerful business corporations has been found to rely on the "third man technique." This involves setting up front organizations to provide opinions favorable to TNCs in editorial and news pages and, conversely, to defuse the opposition (Kachur 2001). Evidence of such important actions is given by the Global Climate Coalition (formed by Burson-Marsteller and consisting of Dow Chemical, Exxon, Ford, GM, Mobil, and Union Carbide, among others), the International Climate Change partnership (comprising BP and DuPont), and the American Energy Alliance (including Edison Electric and the American Petroleum Institute); all three groups are accused of creating fake grassroots organizations to mold public opinion (Rampton and Stauber 2001).

Contributions to the social sciences made by academics and researchers in the area of cultural studies alert us to further involvement of TNCs in cultural activities. One such form involves the "protection" of cultural forms as a way of demonstrating friendliness to the societies in which the TNCs work. In this regard, Texaco has music-based programs in Azerbaijan to protect the restoration of musical instruments and indigenous music and in Kazakhstan to restore a village's crafts in saddle making, metalsmiths, wood-carvers, and jewelry (Dowling 2000). In Venezuela, Cigarrera Bigott, a company that represents British American Tobacco, has been quite creative in maintaining a public presence and corresponding influence. Since cigarettes can no longer be advertised, by creating a foundation (*Fundación Bigott*) devoted to popular culture, *Cigarrera Bigott* not only is frequently mentioned in the media but is even becoming associated with forms of Venezuelan cultural identity. The areas in which the foundation works are related mostly to cultural production: publications that include a regular journal, calendars, and a book per year; a technical support program for farmers and tree planting; and a program to provide financial support for schools, museums, and performing groups. By now, the foundation has produced three generations of television programs. In the view of Guass (1999), the foundation is helping simultaneously to document, present, and redefine Venezuelan popular culture through more than 140 television programs produced since 1985. In the United States, similar roles are being played by major electronic firms: One of the largest sponsors of culture in the United States is Philip Morris. Cisco is helping the development of computer programs in schools, but through its generosity, it is gaining a solid place in the recognition of its logo by new generations.

RESISTANCE TO TNCS

As a whole, TNCs aim at making the world less risky and less expensive for commercial investment rather than seeking democratic or humanitarian objectives. As a whole, TNCs have been gaining so many rights before the state that they are becoming the new citizens of the twenty-first century. To rebut the growing criticism of practices and influences of TNCs, some voices ask, Why do we assume that virtue can be associated only with the nation-state?

One response is that it is not a question of where virtue resides but rather of which institutions are more likely to foster civility and community solidarity. As Petras (1999) contends, the distributive consequence of globalization cannot be separated from the patterns of ownership and control of the institutions, the class structure, and the state. Such dimensions as concentration of ownership have clear consequences on various other aspects of social life. For example, taxes have become regressive, as tax revenues for government come increasingly from wage and salaried groups, while the share from TNCs is declining. This occurs through the continual pursuit of legal loopholes and the resourcefulness of corporate tax lawyers to devise tax shelters that include shifting the locus of earning to countries with lower tax rates, a tactic called "transfer pricing" (Petras 1999).[11] It should be remembered also that although new products and markets are constantly being created, the basic relations of power have remained unchanged (Marginson and Mollis 2001). One may ask, To what extent are states independent today? What are the new meanings and manifestations of sovereignty?

To counter the negative consequences of the concentration of economic power in private hands, globalization requires a new regulation that must be based on a democratic structure of international power. González Casanova (1996) suggests that we devise a new theory of the state where the growth in the power of supranational institutions is recognized. He argues that there has been a "reconversion of dependency" and that it is important to see not only what is new in the world today but also what is old. In his view, "reconversion is in large measure recolonization" (41). Some of the old colonial powers are indeed resurrecting: Spain, for instance, is today one of the most conspicuous investors in Latin America.

The presence of TNCs should not be equated with evil. But how does one break with the lure and logic of profit and capital accumulation? How do large companies recognize decent wages, which so affect the schooling of children? How does one introduce the values of public spiritedness? How does one challenge an unequal international division of labor? Paul Hellyer, former deputy prime minister of Canada, states,

> Globalization is a code name for corporatization. It's an attempt by the largest corporations in the world and the largest banks of the world to re-engineer the world in such a way that they won't have to pay decent wages to their employees, and they won't have to pay taxes to fix potholes and to maintain parks, and to pay pensions for the old and handicapped. (cited ISEC 2001)

Are voices who resist the actions of TNCs paranoid? Perhaps. But there are also solid signs of nondemocratic practices emerging in the global scene. The process of globalization involves not merely the presence of ultramodern technologies; it is also accompanied and facilitated by many regulations imposed by central countries (Weisbrot et al. 2000), some of which burden certain groups of those advanced countries with negative consequences. It should be noted that the MAI was negotiated for nearly two years (1995–1997) within the OECD countries with almost no public awareness. This agreement, quite broad in nature, would require the twenty-nine (mostly developed) nations participating in it to codify the liberalization of international investment, much as the North American Free Trade Agreement (NAFTA) did for North America. It was supposed to be completed by April 1997. So far, grassroots opposition from environmental and citizens organizations throughout the OECD, especially those in the United States, Canada, and France, have forestalled completion of the agreement.

An example of TNC action with clear consequences for culture is the current negotiations on the liberalization of the audiovisual sector (e.g., the film and television industries). This is eagerly advanced by the Motion Picture Association of America (MPAA) and its international organization, the Motion Picture Association (MPA). Some countries, notably France and Canada, are trying to protect their culture by maintaining national film quotas and subsidies (Wheeler 2000), but many developing countries will be unable to stop the onslaught of cultural production emanating from the United States. Will it be possible to generate a North–South alliance against economic forces that globalize culture in unidirectional ways?

Transnational corporations have an interest in a higher international value of the dollar since this allows them to buy assets and labor more cheaply overseas. But a higher dollar erodes the U.S. manufacturing base and increases its trade deficit by making U.S. imports cheaper and exports more expensive abroad; in the process, it erodes the quality of life and diminishes employment of U.S. workers, who have a good reason to be concerned about and become involved in the monitoring of TNC practices and initiatives. Indeed, a number of NGOs based in the North are now engaged in careful monitoring of actions by TNCs such as Nike, Shell, BP Amoco, Rio Tinto (a British mining corporation), and Novartis AG.

A major initiative, one that could have significant repercussions for the developing world, concerns the so-called Tobin tax. This measure would tax by 0.10 and 0.25 percent all international financial transactions, many of which, as we have seen, are speculative and can have destabilizing repercussions in developing countries. The implementation of the Tobin tax would yield about U.S.$166 billion a year (Quebec Network on Continental Integration 2001; other sources estimate the revenue to oscillate between U.S.$100 and U.S.$300 billion per year).[12] Yet how many citizens in the North are aware of its potential for redressing adverse consequences of TNC and individual speculators' excesses? And, more important, how many would, in the end, support enactment of legislation to this effect?

NOTES

1. Some researchers prefer to apply to these corporations the term "multinational" because they have offices in more than one country but retain a very high fraction of their assets in their home base economy. As evidence, Carnoy (2000) mentions the difficult times IBM experienced as a result of the 1990–1992 U.S. recession and how Japanese banks were affected by the slowdown of the economy during a similar downturn in Japan.

2. The 1999 sales of each of the top five corporations (General Motors, Wal-Mart, Exxon Mobil, Ford Motor, and Daimler-Chrysler) were larger than the gross domestic product of 182 countries (Anderson and Cavanagh 2000).

3. López de la Roche (1999) introduces an additional typology, classifying TNCs in terms of either exploiting raw materials abroad or producing in their domestic market and then exporting their products.

4. In this book, I will use indistinctly the terms "core," "central," "dominant," and "hegemonic" countries to refer to those in the highly industrialized world.

5. The four countries with the most corporations in the top 200 are the United States (82), Japan (41), Germany (20), and France (17) (Anderson and Cavanagh 2000). Of the 100 top-ranking TNCs in terms of foreign assets in 1996, only two were from developing countries: Daewoo (South Korea) and Petróleos de Venezuela (Venezuela).

6. According to Sassen (1999), different kinds of capital have their own tempo. Although times are becoming increasingly shorter, they range from one minute for conducting a financial transactions to about nine months for producing many kinds of manufactures.

7. John Malone, the founder of TCI, bought later by AT&T, once remarked, "It is hard to get angry at your competition anymore because you compete in one market

and [are] partners in another market" (McChesney 2000, 5). The president of Bulova reportedly said, "We are able to beat the foreign competition because we are the competition" (Harvey, ca. 2000).

8. Enron, a major TNC in the United States, developed during its existence more than 2,800 subsidiaries, with 882 of them located outside the United States in offshore and banking havens (those with few regulations or reporting requirements). No taxes were paid by Enron during its last four years; it received instead $382 million in tax refunds from the American government (*The Revolutionary Worker,* 2002).

9. Following demonstrations by various civic organizations in South Africa, a number of pharmaceutical companies agreed to give special discounts for HIV/AIDS medicines to African countries.

10. The reduction in biodiversity occurs because the few genetically engineered plants are much more aggressive than the natural ones and are most likely to destroy them.

11. While capable of producing enormous amounts of wealth, it is not clear how much of the revenues of TNCs goes to augment state revenues: Of the U.S. corporations among the top 200 TNCs in the world, forty-four did not pay the full standard 35 percent federal corporation tax during the period 1996–1098 (Anderson and Cavanagh 2000).

12. The Tobin tax was invented by U.S. economist James Tobin, Nobel Prize winner for economics in 1981. The tax would be very small, the equivalent of 10 to 25 cents per U.S.$100 in each transaction; even so, it remains a distant possibility.

6

The University as the Spearhead of Globalization

Romantic visions of universities depict them as independent communities of autonomous and even altruistic scholars. But in fact, far from this perception, these institutions are very much affected by external forces and limited by constraints presented by the world outside (Lockwood, cited in Burton and Robinson 1999). In the era of globalization, a time in which a "knowledge society" is supposed to prevail and a "knowledge-based economy"[1] is expected to be the driving force behind many applied developments, the university becomes a special place from which to advance new visions and ambitions.

The university attains a privileged position under globalization because the university produces and disseminates the highest level of education and is thus able to assign people in the highest possible positions. Its work affects lower levels of education (primary, secondary, and vocational) and strengthens or weakens the role education plays in the representation of society's members.

Some of the external forces wielding a substantial impact on the university are clearly linked to economic globalization trends, such as the development of educational credentials that can move easily across borders and the emergence of fields with relevance essential to the new occupations that demanded a globalized economy. Other forces are related to new communication technologies that make it possible to reach others instantly and massively at low costs anywhere in the world, thus creating new opportunities for teaching and learning. Still other forces impacting on the university seem more linked to neoliberal economic ideologies, such as the reduction in state funding and the notion that universities should become self-supporting and that their students pay for the services they receive. As a result of a confluence of factors, universities throughout the world are facing new power relations and potential conflicts between public and private interests. There is already a visible changing structure in the administration, and new conflicts, such as those regarding the ownership of intellectual property, are creating both possibilities and challenges (Holton 1997).

This chapter intends to show the various consequences of globalization for higher education. It examines the unfolding diversity and differentiation among institutions of higher education. It identifies some of the key manifestations of the growing influence of business over knowledge production and considers the interaction between new information technologies, ownership of intellectual property, and the new forms of leadership that are emerging.

DIVERSITY AND DIFFERENTIATION IN HIGHER EDUCATION

Clark Kerr, a noted expert on higher education, perceives two "shock waves" in the history of U.S. universities. "Shock Wave I" he applies to the acceptance of national responsibility for scientific research and development, university access for all high school graduates, and the demands of politically restless students. "Shock Wave II" he terms the extensive array of forces in existence since the 1990s associated with the "new electronic technology, the DNA revolution, new demographic realities, including the rise in the proportion of historically disadvantaged racial and ethnic groups; competition for public-sector resources . . . ; competition for students from the for-profit sector; responsibility for improving primary and secondary education; globalization of the economy; and contention over models of the university" (Kerr 2001, 10). These surges of changes have brought with them challenges for the established comprehensive university as alternative institutions and forms of delivery are emerging. This in turn will generate competition for students, particularly those who represent new profiles, such as workers and employees seeking occupational mobility via advanced education and the growing pool of older people able to take advantage of expanding forms of lifelong learning.

A clear sign of change in universities is the rapid differentiation in the kinds of existing institutions of higher or postsecondary education.[3] Universities no longer enjoy a monopoly in providing high-status information to adults; numerous other institutions, ranging from minor private universities to technical universities to computer training institutes, compete for students. Access to higher education has become less exclusive, fitting diverse needs for knowledge, degrees, and jobs. But this increased diversity in the provision of higher education has also augmented differences in academic prestige, financial resources, and social power of both its faculty and its students.

The escalation of economic globalization has driven a demand for instrumental education—that which can be clearly tied to the goals of production, productivity, and employment. Instrumental education carries with it a dynamic of specialization: specialization of specific universities and specialization of campuses within large university systems.[4] So, in addition to universities, there are now technological institutions, business and computer academies, community colleges, private institutions (both elite and nonelite), virtual universities, and so on. Some of these institutions, to be sure, pre-date globalization. What is new about them is their accelerated rate of growth and emergence in all parts of the world. The differentiation among centers of postsecondary education is accentuating the distinction between teaching and research. Whereas formerly there had existed an uneasy balance between the two, it has now become more typical for the most prestigious institutions to focus on research. This shift has some unintended negative effects: As teaching becomes less central to a university's reputation, it is increasingly relegated to part-time and junior faculty, particularly at undergraduate levels. Conversely, in institutions in which training prevails, teaching overrides research, and institutions become heavily populated by part-time or temporary faculty and do not develop a strong institutional environment (Finkelstein and Grubb 2000).

Links between economies and the growth of international authority affect the structures of professions at national levels (Orzack 1992). Today we have new supranational and international public authorities shaping higher education. In addition to such established and influential international organizations as the Organization for Economic Cooperation and Development (OECD), the World Trade Organization (WTO), the World Bank, and the International Monetary Fund (IMF), we have now the supranational European Union.

Initially, the European Union had no explicit mandate regarding education. So, a key strategy for Europeanizing higher education has been through the facilitation of recognizing study in other European universities. To this effect, ERASMUS was started in 1987 and later replaced by SOCRATES in 1992. By 1997, more than 100,000 European students were attending universities in other European countries (Van Damme 2001). Beyond making possible cross-European experiences, the European Union is changing the nature of the university in other countries. In particular, it is giving rise to substantial modification of the German university. Up to a few years ago, about 75 percent of higher-education students in Germany were enrolled in universities, institutions that have enjoyed considerable financial support from the state. The other 25 percent attended teacher education colleges, schools of theology, comprehensive technical colleges, and art academies (Fallon and Ash 1999). Today, ongoing discussions in Germany are revising university framework legislation in the direction of increased differentiation within higher education, explicitly invoking the principles of private higher education, greater student choice among types of institutions, multiple sources of financing, local control of admissions, and sanctions against dilatory students (Fallon and Ash 1999).

In contrast to Germany, higher education in the United States has long been a widely differentiated set of institutions, providing many alternatives for students at a wide range of cost and accessibility. In the United States, about 20 percent of students in higher education are enrolled in universities; the rest are in comprehensive four-year colleges or in preparatory or reduced-degree two-year colleges. The important point, however, is that globalization is affecting both countries. Germany is moving into the U.S. model by accepting an increased differentiation of institutions. The United States is shifting toward increasing standardization of its credentials and curricula to accommodate international norms (Fallon and Ash 1999).

To push the advance of globalization in European countries, a number of regional alliances in that region are fostering the homogenization of content among institutions highly diverse in terms of structure, objectives, and location. Notable among these initiatives is the TEMPUS (Trans European Mobility Program for University Staff) project, funded by the European Union, which seeks to facilitate the process of democratization in eastern Europe through the dissemination of the western European curriculum. The Santander Group is an alliance of forty universities that seek to expedite the mobility of ERASMUS/SOCRATES programs within Europe. Universitas 21, a conglomeration of universities worldwide (in the United Kingdom including those of Glasgow, Edinburgh, Nottingham, and Birmingham), is also organized around the principle of easy transfer of course work and credentials. Critics of such facilitated educational exchange and equivalence programs in Europe maintain that the model being transferred is one of the "West as expert," leaving unconsidered how eastern European countries may be able to identify and pursue their own development needs. In other words, they contend that international exchanges may superficially be promoting cultural exposure while in fact strengthening cultural homogenization.

While there is a tendency toward homogenizing content across countries, the simultaneous differentiation of types of universities and institutions of higher education is a globalization goal not only because it caters to different requirements for workers and occupations but also because it opens the educational market to private entrepreneurs and investment. A key tool in accelerating the diversification of institutions of higher education is deregulation, or decreasing the number of rules and guidelines to facilitate the creation and functioning of new institutions. Differentiation of institutions is closely linked to privatization, a path pursued by many countries to reduce public expenditures in education. But cutting back state funding for higher education shifts that burden to students and families, resulting in declining academic salaries and conditions of academic work in many countries (Altbach 2000).

One country that has engaged in high levels of university deregulation is Australia. Through successive measures, the Australian government has abolished previous controls on the number of students admitted to university, granted students the ability to select where to study, instituted a voucher system enabling students to enroll in either a public or a private institution, authorized institutions to set their own tuition fees and standards for equity, provided student loans at market rates, established federal funding for institutions that meet government policy and fiscal objectives, and set up new quality assurance arrangements to facilitate the entry of new providers of higher-education services (Gamage 2000; Mollis and Marginson 2000). The achievement of these goals obligated universities to compete for competition for students and to reframe higher education as a market-driven industry (Gamage 2000). Higher education became an export-oriented institution, specializing in the provision of knowledge to meet consumer demand. Today, Australia evinces a large diversity of institutions of higher education that spend a great deal of time recruiting students from within and from abroad.

Program differentiation within and among universities is now subject to assessment and (when highly positive) to rewards that go to departments and schools that do "better"—that is, those that visibly respond to interests of industry, commerce, and government—and that then become recognized as "centers of excellence" and are given more external and internal resources. Mok (2000) documents the case of Hong Kong, where universities are providing resources for the further strengthening of well-performing centers and are closing those considered "weak."

CHANGING FIELDS AND STATUSES

Taking a philosophical look at the university, Santos (1995, 223) considers this institution to be one of the key vehicles for modernization, typically resting on three pillars: the cognitive-instrumental, the moral-legal, and the aesthetic-expressive. But he finds that of these, the cognitive-instrumental dominates at present. In his view, there is now an atrophy of the cultural dimension of the university. In the traditional context of the university, its key contributions were research, training of qualified and highly specialized labor, high levels of credentialism, service provision for region and community, social leadership, and social mobility for children of factory workers. With the new emphasis on pragmatic ends, some of these functions are becoming mutually incompatible; salient among these is the function of teaching versus research and the function of serving the community versus serving the business firm.

The instrumental facet of the university will lead to a preference both by the state (when it funds the university) and the university itself (as it moves to self-sufficiency) to promote research on such topics as new materials, biotechnology, artificial intelligence, robotics, and energy (Gidley 2000; Santos 1995). This prediction is clearly realized in countries in which natural resources are limited but in which their human capital can be further developed. Thus, Singapore, China, and Korea evince exceptionally strong government support of science and engineering.

In several countries, public universities are facing serious cuts in their budgets, especially in the social sciences and the humanities, which now have to face the competition of private universities subsidized in part by the state (Santos 1995). Given their relatively low market value, the humanities are finding it difficult to exist in many universities.

There is no question that under globalization, universities are becoming more entrepreneurial. Rowan (2000) contends that this will lead to epistemological diversity and diversity of fields because diversity increases the possibilities of securing new resources and attracting new students. Rowan's analysis brings an important argument. As do several others, he predicts that universities will look for fields likely to yield high revenues. But he predicts also that fields that are low cost (i.e., no labs, expensive equipment, or other components are needed) but also low revenue (e.g., music and Latin) are likely to survive mostly through political bargaining. He argues that there will be a tendency among all fields, including professional schools such as education, to portray themselves as scientific (Rowan 2000). The negative implication of this for the field of education is that its knowledge, in the attempt to become scientific, may be artificially decontextualized or that the "scientific" nature of education may result in the sacrifice of a number of disciplines. Examples of this narrowing of concerns can be seen in the increasingly few schools of education that offer such courses as history, philosophy, and even sociology of education. Other manifestations of the same phenomenon can be seen in initiatives in several highly prestigious research universities to merge all language departments into a single division and combine language teaching with culture and literature. Reasons for these mergers reflect a vicious circle: Since the language and literature departments are now receiving reduced funding, the number of enrollees has decreased, making these departments in turn no longer cost effective. Amid the sea of changes affecting in negative ways those fields whose nature is not of immediate or practical relevance to production are some encouraging developments, such as the establishment of the Canada Research Chairs Program in 2000 to create 2,000 research chairs by 2005. Although this program will allocate 45 percent of the chairs to the natural sciences and engineering, it also assigns 35 percent to health and 20 percent to the social sciences and the humanities (G. Jones 2000).

While an important characteristic of universities in central countries today is the increasing proportion of their international students, little has changed among the students of Northern origins vis-à-vis their recognition of cultures, countries, and students in the South, thus making globalization an asymmetrical phenomenon. In the United States, less than 1 percent of the postsecondary student population studied abroad in 1999. Currently less than 3 percent of U.S. students study abroad over the course of their higher-education programs (Engberg 2001), and most travel to Europe (Altbach and Peterson 1998), indicating a weak interest in learning more about other cultures.[5] A fourteen-nation study conducted by the Carnegie Foundation of the academic profession found that while more than 80 percent of the faculty in thirteen countries valued connections with scholars in other countries, slightly over half the U.S. professors thought so, and only 45 percent considered that the curriculum should be further internationalized (cited in Altbach and Peterson 1998). Moreover, federal funding for international education has declined; the Fulbright program, a key vehicle for academic exchanges with other countries, has been reduced by 43 percent in constant dollar funding since 1994 (Engberg 2001).

As anticipated, new fields of study are emerging in institutions of higher education that have experienced veritable explosions of scientific and technical specializations. There are now also university programs in environmental education, multicultural education, women's studies, ethnic studies, cultural studies, and human rights education, all supported by global frames of reference (Williams 2000). These latter fields operate with limited resources and are relatively marginal to the teaching and research life of the university.

A correlate of the affluence that globalization is creating in the North is the brain drain that many developing countries are experiencing. Many of the best professionals in developing countries are going to central countries, motivated by the possibility of a better life. This calculation also crosses the mind of international students, many of whom decide to stay in the country in which they conducted their university studies. The stay of international students in Northern countries creates two effects: First, Third World countries are not able to benefit from increased knowledge and skills; second, there continues to be a centralization of knowledge and research in the North.[6]

An outcome of a serious nature is the decreased attention to critical thinking within the university across countries. Simultaneous with the growth in the status now enjoyed by instrumental disciplines and professions has been a decreased importance attached to the development of critical thinking. We define this skill as the recognition of awareness of one's surrounding as fundamental to education and as the understanding of political and economic forces as central to knowledge acquisition.

With the advent of globalization, English has emerged as the dominant language of communication. This means not only that the major research journals and academic books are in English but also that the dominant research prioritizes models of thinking predicated on Anglo-American scholarship, more likely to be functionalist in nature (i.e., framing problems as technical rather than political), quantitative, and willing to take for granted current sociopolitical developments in the world (Luke 2000; Marginson and Mollis 2001). This perspective tends to leave some issues out, including problems of significant importance. As David (2000, 12) and others argue, many of the scientific challenges of the twenty-first century require our understanding of the "*global* environment and eco-systems." Ironically, universities are becoming more global than ever in terms of students and marketing interests, but at the same time their concerns focus increasingly on material aspects.[7]

INFLUENCES OF BUSINESS ON THE UNIVERSITY

In the same way neoliberalism has influenced lower levels of education (which we saw in chapter 1), it is shaping objectives, procedures, and outcomes at the university level. A detailed look at university practices since the 1980s reveals patterns similar to those found in business firms.

Performance Assessment

As noted earlier, a typical feature of reforms in higher education is the encouragement of market differentiation among institutions. Both a means to achieve this and a consequence of the same policy has been the emergence of ranking systems comparing universities by degree of "excellence." Criteria for performance involve several indicators, all of which reward exclusivity in student selection and the ability of faculty to secure research funds; the criteria also give positive valuation to the existence of supportive conditions, such as library resources and faculty-to-student ratios. None of these indicators is sensitive to the specific objectives of particular universities or to the extent to which students may be gaining knowledge and skills to become better citizens.

In countries with strong government funding of public education, performance criteria result in the establishment of a performance-based distribution of research funds among universities. This practice is perhaps most entrenched in the United Kingdom, where, as a result of the Research Assessment Exercise System, universities are ranked in terms of performance along selected criteria and then receive research funds on the basis of this ranking. The criteria are based on the proportion of research faculty and the amount of research they perform. But the actual assessment is soon reduced to quantitative indicators, such as scores on admission tests, teacher-to-student ratios, amount of research dollars obtained from federal grants, and length of time to graduate. The assessment indicators do not measure the relevance of what is being taught or the quality of content (Tikly and Crossley 2001).

In the case of the United States, there are no formal mechanisms for the evaluation of universities, but the annual ranking exercise conducted by the popular magazine *U.S. News and World Report* produces significant consequences in the operation of universities. The ranking, based on several indicators, assigns great importance to the university's ability to obtain external research funds and to the stringency of student admissions procedures; it also gives substantial weight to the "reputation" the university and its various departments enjoy in the views of such persons as presidents, deans, and admission officers.[8] That such rankings have significant consequences for research funds is reflected in the fact that nonrefereed federal research dollars in the United States increased 250 percent from 1996 to 2000 (O'Meara 2001).

Universities in the newly industrialized countries of Asia have been eager to follow assessment practices. In Korean universities today, new types of incentives, such as contract-based appointments, a yearly stipend system, and additional benefits to the best researchers and teachers, are at work (Tikly and Crossley 2001). This is also the case in less industrialized countries. In 1999 in Brazil, the application of standardized criteria resulted in universities in the northeast of the country, an economically impoverished area with a serious deficit in advanced education, to be found weak and thus ineligible for federal support.

While assessment procedures could be devised to gain greater understanding of the contribution of universities to the overall improvement of their societies, this is not the case. The assessments focus instead on quantitative indicators that pit one university against others. Moreover, the focus on performance and the consequent competition that it generates among universities result ultimately in taking away the autonomy of purpose and the function of those universities. Marginson and Mollis (2001) maintain that a key feature of the entrepreneurial emphasis within the university has been the shifting of student identity from pedagogical or democratic subjects to consumer subjects.

Some of the performance assessments borrow from business the notion of total quality management (TQM). Applied extensively in Australian and Asian universities, TQM is concerned with improving the quality of a product as determined by customer satisfaction in universities. But typically, the "customer" is not the student but rather the business firm. Rooney and Hearn (2000) note that TQM focuses on quantifiable indicators rather than on qualities, which are more difficult to measure, and seeks to reduce costs. Rooney and Hearn contend that TQM is about eliminating "error" (variance) despite the fact that diversity should be an objective and a sign of success rather than failure in universities. Echoing the same concern, Mollis and Marginson (2000) found that current assessment practices in Argentina and Australia favor the use of numerical indicators but avoid expert judgments.

A variation of TQM is at work in Hong Kong, where it is called the quality process review (QPR). Described as an "externally driven meta-analysis of internal quality assurance, assessment and improvement systems" (Mok 2000, 158–59), QPR is said to be better than the TQM exercise carried out in Australia. According to Mok, QPR considers quality but also pays attention to the processes that are assumed to produce quality. QPR has been used to examine curriculum and pedagogical designs, the implementation of teaching, student outcomes assessment, and the resources the institution has in terms of human, technical, and financial assets (Mok 2000). Typically in the hands of professionals, and although believed to promote autonomy, one of the main consequences of these micro-level evaluations seems to be the shifting of institutions into a convergence of goals and functioning—something that is not always desirable, especially if the university seeks to serve particular needs and populations. As Mollis and Marginson (2000, 29) note, challenges to TQM and its variations are very difficult to mount today because "the indirect effects of assessment on academic work [are] scarcely capable of political challenge from internal agents, for to resist the technologies of assessment is to appear to stand against accountability itself."

Competition

The competition that operates in higher education positions university against university, department against department, and professors against each other. While competition has always existed, today the concept has been extended to new frontiers. This competitive ethos characterizes both faculty and students.

The essential piece in the edifice of competition is the individual scholar who, working at higher levels, may engender departmental or university levels of competition. As university professors are placed in an educational market, they are obliged to sell their skills and knowledge. The constant search for external research funds goes against collegiality and mutuality among professors as colleagues, especially those in very similar fields, are seen as potential rivals. Competition for grants often ends up pitting personal productivity and creativity against attention for students (Currie et al. 2000).

In many universities, researchers concentrate on their own department and, frequently, on their own research to the detriment of other university-related concerns. Students are still needed to bring in revenues, and weak students are sometimes admitted because more bodies are needed. But since the best professors are concentrating on their own research, they are not available to supervise doctoral dissertations or can provide only limited assistance. Consequently, some argue that poor doctoral work is more frequent than in the past. Competition within universities is introducing little incentive to collaborate on knowledge production. This has been termed the "balkanization of faculty," and the principle "I market my program, I win" prevails (Gumport 2000). Describing universities in the United Kingdom, Morley (1999) holds that a new culture has embraced these institutions, as there is now "constant preoccupation with finances, measurement, marketing, and accountability" (189).

Competition among universities is emerging also through disguised forms of decentralization mechanisms and in the diversification of income generation. Data from China, a former communist country and thus previously characterized by a large amount of centralized planning, has now applied the principle of decentralization to many institutions, permitting universities to establish and run their own programs. At the same time, however, it seems that the state's role as a "regulator and overall service coordinator" has been strengthened. While the state has been diversifying sources of educational financing (e.g., surcharges, tuition and fees, profits from school-run enterprises, and tax-deductible contributions from businesses and individuals), it has developed a scheme that will give it considerable room for influencing institutions of higher education by creating and then manipulating competition among them. China's Project 211 will target the best 1,000 institutions of higher learning and support their development to become "world-class universities." Project 211 seeks to reform the universities to create a solid base for scientific, technological, and social development. Central to the scheme is the introduction of competition among universities according to international benchmarks and through focused promotion of engineering and technology (Mok 2001).

Many central countries have been pursuing diversification of income generation through distance education and offshore programs. The dominance of English as the research lingua franca has resulted in a major advantage for Anglo-Saxon countries such as the United States, the United Kingdom, Canada, Australia, and New Zealand. They can easily market higher-education programs abroad, as many students from developing countries will seek instruction in English, a process perhaps best illustrated by Australia, which increased its international (or overseas) students from 5.5 percent in 1991 to 13.7 percent by 2000, greatly surpassing the overall rise in higher education over the ten-year period (Turpin et al. 2001).[9] The marketing of university programs abroad is examined in the following sections dealing with increasing ties with business firms and the use of new technologies in higher education.

Taken to its extreme in the global context, competition leads universities no longer to seek preeminence within their own country but rather to become the leading research university in a global higher-education economy (Newby 1999). This global standard, in turn, leads to the homogenization of practices and topics. Gonzalez and Menendez (2001) have seen increasing similarities among Argentinean universities in terms of reading materials, the priorities they assign to disciplines, and the conduct of their own professional practices. For instance, researchers in Argentina must publish at least one article per year in English, which means publishing in a Northern journal to be read by others, mostly non-Argentineans. This example illustrates the growing domination of a powerful symbiosis emerging between language, particular ways to see the world (e.g., research models with easy currency), and globalization. Aghion et al. (2000) note that "no part of the world stands more to gain from biotechnological progress than Africa, which has been ravaged by AIDS and malaria in the last part of the 20th century and where severe agricultural conditions enhance the payoff to new genetically designed seed and livestock varieties" (17). Under current Northern-dominated research trends, one may wonder how research on these topics can be endogenous, especially if it is produced in an indigenous language and through data-gathering methods and rules of evidence not endorsed by elite research journals.

Incipient evidence regarding the impact of competition among students, though still more anecdotal than carefully researched, is indicating that young university students in elite universities in the United States tend to be more individualistic and less likely to become concerned with larger social issues (Brooks 2001). The new meritocratic elite seems more interested in efficiency and success in their future jobs than in any social concerns. To support his assertion that elite university students are today different from those in the past, Brooks refers to time-analysis studies carried out by the University of Michigan's Institute for Social Research, which found that the amount of indoor play by children ages three to twelve declined by 16 percent from 1981 to 1997 and that the amount of television watching (surprisingly) declined by 23 percent. In contrast, these studies found that the amount of time spent studying increased by 20 percent and that the amount of time in organized sports increased by 27 percent during the same period. Brooks goes on to argue the emergence of the "organization kid," one who rarely questions authority and who readily accepts his or her elite position as part of the natural order of life.

In response to Brooks, it must be noted that while elite universities may be fostering narrow individual identities, in other universities there are important signs of social awareness and concern. An example is provided by students at the University of California at Berkeley who fought the Board of Regents' 1995 decision not to consider affirmative action favoring minorities in student admissions. As a result of a protracted struggle by students, with the support of some faculty members, the Board of Regents rescinded such a policy in May 2001.

A consequence of the growing culture of assessment and competition is the inordinate importance given to "excellence." Although, of course, everyone would like to excel, the use of rankings makes it an unattainable goal for most since by definition this procedure produces a hierarchy, with the implication that those below a certain position (perhaps below twentieth or thirtieth place in the case of U.S. universities) are less-than-excellent institutions.[10]

Productivity

A logical sequitur of a definition of higher education based on instrumental terms is the measurement of productivity in terms of the ability to attract external funds. University professors are now placed in an educational market where they are obliged to sell their skills and knowledge. This means two things: First, they have to respond to issues that external funders (government, foundations, or business firms) deem important; second, they must refrain from proposing critiques that funders find irrelevant or contrary to their interests. Furthermore, the pressure to conduct research is forcing academics to buy out their teaching assignments with consultancy money or research grants, freeing them to "prioritize research for promotion purposes" (Currie et al. 2000, 283).

If productivity is defined primarily in terms of ability to attract funds, questions may be raised about the future of such endeavors as social transformation or social justice, efforts that by their very nature are controversial and not immediately or directly revenue producing. Who will readily find educational studies that seek to probe the continuing, persistent forms of ethnic discrimination or gender segregation? What will happen to fields that are less prestigious than science and technology, such as those dealing with adult literacy or vocational education? As Currie et al. (2000) observe, globalization presses academics to do types of research that have more prestige or better funding than others. Speaking of the United Kingdom, Tikly and Crossley (2001) maintain that emphasis on utility and "relevance" has led to a critique of theory in favor of teaching and "evidence-based research" that is concerned exclusively with developing and disseminating "good practice," that is, focusing on micro-task efficiency and disembedded from larger contexts.

User Fees

One principle with obvious origins in the business world is that one pays for the service one receives. This logic is at odds with socially accepted definitions of education as a common good. Since most countries in the world have not attained mass higher education (defined as enrolling a minimum of 40 percent of those of ages eighteen to twenty-four), higher education cannot be considered a free good as would basic education. Yet the charging of tuition fees, one of the most exclusionary practices, is contentious in many developing countries because it is seen likely to lead to further discrimination between the poor and the rich in access to higher forms of knowledge.

Those that favor user fees for universities, primarily the international financial institutions and notably among them the World Bank, argue that public universities with no or low tuition amounts to having the state subsidize the rich because many of those who attend public universities belong in fact to middle and upper social classes. There is indeed evidence that most of those who attend public universities derive from middle and upper social classes. In Argentina, for instance, more than 50 percent of the students in public universities belong to the highest 20 percent of the income distribution (González and Menéndez 2001). The international lending agencies, which have successfully influenced governments, invoke the need for user fees on the principle of social equity. To minimize negative impacts of tuition fees on the poor, they suggest a system of loans, often designed on the basis of student need. From the perspective of many students, user fees is a very disputed notion not simply because the students will be asked to pay tuition but because they fear that once fees are established, they may jump in the future to the point of creating considerable exclusion of low-income students.[11]

Another development linked to the need for user fees is the response by universities in the North that are now promoting "internationalization." This initiative usually amounts to seeking overseas students as new sources of income. Internationalization policies do create new opportunities for students of developing countries. In several Asian countries, for instance, some lower-quality colleges are currently functioning as brokers to backdoor entry to Australian universities (Gamage 2000). On the other hand, as noted earlier in this chapter, there is scant evidence that the increased presence of international students is serving to sensitize the curriculum to Third World needs or that the student environment in those universities is becoming more multicultural.

Consumerism

Further impacting higher education is the growing trend to define students as clients or customers. In the words of one research university president, his institution is the "largest export industry," a phrase that implies that students come to the university from abroad to buy knowledge.

There are several manifestations of consumerism. At one level, there is the student who feels that he or she has entitlements similar to those of the buyer in the marketplace. So in many universities, particularly at the undergraduate level, class attendance and participation are increasingly becoming voluntary, arrival and departure times are self-determined, and a passing grade is a typical expectation (O'Meara 2001). At another level, there is a noticeable presence of business firms in university life because universities have to find sponsors for many of their activities. At present, it is estimated that more than 20 percent of all voluntary support for U.S. universities comes from corporate sponsorship, which includes the practices of college and universities to license logos and trademarks for clothing and other goods. More than 300 U.S. colleges have agreements with for-profit vendors to carry commercial advertisements on their Web sites to defray design and maintenance costs and to generate additional revenue (O'Meara 2001).

Changing the Nature of Governance

As business norms penetrate the university, traditional modes of leadership, with governance by professors, are giving way to decision making by professionalized management focused on economistic principles (Currie et al. 2000).

In Australia, significant changes have affected governance. As its university system fell from full public funding in 1974 to 51 percent in 1998, governance shifted from elected heads of departments and deans to appointed vice-chancellors engaged in limited consultation with faculty (Gamage 2000). A similar pattern is at work in many other countries, with the result that vice-chancellors (provosts in U.S. terminology) possess greater autonomy than in the past to determine their institution's own priorities.

In the U.S. university, decisions now guided by revenue concerns have led to the establishment of for-profit subsidiaries to function as financially self-sufficient teaching or research entities with streamlined governance structures (O'Meara 2001). Other strategies affecting governance practices, being followed in China, are the provision of exclusively short-term contracts, frequent "management audits," and the creation of subcommittees for "quality assurance." All these mechanisms operate to create quick incentives and punishments linked to performance, with "performance" predicated on revenue raising (Mok 2000).

Conditions of Work

The sense of community is changing in universities in several ways. The restructuring of university management along more efficient, revenue-linked processes is fostering changes in the composition of faculties, now characterized by a reduced set of tenured professors and many part-time faculty members. "Faculty may become in the future a gypsy faculty, with the expectation that they provide the equivalent of part of their wages through 'consultancies'" (Gidley 2000, 240). There has been a steady increase not only in part-time faculty but also in hours of work per capita for all faculty. Empirical studies indicate an increase of three hours of work per week per year since the 1970s, reaching in the late 1990s almost forty-eight hours a week in Australia, fifty-three in New Zealand, fifty-three to fifty-six in the United States, and fifty-four in Britain (Currie et al. 2000). Within academic circles, there has been a traditional expectation to work long hours. But what Currie et al. find worrisome is the constantly increasing amount of time taken by new administrative tasks and the resulting fragmentation of work time.

This increase in expected work time seems to be having especially negative impacts on women. A study in the United Kingdom found that women professors average 64.5 hours a week compared to an average of 58.6 hours for male professors (Morley and Walsh, cited in Currie et al. 2000). Studies in Australia indicate that the large majority of academics (about 72 percent) see universities as demanding significant personal sacrifices, especially in the area of family life (Currie et al. 2000). Since it is still women who carry the main responsibility for home and family, they find this to be a greater challenge than do men. And since in requiring more time the university does not consider the differential impact on men and women, current trends are strengthening the divide between private and public worlds, thus indirectly weakening any effort to balance the participation of women and men in family life. From a gender perspective, the new economic emphasis of the university goes against the values of collegiality and mutuality. Ongoing research by Acker and Wyn (2001) has found significant time constraints and stress among women academics in Canada and Australia. Examining the current panorama, Currie et al. (2000) conclude that "under globalization, there is a tendency not to question the masculinity discourse of the university" (289)—a discourse that normalizes high workloads and foremost commitment to the institution.

Although never a prevailing practice, the tradition of providing benefits to the staff, including those in nonacademic service, such as free or subsidized tuition of their children as university students (assuming that they meet admission requirements), is practically gone. Today, most of the work done by janitors, cleaning personnel, and other workers in university cafeterias and dormitories is done through outsourcing or subcontracting. Social mobility through university employment—which used to give those unable to afford it access to courses and even degree programs—is becoming a thing of the past.

Another feature of the university that is undergoing change is the principle of tenure. An increasing number of voices (e.g., Keith 1998) no longer see tenure as needed to protect faculty autonomy but consider it rather as a source of low productivity. Not surprisingly, several initiatives to move into "posttenure review" practices are now being tried. These initiatives subtly but relentlessly erode tenure by bringing faculty into review procedures that may find them incompetent or "neglectful of duty" and thus subject to termination procedures.

CONNECTIONS WITH BUSINESS

With the growing importance of business support, institutions of higher education are becoming more sensitive to market needs and focusing on producing graduates to suit employers' needs. The response of elite universities has not yet been uniform, however, as reflected, for example, in Oxford University's three endowed chairs in business, in contrast with Harvard, which has nearly ninety (*The Economist,* cited in Pitt et al. 1997).

Some positive consequences ensue from this close business–university connection. The need for more highly educated workers is leading universities to provide programs for continuing professional education and certificates through part-time study, as manifested in graduate students now outnumbering undergraduates in the United States, Canada, and the United Kingdom (Jarvis 1997). More older and retired people are pursuing higher education, seeking fuller and richer lives. Also positive is the number of very successful business–university partnerships that have provided synergistic support for efforts that neither side alone would have been able to accomplish. Examples of this are the successful effort to map the human genome and the strategic alliance between microelectronic firms and universities in Silicon Valley in California. The genome project, which brought together the academic and corporate worlds, was responsible for the productive "marriage of two cultures." The increased presence of transnational corporations in many countries, supported by mergers and acquisitions of firms, has led to frequent relocations of qualified personnel, growing reliance on electronic data storage and processing systems, and the transfer of knowledge across national borders (Orzack 1992). This has greatly influenced a more comprehensive definition of certain professions and, in balance, has had a positive effect on higher education.

On the negative side, the current numeric expansion of universities, occurring as it does under the forces of globalization, is producing a standardization of knowledge in the sense that higher education responds to the pressures of a globalized professional labor force (Jarvis 1997). There is already a large number of international students in business and information technology. This group creates "a global elite steeped in American talk and business practices" (Marginson and Mollis 2001, 599). Moreover, the research of doctoral candidates tends to be more work based or instrumental when students are funded by their employers. In addition, it is quite likely that employers will fund only certain fields.

An important manifestation of the business–university connection, the
value of which may be either positive or negative, is the emergence of distance education programs with heavy business influence. A number of high-
ranking American research universities, such as the University of California at
Berkeley, the University of Michigan, and Columbia University, have established ties in the private sector with major media and information-technology
companies, such as Time Warner, Disney Corporation, Microsoft, and Cisco,
to develop the software and support needed for the global market in higher
education (Newby 1999). Universities, therefore, are providing academic expertise and their "branding" for market credibility, while the partners provide
production facilities, distribution, marketing skills, and much of the underlying technology (Newby 1999). Institutions such as New York University and
Columbia University have entered into commercial activities that in the view
of some "compromise their traditional roles" by setting up for-profit subsidiaries (Altbach 2001). Other universities, such as Monash University in Australia, are establishing profit-making branches overseas.[12] Similar patterns
have been reported in the developing world. For instance, universities in
China are directing much of their attention to providing consulting services
and setting up technology companies. Many academic institutions in general
have gone on-line to sell their courses and degrees for money to customers
throughout the world.

Universities in industrialized countries, confronted with fiscal challenges
to their budgets, are developing partnerships with global media businesses.
In the case of some institutions in Australia, for instance, the Microsoft On-
Line Institute, the Virtual On-Line University, and Phoenix University will
likely become major players not simply for the technology of educational delivery but also in the ownership of intellectual property. So far, when corporations allocate funds for universities, they behave in ways different from traditional donors—the foundations and other philanthropic organizations.
While the latter did establish research priorities, they were willing to deal
with broader time frameworks in terms of social impact. In contrast, the corporations are developing a reputation for funding research closely tailored
to their needs and predicated on a narrow definition of major chronic social
issues.

The impact of globalization on the university does not mean that the market takes over higher education. But it does mean in many cases that the
state takes measures to ensure that the market is well served, as is happen-
ing most notably in small, resource-poor states highly dependent on industry for their survival, such as Hong Kong and Singapore—a process that Mok
(2000) terms "re-regulation" as opposed to "deregulation." As a whole, the
predominance of business norms and principles is creating a new ethos in
many universities. As Mok (2000) observes in the case of Singapore, serving
industry is not enough; now universities must also "take on the new role of

fostering an entrepreneurial climate" (164); that is, the universities them-selves must change their functioning to become more industry-like.

A development with mixed consequences has been the expansion of higher education through private initiatives. In recent years, for-profit or publicly traded corporations have entered higher education. This has taken place in two ways. First, multinational corporations are setting up a number of colleges abroad through the participation of regular universities in several developed countries (e.g., Sunday College in Malaysia). A common charac-teristic of these universities is that they emphasize instrumental fields linked to economic globalization: economics, commerce, computer science, mass communications, business administration, engineering, and law. Second, in many other cases the corporations are creating their own programs, mostly in their own country. Major players in the United States are IT&T, Jones In-ternational University, the DeVry Institute, Sylvan Learning Center, Harcourt Brace, and the Apollo Group. The Apollo Group, which operates the Uni-versity of Phoenix, is expected to have an earnings growth rate of 25 percent over a five-year period. The University of Phoenix enrolls 75,000 students, of whom about 14,000 are attending courses exclusively on-line. It has fifty-one campuses and eighty learning centers in fifteen states, Puerto Rico, and Canada; it is currently the university with the largest student enrollment out-side the public state system and is listed on the New York Stock Exchange. During the first quarter of 1998, it posted profits of U.S.$12.7 million on a turnover of U.S.$85 million (Newby 1999).[13] Investors in higher education recognize the existence of a huge market for "offshore" academic programs and are actively seeking sites in developing countries. The Western Gover-nors University, a consortium of public universities in the Midwest and northern Rocky Mountain region of the United States, is a case in point. West-ern Governors is a partner of the Open University of the United Kingdom and will soon offer American degrees by distance learning across the United States and to overseas students (Newby 1999).

For-profit universities offer degrees that require minimal laboratory equipment and that respond to current market needs. They charge tuition fees that are lower than established universities and offer schedule arrangements that permit greater flexibility in student access to courses. In so doing, they are presenting serious competition to traditional univer-sities. For example, while most universities are reporting a drop in the number of bachelor's degrees awarded in business, similar programs at for-profit institutions relying on distance education have increased their enrollment by as much as 180 percent and tripled it at the master's degree level. In 1997, the University of Phoenix accounted for 58 percent of bachelor's degrees in business in the United States (O'Meara 2001). In Australia, the established Auckland University is being challenged by the newer Massey University, a "different style of university that provides flexible study options (extramural, internal, or block courses), a wider range of university programs, extensive research expertise and established centers of excellence," according to Massey's own advertisements (Boshier 2000, 12).

The presence of entrepreneurs in higher education provides increased access at lower costs. In large part because of private involvement, eastern Asia has become the region with the highest growth rate in tertiary education in the world. Particularly because of the incorporation of China into the global market, Asia will produce a demand for forty-eight million university places from 1998 to 2020, which represents a growth of 37,000 places per week, meaning that Asia will need a new university every week (Blight, cited in Lee 1999).[14]

The World Bank has actively supported a number of higher-education projects to liberalize and privatize this level of education, from Senegal to Mexico. As remarked in an earlier section of this chapter, the Bank justifies the privatization of higher education on the grounds that this promotes equity and thus democratizes it. Yet both privatization and liberalization policies contain aspects that raise concerns about curriculum, program standards, faculty attributes, and program requirements since these are almost solely decided by the commercial institution. Altbach (2000), long an observer of institutions of higher education, predicts that the profit motive will blind providers to other issues and that knowledge products will be sold across borders but with little mutual exchange of ideas, long-term scientific collaboration, and exchanges of faculty or students. There is already evidence of this: GATE (Global Alliance for Transnational Education), while created to foster cross-border higher-education enterprises, leaves regulation in the hands of those who own and control the new multinational and distance education institutions (Altbach 2000).

Operating procedures of universities such as Phoenix produce enormous personnel and governance implications for other institutions of higher education. Phoenix provides access to courseware over the Internet and to course assistants in their local study centers. By extending these mechanisms to a wider market, the University of Phoenix estimates that the entire future U.S. higher-education system could be supported by about 250,000 course assistants (as opposed to 750,000 fully tenured professors at the present time). Courses would be held with on-line performances from 1,000 star performers—the leading researchers and teachers who would appear in front of a television camera and who would have sold their courses to Phoenix (Newby 1999). Decisions about courses would depend only on Phoenix's management.

Accompanying globalization and the emergence of the private sector has been a noticeable expansion of higher education. At the same time, the expansion gives rise to new, weaker institutions with less prestige than the established ones. A de facto bifurcated system of higher education is created, so that although more people are gaining access to those levels, the distinction now emerges among these new programs and the degrees offered by elite universities or institutes, with the latter carrying more prestigious recognition.

A number of courses in universities have gone for sale in the sense that corporations are asking to sponsor courses in which students conduct market research or related work for the client. Universities enter into deals with corporations to provide on-line, accredited MBAs for their employees. Pharmaceutical companies are funding biological research budgets and faculty positions in return for first rights to license agreements on research discoveries (O'Meara 2001). The emergence of an elite linked to technological firms and with influence in many sectors has earned them a new name in the media: the digerati.

Not only is private enterprise entering into the provision of higher education, but higher education as well is creating courses to further foster an entrepreneurial spirit in education. Some universities are working on the notion of the "education industry" and thus looking into what are called "emerging educational enterprises." A number of schools of education are offering courses to design and implement business plans to create for-profit educational organizations; typically, these courses include developing "pitches" to sell these plans to "members of the investment community."

The privatization of the higher-education system, which as we have seen is greatly aided by the twin forces of globalization and neoliberal philosophy, creates a number of unknowns. Some observers predict that privatization—and the concomitant expansion of institutions of higher education—will create educational inflation without contributing to the growth of its economy. It is also believed that privatization will contribute to the formation of a student body that is less dependent, financially and politically, on the state and thus more critical of the public educational institution (Mojab 2000). However, we have seen that a growing trend is the diminishing importance of fields of study based on critical thinking, as history and philosophy tend to be; this may not result in a significant questioning of the new private educational system that is emerging.

As higher education becomes more dependent on business for its subsistence, what will happen in countries where there is no tradition and little material base for corporate-funded research and for donations from alumni and foundations? What will happen also in societies where poor families cannot contribute to the tuition of their children?

In affecting the definition and structure of professions, the internationalization of economies is moving fields of study toward convergence. Becoming increasingly similar are the processes through which abilities are acquired and appraised; the rigor, nature, and duration of supervision during preparatory practice; and the nature of assessment procedures that evaluate the mastery of skills (Neave, cited in Orzack 1992). Frequent exchanges of high-level personnel across countries demand uniformity of skills. The free movement of qualified personnel, common in the European Union, requires harmonization of professional standards, such as restrictions in services offered, requirements for membership, quotas on educational programs, subsidies, fees, insurance payments, ethical norms, and professions requiring formal education. Orzack (1992) predicts that there will be a push toward greater regional/global regulations, not less. He cites the case of modifications in the engineering profession in Denmark, where at one time this occupation was not regulated (i.e., subject to a well-specified curriculum), in contrast to France, where it is. He also envisages likely disputes regarding occupations such as pharmacy (vs. medical doctors), optics (vs. ophthalmology), and accountancy (vs. bookkeeping). The process of homogenization of content and definition of occupations is in itself not bad; the problem would arise if this process were to redefine fields in ways that exclude degrees from other countries.

In this regard, a process of marginalization has been noted to accompany the homogenization of higher education. The 1990s witnessed widespread international scientific collaboration, with scientific work accomplished through networks and teams whose members resided in geographically separated institutions, reflected in the increase in international collaboration in selected scientific journals covering mathematics, physics, chemistry, and biology from 6 percent in 1981 to 11 percent by 1991 and 15 percent by 1995 (David 2000, 10). This increase, David argues, is not entirely due, as some might expect, to greater computer-mediated communications but was also facilitated by the end of the Cold War.

To what extent will the Third World benefit from this increased collaboration? A survey of institutionalized research capabilities found that only about forty among the 130 developing countries possessed a "solid" indigenous science and technology base sufficient to create the "grounds for endogenous technological innovation and the capacity to enter into collaborative agreement with international scientific projects" (David 2000, 11–12). Collaboration depends on access to libraries of international working papers, current databases, high-speed communications with distant collaborators, and (in the case of scientific fields) expensive equipment. In the absence of these resources, highly competent researchers will experience "marginalization, rapid obsolescence of their expertise, and frustration in their chosen lines of scientific investigation" (David 2000, 12).

NEW EDUCATIONAL TECHNOLOGIES

According to the International Data Corporation, by 2002 some 2.2 million college and graduate students throughout the world will be taking courses on-line; this contrasts starkly with 700,000 such students three years ago. It is projected that 80 percent of higher-education institutions in the United States will be offering on-line instruction in a few years (Schevitz 2001).

A combination of technological developments and economic globalization tendencies is at work in the creation of programs using distance forms of education. A growing convergence of business interests emerging among companies serving distinct markets and market segments has resulted in an explosion of partnerships and alliances between educational institutions, corporations, and Web-based business (Evans et al. 2000).

Among such ventures now in existence is the International Space University (ISU) with almost thirty interactive or satellite campuses electronically connected around the world. Students and faculty of ISU work in teams, conduct interdisciplinary design studies, and simulate future space missions through collaborative electronic networks (Pelton 1996). There are also such companies as Jones Intercable and the Mind Extension University that offer a mixture of videotapes, readings, interaction with CD-ROMs or Web sites, and e-mail chat groups that may teach more than a lecturer in a classroom can (Pelton 1996). Some countries are taking firm steps to benefit from the new communication technologies. South Korea is streamlining the country's computer networks to help promote the expansion of on-line learning in the country's universities. The plan, by the Ministry of Education, will also promote the use of English as the second language of instruction. In the United Kingdom, the British Aerospace Virtual University and the Unipart University are rapidly expanding their capability and offerings.

A recent and rich example of new partnerships is the coalition of the University of California, Los Angeles, School of Theater, Film and Television; the Australian Film, Television, and Radio School; and the National Film and Television School of Great Britain. This cross-continental partnership will offer a three-year certificate with a sequence of on-line courses focusing on making movies with digital technology. It will also offer courses for elementary and secondary students, professional training courses on integrating audio and video into business, and general interest courses on the history and making of films (Schevitz 2001). This partnership is expected to cost between U.S.$20 and U.S.$30 million, money that will be raised "through partnership with industry." Already more than 90,000 students have reportedly contacted UCLA expressing interest in the on-line program (Schevitz 2001). As Newby (1999) comments, "Why should a mature, part-time student enroll in a mediocre MBA course at the University of Poppleton, when he or she—possibly supported by their employer—could take an MBA from Harvard or MIT over the Net?"

To help African higher education, the World Bank established in 1998 the African Virtual University (AVU). At present, it connects twenty-five African universities through the Internet using satellite broadcasts. Thus far, it has

been offering undergraduate and remedial courses, but soon it will grant
B.A. degrees in computer science, computer engineering, and electrical engineering. The AVU's objectives are "to provide quality, cost-effective, mass
education at the tertiary level in a resource deprived environment" (Oberle
1998, 55). This virtual university offers courses designed by the University of
Massachusetts and the New Jersey Institute of Technology in the United
States and by the University College Galway in Ireland (Okuni 2000). So,
while it provides new knowledge to African countries, at the same time it
presents knowledge conceived in the North and most suitable to its own
conditions.

As Web-based education becomes more widespread, this will affect a
number of current regulations governing higher education, typically including "full-time," defined as one attending twelve or more hours of classes
each week; the classroom as the site of at least 50 percent of instruction in a
course; and "residence" requirements (which, although they vary across universities, still need the student's presence on campus at some point). Some
problems that have surfaced include students in institutions that offer on-line
master's degree programs in electrical engineering who do not qualify for
federal financial aid because they do not meet campus residence requirements. Some international students will also encounter problems to obtain
student visas as the definition of "full-time" enrollment changes (Kirby 2000).

Some consequences of education by Internet remain to be fully assessed.
What will happen as students spend less time in social interaction and more
time in front of computer screens? Very limited evidence is provided by a
study at Kings College (London), which began offering virtual learning environments in 1998, at which time module tutors (i.e., instructors) were en-
couraged to rewrite modules for this method of teaching and learning. An
evaluation of the program in 1999–2000 focused on one element of the virtual classroom: the interactive communication system that gives students the
opportunity to communicate and discuss their courses asynchronously (at
times of their own choosing). The findings showed that most interaction
lacked the sociolinguistic conventions to guide the initiation, development,
and closure of group discussions. In consequence, effective communication
did not occur, leading to the "fragmentation of a learning community with
feelings of isolation and confusion among some students" (Richardson and
Turner 2001).

INTELLECTUAL PROPERTY RIGHTS AND
THE COMMODIFICATION OF KNOWLEDGE

While advocates of globalization praise the enormous development in communication technologies and call the current era the "knowledge society,"

never before has knowledge been so protected. A Baltimore inventor is said to have received a letter from Thomas Jefferson in 1813 in which Jefferson writes, "He who receives an idea from me, receives instruction himself without lessening mine; as he who lights his taper at mine, receives light without darkening me" (cited in David 2000, 13). This view of ownership of information ("infinite expansibility") is seen as a central feature of commodities known as "pure public goods." But under today's market economics, certain information and knowledge does not circulate to be shared freely among the many. Rather, much information and knowledge is being increasingly protected through commercially driven exploitation by means of patents, copyrights, and privatization.

A major mechanism for the protection of knowledge, especially that which can be sold in the labor market, consists of the agreements on trade-related intellectual property rights (TRIPS). At present, intellectual rights agreements posit an asymmetrical definition of the private domain, engaging mostly in rhetorical reference to the power of individual "rights." As David (2000) puts it,

> [Intellectual] property rights both delineate and convey to the holder the legally sanctioned conditions for excluding others from trespass: they do not establish for others any positive rights not to be excluded. Although the concept of a distinct sphere demarcated as the "public domain" is well recognized under conventional intellectual property laws, what it contains is not defined and legal "rights" to its use are not delineated; "property" is what is defined by the law, and the public domain holds the residuum. Thus, the exemptions permitted for "fair use" of copyrighted material (under U.S. copyright law and the Berne Convention) do not convey to researchers, educators or literary commentators any positive rights to reproduce expressive material without license from the copyright holder. Instead, they offer simply a legitimate ground for defence against suits brought for copyright infringement. . . . As "fair use" is not then a legally established "right," there is nothing in the law that reciprocally secures reasonable conditions of "fair use" access to legally protected texts and data for a purpose such as research or evaluation. (17–18)

Consequences of this attitude toward the protection of knowledge are emerging in academic institutions. One account, coming from an academic in a major U.K. research university, states that research faculty members who have developed or invented a creative product that may be capable of exploitation have been instructed by university administrators not to publish a paper concerning the invention, not to deliver a lecture at a conference on it, and to avoid talking about the invention to industrialists—all clearly forms of academic conduct much at variance with traditional forms of sharing knowledge and discoveries. UCLA, a major U.S. university, is currently requiring faculty in arts and sciences to place their course content on the Web. It did so without any prior consultation, thus challenging the intellectual property rights typically held by individual professors. In Canada, faculty at York University went on strike to prevent such a requirement. Note that these examples of university protection of property rights invoke the right of the institution, not the individual. The ultimate purpose is the commercialization of knowledge, not its free and wide dissemination. However, pressures to protect one's knowledge are also emanating from the academic researchers themselves. In fields such as biotechnology, where large revenues stand to be obtained with new products, there seems to be a shift from "publish and perish" to "patent and profit" (Abate 2001).

The application of intellectual property rights to university work is making academic institutions increasingly secretive and modifying the scientific culture of sharing and exchanging points of view. Disclosure will occur, therefore, primarily under market conditions. A patent gives monopoly over knowledge to the creators (individual and institutional) of the invention, and the sharing of that knowledge is possible only to those who pay for it. This principle has protected many worthwhile scientific and technical advances in the past. What becomes problematic today is its excessive extension to so many areas of life and thought. The new situation may produce what David (2000, 8) calls the "tragedy of the commons," or the potential destruction of public knowledge from "over fencing," namely, the creation of artificial barriers whose purpose is the extraction of economic rents.

RECAPITULATING

The possibilities and challenges facing the university in these globalized times are many. Among the welcome possibilities is a new window of great creativity, aided by new technologies and the presence of social actors with innovative perspectives. The expansion of access to higher education in many countries and greater connectivity between ideas and use are positive developments.

The challenges are, unfortunately, numerous. Speaking in the context of higher education in the United States, Kerr (2001) identifies four challenges: ensuring that cooperation with industry does not intrude on the basic science activities and the integrity of the research university, developing admissions and tuition policies to serve the expanding number of students, improving the performance of schools of education in training teachers, and selecting able university presidents. In this appraisal, it is clear that issues of student access, academic content, and governance are at play. On a broader scale, many fear that today we face the emergence of social Darwinism—people being pressured to compete as profit maximizers rather than to co-operate as citizens, accompanied by a splintering of progressive causes (Schugurensky 2000).

An increasing number of universities are engaging in expansion and exchanges with other countries. Unfortunately, the prevailing motivation these days is profit rather than human solidarity. How can the curricula of higher-education institutions consider the distinct perspectives and issues generated in many fields and in other countries? How do we prepare faculty and students to become global citizens? Global expertise should consider leave programs for development work abroad, faculty exchanges, and financial resources for professional international travel. It should include the development of internal and external partnerships that promote a vision that recognizes diversity and the preparation of students from a cross-cultural perspective around values such as tolerance, respect, and appreciation of ethnic differences (Firebaugh and Miller 2000).

As fields of study expand and there are large flows of students across countries, one likely outcome is that comparative and international education will attain greater importance. Altruistic and self-serving reasons will operate: The importance of knowing other groups and cultures and the perceived need to foster social justice and sustainable development but at the same time the need to become more competitive will require universities to learn what others are doing and to seek ways to increase the enrollment of international students. The development of comparative insights across situations and countries will improve our understanding of current and evolving trends, but how much room is there today for comparative reflexivity?

A desirable direction for comparative and international education should be to deal with problems that go beyond the nation-state, such as AIDS, awareness of ethnic conflict, asymmetries along gender lines, and environmental impacts, such as ozone depletion and ocean/land pollution. Williams (2000) gives a positive example of the conceptual changes taking place in some parts of society, noting that the concept of "global security" is being redefined from ensuring human safety through military means alone to including the understanding of threats to human well-being from development (meeting human needs), environment (damage to the environment), and violence (human rights, civil unrest, and terrorism). The university is responding to these changes, but its curricula are undergoing modifications slowly. Some subjects can serve to make the university more internationalized than globalized,[15] such as the use of a second or third language and the study of history, particularly global history, to understand rapid social changes and uncertainties linked to globalization.

Marginson and Mollis (2001) identify a clear agenda for comparative education that involves engaging in research on the global agencies and other global institutions, on the new geopolitical-educational structures of power in a globalizing world of international education including on-line education, and on the implications of new forms of governance and identities other than the national. They also recommend the use of more qualitative research approaches to move researchers beyond positivist frameworks and static categories.

While there are many challenges for the university, we need to recognize a crucial fact: In terms of social understanding and praxis, the university may not be developing the most important knowledge for the creation of a new social order. New competitors have emerged from within civil society in the form of social movements.[16] Hegedus (1990) calls these movements a "self-creative society." A noticeable difference in the knowledge held by these movements is their widening coverage of issues in contrast to the discreteness and narrowness of the research fields of the university, a consequence of the different analytical perspectives, epistemological bases, and research methodologies in use. In this respect, Hegedus notices that some formal research endeavors are based on theories that emphasize change at the individual or micro social order (such as those proposed by the economist Milton Friedman [1962]), while others consider primarily the organizational and/or political level (such as those put forward by the sociologist Claus Offe [1984]). Social movements, in comparison, are producing more holistic knowledge based on ongoing practice and exchange with their immediate environment.

The university's attainment of its positive potential will require a social protagonism most intellectuals have seldom had to engage in. These persons have a social responsibility to create and offer learning environments that foster the students' development of intercultural adaptability and human solidarity; they also have a responsibility to engage the rest of society in a critical understanding of ongoing economic and political developments throughout the world. Yet can faculty help mobilize public opinion and understanding when many professors themselves are not reacting to the corporatization of the academy in the first place?

NOTES

1. The reference to the "knowledge-based economy" is somewhat misleading in that most workers will not be those with high levels of skill. In the United States, the country at the vanguard of globalization, less skilled workers constitute the majority of its labor force.

While it is true that these workers have experienced zero or even negative real-wage growth, it remains inarguable that any economy requires workers/employees at all skill levels.

2. Education serves to stabilize society by holding the possibility of upward mobility and opportunity through schooling and credentials, all the more at higher levels of education. But the greatest portion of upward mobility has been found from changing job structures, not through education or human resource planning.

3. It would be erroneous to assert that there is a single university model in the industrialized countries. The countries of Anglo-Saxon origin have a liberal/pluralist/federalist model, while France has a unitary/statist model. The latter is characterized by free education for all high school graduates by right with no unmet student demand, greater decentralization of system administration, more university autonomy, creation of stand-alone campuses, increasing government resources, and steadily rising standards of pedagogical practice and innovation. The former, especially evident in Australia, is currently characterized by increasing privatization, increased accountability, and, consequentially, greater stress and lower morale in the faculty (DeAngelis 1996).

4. In the larger institutional context, several U.S. universities are withdrawing from comprehensive full coverage of fields, as their campuses are being asked to complement each other and create a specialization niche (Gumport 2000).

5. In the United States, a key country in the marketing of programs abroad, foreign-language study and competence has decreased in requirements in four-year institutions from 34 percent in 1965 to 22 percent in 1995 (Engberg 2001).

6. I owe this point to Raymond Morrow (personal communication, November 2001).

7. More universities are adding global tracks to their marketing curriculum, but mainly so that students learn how to negotiate and develop relationships in other cultures (Schmidt 2000).

8. *U.S. News and World Report,* the dominant source of U.S. university rankings, uses seven criteria: academic reputation (obtained through comments by presidents, provosts, and deans of admission), student permanence in the university, faculty resources (class size, faculty salary, proportion of faculty with highest academic degree, and full-time faculty), student selectivity in admissions, financial resources spent on services and programs, student graduation rate performance, and alumni donations. This magazine sets de facto higher-education policy, sending all universities into an array of short- and long-term activities to move up in the hierarchy. Departments unable to improve their rankings are perceived as incompetent and even subject to closure. According to anecdotal information, one prestigious university whose history department was found to rank tenth told its external evaluators to verify whether such ranking was correct, in which case the department was to be closed. As it turned out, the evaluators gave the department a very strong recommendation.

9. Perhaps as consequence of the international student expansion, both Australia and New Zealand have announced their intention in 1999 to develop an "Asian focus" in their curriculum (Dale and Robertson 2002).

10. Moreover, there will always exist mediocre and poor institutions. The challenge is to help weak institutions improve and to give them the resources to identify their weaknesses and correct them. Further, rankings that locate universities and departments in positions according to a single set of criteria are not sensitive to alternative missions or differential institutional phases or sizes; they condemn weak or incipient institutions to premature failure.

11. Schemes to introduce tuition fees are typically accompanied by the provision of student loans to low-income students. This option is not considered very attractive since loans become due at graduation time and if the student has not been able to find a job, he or she faces payments that cannot be made.

12. This instance of internationalization, via a marriage of convenience between universities in the First and the Third Worlds, is a purely finance-driven response to globalization. Universities will go most likely in the direction of airlines—developing global alliances to attract the requisite investment and enrollment.

13. The University of Phoenix requires higher tuition fees than other universities. The cost of its courses (as of 2001) was between U.S.$1,200 and U.S.$1,300 per unit. This higher cost is offset by the convenience in schedules and the fact that physical presence of students at the university is kept to a minimum. Not surprising, most students have regular jobs; 65 percent of the students at the university are subsidized by their companies. It currently offers twenty-three degrees, primarily in business, education, and health. Its "classes," or rather work groups, typically have ten students. Each course is led by a professor who is a well-recognized leader in the field. The university has 1,600 faculty members and 21,000 students (2001 data).

14. The higher-education expansion in Asia is due to its previous low third enrollment ratio in Asia, in contrast, for instance, to that in Latin America.

15. P. Jones (2000) makes a distinction between globalization and internationalism that is helpful to consider. He considers globalization the emergence of a world economy and internationalism the development of global solidarity through democracy and peace.

16. Social movements are loose coalitions of groups seeking to create an oppositional discourse on human rights, social justice, equality, and global well-being. The literature differentiates between the traditional social movements, mostly Marxist inspired, that sought resolution to social class conflicts from the "new social movements," which are not class based but rather are formed around important social issues, such as the ecology, the possible use of atomic weapons, rights for indigenous peoples, women's rights, and the defense of gay/lesbian identities.

7

Gender within Globalized Education

This chapter considers the consequences of the globalization process for women and men. More conceptually, it asks, What consequences has globalization brought on the social construction of gender?

The second women's movement in the 1970s[1] aspired to more than equal political rights; it sought also to bring an end to the oppression by men and gain new freedoms for women (Reinalda 2000). Though their position is generally better than in the past, in no country do women have power equivalent to that of men. On the basis of a still rough statistical indicator used by the United Nations—the Gender Empowerment Measure (GEM), which considers the political and economic decision making of women in addition to their per capita income—it can be seen that in no country do women have the economic, social, or political power of men; the highest score (in a system in which 1.0 indicates parity with men) is 0.825 for Norway. Of the eighty countries for which the pertinent indicators are available, thirty-two show GEM scores less than half that expected under conditions of equality (United Nations Development Program 2000, 165–68).

In balance, what have been the consequences of globalization on women? It will be shown that the gendered nature of market forces and public policy are attributes that globalization has not been able to alter. In fact, it has built on them. Conditions in the process of formal education continue to present features that produce and reproduce a subordinate status for women in society. At the same time, new possibilities for change are emerging, notably through organized women's groups in civil society. To analyze the conditions of women and the situation of gender in times of globalization, this chapter follows an approach that builds on four streams: the economic, the communications, the cultural, and the educational. In doing so, the objective is to present a balance of positive and negative consequences of globalization for women as well as for the political project that women are following (or can follow) to attain liberation from sexism and patriarchal domination.

CONCEPTUALIZING GENDER IN DEVELOPMENT

Feminist scholars have made substantial progress in the understanding of how gender functions in society. Over the past thirty years, they have moved from seeing the problem of women as one of *exclusion* from access to social benefits to identifying and exploiting the resources and opportunities needed for their integration and then to recognizing the key problem as being precisely their *integration* into a process that relies on a gendered division of labor and power (Elson and McGee 1995; O'Brien et al. 2000).

As an analytical model, gender implies the interconnection of different structures on which inequalities between women and men are built. It considers phenomena of symbolic and sociostructural character and is alert to questions of material and ideological production and reproduction (Maquieira and Vara 1997). The axes of discrimination and disadvantage in society are multiple. They include patriarchal gender relations, racial hierarchies, and class inequalities, all of which create differential access to means of production, distribution, exchange, and communication. While these axes of discrimination include more than gender, their combined power makes the situation of women one of the most deprived in the world, regardless of class, ethnic, and "race" affiliation.

Feminist scholars made a significant advancement when they realized that the intimate spheres of social life play a central role in the creation of gender relations and representations. This leads them to argue, as Fraser (1989) does, that families are sites of labor, exchange, calculation, distribution, and exploitation and to maintain that it is a "grave mistake" to restrict the term "power" to bureaucratic contexts, for there is domestic-patriarchal power as well as bureaucratic-patriarchal power. Fraser contends that perhaps symbolic and material reproductions are not totally divided since the production of food and objects in themselves produces social identities. Finally, she asserts that the worker-breadwinner role integrates the family with the economy and the state and confirms women's dependent status in each.

Theoretical advances in the connection between gender and society on the one hand and gender and social development on the other unfortunately have not been matched by progress in other public arenas. More women than men experience poverty, and this increases over the life cycle of women, as they have family responsibilities that men do not (Townsend 1993). While all international institutions and most governments see the need to address gender concerns today, their arguments in favor of women are usually framed in terms of women as mothers, housewives, caretakers, and workers. This is reflected in a recent and important speech on the new millennium by Kofi Annan (2000, 23), current secretary-general of the United Nations, who argued that "extending equal opportunities to women and girls has multiplier effects for entire families and even communities," thus, perhaps unwittingly, reiterating the argument that women are important not on their own merits as citizens but as individuals who will facilitate the lofty pursuits of others.

The State and Social Welfare

An extensive body of feminist theory recognizes the complexity of state formations (Blackmore 1999; Eisenstein 1979; Franzway et al. 1989; Ruggie 1984; Walby 1990; Watson 1990). While the state is the primary site of policy and regulation, it does not always deliver for all its citizens, and often it does not deliver equally. But regardless of differences among states and their commitments to the solution of gender differences, the less the state provides in welfare, the more that is done by women.

There is agreement among feminists and other scholars that the emerging global economic mechanisms—notably deregulation, liberalization, and privatization—are gendered in conceptualization and effect (O'Brien et al. 2000, 84; see also Mittelman and Tambe 2000; Sen 1998). Market reforms have accentuated geographic, ethnic, and gender disparities in educational access and achievement in many countries, from China to Chile.

The burdens imposed in developing countries by structural adjustment programs (SAPs), a prominent feature of neoliberal policies, have been felt by poor women more than any other group, given their socially circumscribed access to and control of land, labor, credit, and extension services and even control over their own physical mobility (O'Brien et al. 2000). A common requirement of SAPs is the closing of state-run firms and the curtailing of expenditures by the state, primarily in social welfare areas such as health, agricultural subsidies, and education. Increases in the prices of food, fuel, and essential services such as water and electricity have placed extra burdens on women in low-income households. Because welfare is still very much associated with women's responsibilities, these measures have reduced state support for women, who then have had to engage in self-help activities. Cuts in social provision have also affected women's employment since a large number had been working in government bureaucracies. For many poor women, indeed, the boundaries between the formal and the informal sector of the economy are becoming blurred as they are obtaining "flexible" jobs, a euphemism for work with little employment security and weak or limited benefits regarding sick leave, maternity leave, and pension plans. Despite these negative effects, the official discourse on structural adjustments is notoriously silent on gender issues.

A series of world conferences over the past decade dealing with a wide range of social issues (population, human rights, housing, education, health, and the environment) have progressively heightened international awareness of the multiplicity of actions that must be taken to improve social conditions. Unfortunately, governments sign declarations but often do not honor their commitment. Copehagen+5, as is termed the five-year assessment of the World Social Summit (held in Copenhagen in 1995), found that only four of the 186 signatory countries had honored their commitments (United Nations Commission for Social Development 2000). Similar conclusions about the poor response of states to commitments were reached in the midevaluation of the Fourth World Conference on Women (held in Beijing, also in 1995). Even today, after more than a decade of conferences to advance the condition of women, internationally accepted indicators of income-related poverty do not provide information on the particular incidence of poverty among women. Gender concerns have become a voluntary matter.

Weakening the state response to women is the position taken by large multinational and bilateral agencies that do not acknowledge groups of civil society as possible partners but that deal almost exclusively with the state. Typically, development program assistance makes no connection between gender equity objectives and economic policy reform (Elson and McGee 1995). The World Bank, the largest and most influential of international agencies, does not recognize women as legitimate interlocutors in economic policymaking. In 1997, the World Bank attempted to correct this shortcoming by setting up a Gender Sector Board in one of the four new Technical Networks that represent restructured thematic support service to countries. But parallel changes in World Bank organizational procedures now make it necessary for specialists to sell their services to project designers (O'Brien et al. 2000). In other words, gender specialists can intervene only if they are requested to do so.

In industrialized countries, under current notions of economic competitiveness, gender policies, and equity policies in general have taken a very marginal position. There has been a downgrading and downsizing of affirmative action and equal employment opportunity machinery in many central countries (Henry 2001). In the United States, the country leading the globalization movement, welfare has been replaced by "workfare" schemes, making it impossible for poor women to attend school. Even though an educational attainment gap between women and men no longer exists in the United States, women do not have access to equivalent jobs or to well-paid jobs. Having more years of schooling has not resulted in correspondingly better jobs for African American and Hispanic women (Weis 2000). In Australia, a country with a distinguished record of support for gender issues, funding for the Human Rights and Equal Opportunity Commission—a com mission central to the advancement of women—has been reduced, and there is no longer a separate commissioner for sex-based discrimination (Henry 2001). The U.S. government disbanded the Office of Women's Issues at the White House in March 2001. Although this office never had a large staff or substantial charge, its disappearance signals a reduced symbolic recognition for gender issues.

In developing countries, gender is also losing its specificity and importance. While it is recognized that poverty is an outcome of the interaction between globalization, marginalization, and gender (Mittelman and Tambe 2000), dominant neoliberal perspectives believe that poverty will be eliminated through integration of workers—men and women—into the international capitalist economy because, they argue, poverty is essentially underutilized labor. Poverty is also defined as evincing low consumption levels. In this framing of poverty, overconsumption by others (and thus the tendency to offer low wages to workers, particularly in Third World countries) is not seen as a cause of poverty.

THE ECONOMIC STREAM

Ward (1984) observed, "The intrusion of the world-system through foreign investment from and trade dependency on core nations has operated to reduce women's status relative to men's" (3). She perceived that more men were gaining access to new agricultural technologies, that women were being relegated to local trade routes while men controlled national and international trade relations, and that men were having access to capital-intensive investment and new industries from the core countries.

The situation in 2002 is no different. Traditional gender ideologies continue to pervade the social relations of production. The articulation of gender ideology with globalization ideology creates and sustains persistent poverty (Mittelman and Tambe 2000, 80). Neoliberal principles such as deregulation, liberalization, and privatization are gendered because they simply assume women's ability and willingness to bear increasing demands on their labor, in household obligations of food provision, for child rearing and educating, and as caregivers for the elderly. They are gendered also because they ignore that self-regulating markets and the privatization of land restrain women's access to previously community-held productive resources. They are gendered because they continue to assume that women's domestic duty, food provision, and caregiving for the family are activities rewarded through love and the gratitude of family members (Mittelman and Tambe 2000, 84–85).

Under neoliberal economic philosophies, women are being negatively impacted in both urban and rural production. In Africa, rural women represent 60 to 80 percent of the agricultural workforce (Arrighi and Silver 2000), but few, if any, government policies consider this group worthy of significant and sustained intervention. A case study of Mozambique showed that privatizing land and raising cash crops works against the interest of women farmers (as communal lands are lost and growing for the market leads to cultivating agricultural products for export, not domestic consumption). Decreases in state funding of health and rural transport further affect rural women. And in communities that manage resources on the basis of common property and indigenous knowledge of biodiversity, women are increasingly being squeezed out (Sen 2001). Trends toward industrialized production in rural areas are affecting women's ownership of and access to land. Further, the loss of local plant and animal species to large-scale, commercial production is a particular challenge to women since they rely on seasonal diversity and variation to ensure food, income, and health for their families.

Many urban women, particularly at lower levels of education, are being incorporated into export industries that are labor intensive.[2] A case study of the Philippines (Mittelman and Tambe 2000) found that women in export-processing zones (EPZs) earn wages below the minimal requirements. In many countries, women are operating under subcontract arrangements that place them at the mercy of brokers who determine production and compensation rules. When subcontracted and thus physically dispersed, women cannot organize themselves in unions or associations. Even workers in EPZ firms cannot be unionized because employers can fire them quickly. In some cases, the production technology of many such firms has become highly mobile, as physical plants operating in portable modules can move out of certain neighborhoods, as is reported to be the case in the Dominican Republic. Under such conditions, women are not available for unionization; they are not even available for training using nonformal education approaches.

No country in Asia has been able to expand its manufacturing capacity without pulling an increasing proportion of women into industrial wage employment.[3] In the early 1990s, women accounted for more than 43 percent of the manufacturing workforce in Indonesia, Malaysia, the Philippines, Singapore, and Thailand. In countries making the transition from socialism to capitalism, such as Cambodia, the Lao PDR, and Vietnam, women's labor is a significant element of their "comparative advantage" in export-oriented manufacture. Few governments have or are willing to enforce legislation that ensures women workers in the manufacturing sector fair living wages, benefits, occupational safety, and opportunities for upgrading skills (Guttal 2000). Poverty, however, is so great that, for many women, low-paying jobs in the EPZs are better than unpaid service within the family. Mittelman and Tambe (2000) consider that in those situations, "the resolution of poverty lies in establishing a social market—resubordinating economics to society but without maintaining the gender ideologies that helped to animate these inegalitarian and hierarchical social structures in the first place" (89).

Given the low level of attention paid to social and collective economic development of rural areas (since globalization is based on industrialization), in many countries women migrate from rural to urban areas and then become hawkers and vendors in the urban informal sector or work as factory workers, as domestic workers, and increasingly as prostitutes. This is a pattern documented in case studies of Thailand and the Philippines (Guttal 2000) but also noticeable in countries in Africa and Latin America.

A high expectation of globalization was that the new technologies of production would create a new division of labor and emphasize flexibility and cooperation, thus generating exceptional opportunities for women (Valdes 1991). The world's economy is frequently described as post-Fordist. Yet for many low-income women, the Fordist model (fragmented tasks and assembly-line production) continues to prevail.[4] Agro-industries tend to hire young and unmarried women, many in temporary jobs with very discrete tasks. Eighty-four percent of the jobs in the fruit industries in Chile are seasonal jobs (Maquieira and Vara 1997). Women in garment and electronic factories perform tasks heavily linked to assembly-line features. Women indeed have gained much more access to paid employment, but many jobs remain characterized by uncertain terms of duration and low wages. More women can be found in the service economy, but they occupy low-level positions (Sen 2001). In the area of educational jobs, more women can now be found as schoolteachers and in university positions. At the same time, the competitive globalized economy is pressing institutions to become efficient by doing "more with less." One of the strongest trends in U.S. higher education is part-time employment; women hold one-third of the full time jobs and half the part-time appointments.

A popular principle guiding countries as they seek to reposition themselves in the global economy is to increase their human capital, particularly in science and technology. This objective should work to favor women, but since competition has a strong time dimension, governments are exerting little effort to develop potential resources, preferring instead to work with groups that are more easily available. In the race to make their countries economically productive, they see no time to spare preparing women—or minorities—to fill those positions. The pattern characterizing industrialized countries is to emphasize the short-term fix, importing human resources from other countries (notably India and China) and leaving unattended (sacrificing in a sense) their own potential domestic pools.

Economists have seen that an increased demand for more highly educated, low-cost labor tends to expand women's educational opportunities (Carnoy 2000). On the other hand, women's incorporation into the labor market in conditions of wage and leadership disadvantage compared to men may not suffice to generate changes in the social relations of gender. Career and pay equality for women and men function as a structural precondition for the development of equality between husbands and wives in the family: When women earn less than men, they are not in a position to bargain with their husbands for a more egalitarian division of labor in the home (Messner 1995).[5]

Despite the rhetoric that globalization brings the emergence of a "knowledge society," many jobs at menial and low-skill levels still need to be performed, whether in the informal sector or through domestic work. Globalization has modified neither the social nor the sexual division of labor. Paradoxically, working in a different setting, outside the home, and earning an income, however small, becomes a source of change for women as new social spaces and less financial dependence on men widen one's self-esteem and mental horizon. These small interstices offer some unintentional potential that some women have been able to exploit.

THE COMMUNICATIONS STREAM

Changes in communications technology, mainly the widespread growth of the Internet and cable television in many urban areas of developing countries, have had mostly positive impacts on individual women and women's groups. Through capabilities afforded by e-mail (including attachments) and Web sites, the women's movement and its many constituent organizations are now better organized and more quickly mobilized than in the past and increasingly capable of articulating local with global issues. Constant communication rapidly distributes pertinent information among women activists, keeping them knowledgeable of current issues, actors, and outcomes.

Expeditious dissemination of information on events and outcomes occurring in distant parts of the world or in the corridors of international organizations is both a form of transnational action and the cornerstone of quick response and mobilization and thus a means to strengthen the women's movement. The global forms of solidarity that ensue are expressed in both comprehensive and specialized networks on national, regional, and global scales. Ideas of equality and equity, popularized by the international mass media, now reach and permeate many societies. Even when recognition of these principles operates primarily at the level of lip service, "gender" has entered the official discourses of dominant political institutions.

At the same time, it must be recognized that increased communications cannot by themselves alter power relations. Information about events or knowledge about what lies behind such events and their implications are several steps removed from having the capacity to influence them. Further, an internal debate that remains unresolved among women's institutions is a set of basic contradictions in North–South alliances of women. This point is explored in the section "Toward a North–South Alliance?" later in this chapter.

THE CULTURAL STREAM

Culture is an area in which regional and global agreements and the mass media have played a major role. To a large extent, both have produced positive results, yet negative consequences in the case of the media are also discernable.

In Europe, the Treaty of Rome, signed in 1958 (the precursor to the European Union), affirmed through Article 119 the principle of "equal pay for equal work," obliging all signatory nations to comply with this concept. By the swift power of law, countries such as Spain, Greece, and Turkey, whose cultural values were much more conservative than those in Germany, France, and the Netherlands, have had to implement significant changes in gender relations. Yet the European Union, in acting on gender issues, chose to focus on women in a narrow way, attending only to equal pay and sexual discrimination, a posture that Egan (1998) argues favors "role equity rather than role change" (25). Nevertheless, these are two important issues. While Europe is one of the wealthiest regions of the world, it also experiences unemployment and maintains a clear commitment to neoliberal economic policies. Consequently, European countries have implemented cost reductions in social welfare, thus making it difficult for governments to address gender equity concerns.

Along the same vein, the several global summits sponsored by the United Nations in which a large number of feminist and development-oriented nongovernmental organizations (NGOs) have participated have been a source of knowledge for new values, common problems, and consensual resolution regarding the condition of women throughout the world. As in the case of the European Union, rhetoric has gone far ahead of actual implementation, but many women's groups have endorsed new agendas for action and liberating ways of framing traditional gender issues.

The mass media play a formidable role in gender issues. This area of human relations is one of the most resistant to change, given the deep and pervasive nature of ideological beliefs in many societies. The world media, particularly those reaching many homes in both culturally conservative and progressive countries via television or syndicated programs that receive instant translation, repeatedly portray women in new roles and thereby increase their potential for protagonism. It is easy to learn about women scientists, women presidents, and women chief executive officers. Through the onslaught of advertisements contained in these media (television and journals), new images are constantly presented, often showing men in domestic situations, for example, changing diapers, washing dishes, cooking, or baby-sitting. Yet the media (especially the music recording industry) tend also to present highly sexualized and erotic views of women. Two examples from Latin America reveal these prevailing conditions: Inexpensive, popular tabloids in Peru now feature centerfolds of nude women with full close-ups of genitalia. Most of these women are blond and blue eyed, which means that a transnational industry is behind this production. The Spanish version of the U.S. magazine *Glamour,* which is edited in Miami and enjoys wide distribution in Latin America, offers such self-help articles as "10 Ways to Excite Him in Five Minutes" (December 2000) and "Be the Star on Your Bed" (March 2001), the latter of which deals explicitly with the best position to maximize or hide a particular body feature (bust, derriere, legs, or tummy) while engaging in sexual relations. These articles are mostly translations of English versions. They communicate information and knowledge about practices that acknowledge women's sexual desires—a positive development in the quest for transformation in gender relations—yet they seldom address women as citizens, which would take them into issues of political participation, gender equity policies, women's rights as human rights, and so on. In other words, global magazines consumed by women are a prime source of an imaginary that reproduce an apolitical but increasingly sexualized identity.[6]

The cultural stream produces a serious delusory subjectivity in many young women, causing them to think of themselves as already free and equal to men. They do not see the need for political struggle and consider that women's discrimination and subordination are things of the past. This perspective has been aided by globalization norms spread by the school and the mass media, which convey notions of oneself as classless and apolitical and leads to the demobilization of young women, many of whom exhibit an individualistic approach to problem solving and lack a political consciousness and commitment to truly emancipatory sexual rights; they view sex issues principally as a matter of personal choice, not a collective construct and consequence, thus taking for granted many rights that took considerable struggle to obtain (Kamen 2001).

It has been observed that gender ideologies tend to prevail regardless of technological and educational changes. Luke's (2000) qualitative study of highly successful businesswomen in several Asian countries found that local forms of oppression have not been weakened and that global modern discourses merely coexist with oppressive traditional practices. Traditional notions of saving face, the ethos of patronage, and the social debt economy in Asia lead many professional women to be highly deferential to male mentors, protectors, and family members and thus to maintain separate existences as professionals and as women. In this second role, they absorb—without contestation—many domestic tasks and roles that go counter to their own professional advancement. Luke (2000) concludes that Asian patriarchy, with its strong values of family loyalty and obedience and women's quiet demeanor, is very effective in teaching women "their place."[7]

THE EDUCATION STREAM

Gender is an area where culture, power, and structures intersect at full strength. In the school, therefore, "any individual student's voice is already a 'teeth gritting' and often contradictory intersection of voices constituted by gender, race, class, ability, ethnicity, sexual orientation, or ideology" (Kelly 2000, 167, citing Ellsworth).

Gains in school enrollment—indicators of *access* to education but not indicators of *success*—have been reported in recent years in many developing countries, except in those sub-Saharan countries heavily affected by poverty and illness (primarily HIV/AIDS and derivatives) (United Nations Development Program 1999a). Between 1970 and 1997, women have made gains at all levels of schooling, although only a handful of countries have implemented policies specifically designed to reduce the gender gap.[8] According to UNESCO statistics,[9] Latin America has had gender parity in primary and secondary education since the 1970s, in contrast with regions such as the Arab states and southern Asia, where disparities are still considerable. Women's access to tertiary education remains problematic in all developing regions, except in Latin America, where about seven countries report having slightly more women than men enrolled. Girls' enrollment in rural areas continues to be, for the most part, exceedingly low.

While the UNESCO statistics clustered by region generally show enrollment gains over time, an alternative analysis (Weisbrot et al. 2001), comparing 116 countries before and after the application of neoliberal policies and categorizing those countries by their educational spending as a proportion of the gross domestic product, finds that most countries reduced their public spending on education between 1980 and 2000 (see figure 7.1) and reported a slowdown in the primary and secondary enrollment of girls and boys. (See appendix A for figures 1–4 showing the average yearly change in boys and girls primary school and secondary school enrollment.)

It is estimated that providing primary education for the 130 million children (60 percent of whom are girls) who are now out of school in developing countries would add an estimated U.S.$7 billion a year to educational costs over a ten-year period (Annan 2000, 24). Table 7.1 shows enrollment trends for the past three decades.

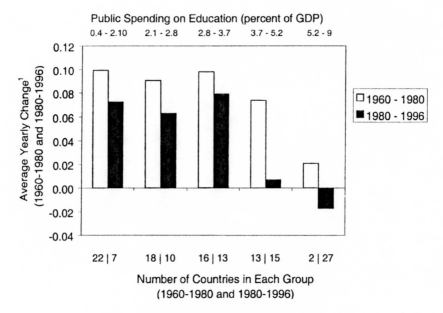

Source: World Bank, World Development Indicators, 2000

[1] In percentage points

Figure 7.1.   Average Yearly Change in Total Public Spending on Education

Observing that the poor educational treatment of girls is "not only a matter of gender discrimination; it is bad economics and bad social policy," the
secretary-general of the United Nations stated in a crucial speech considering the next 1,000 years that "I urge the Millennium Summit to endorse the
objectives of demonstrably narrowing the gender gap in primary and secondary education by 2005 and ensuring that, by 2015 all children complete
a full course of primary education" (Annan 2000, 24–25). Annan urged both
donor agencies in the North and governments in the Third World to comply
with commitments specifically made in 1990 through the Education for All
initiative to attain universal primary education by 2000. What Annan's appeal
failed to note is that these commitments fell considerably short of intended
goals and that the new timeline has not been accompanied by solid analysis
of the conditions under which they would be reached.With the imposition of
neoliberal notions that the state should reduce its intervention in
social spheres, including education, gender policies are being weakened.
Many girls in low-income families, particularly in sub-Saharan Africa and
eastern Asia, drop out of school because their families cannot afford to pay
all the school fees and, when a choice must be made, would prefer to send
their sons. In some countries, the majority of a whole generation, most of

Table 7.1 Enrollment Trends by Sex—All Levels of Education, 1970–1997 (thousands)

Developing Region	Primary Total Enrollment	Proportion Women	Secondary Total Enrollment	Proportion Women	Tetiary Total Enrollment	Proportion Women
Sub-Saharan Africa						
1970	25,318	41	2,640	33	199	20
1980	50,463	44	9,010	36	562	22
1990	64,422	40	14,677	43	1,362	32
1997	81,035	45	21,015	44	2,177	35
Arab States						
1970	12,958	36	3,552	30	446	23
1980	20,744	41	8,762	37	1,487	31
1990	30,353	44	14,991	42	2,449	37
1997	36,625	45	18,710	45	3,906	41
Latin America and Caribbean						
1970	43,963	49	10,740	48	1,639	35
1980	65,414	49	16,969	50	4,908	43
1990	76,552	48	22,656	51	7,410	49
1997	85,177	48	29,153	52	9,448	48
Eastern Asia						
1970	152,767	45	38,167	34	1,435	41
1980	210,902	46	79,037	41	5,293	34
1990	194,867	47	81,963	43	10,603	38
1997	214,682	48	113,404	46	16,790	41
Southern Asia						
1970	71,905	36	26,472	28	2,818	21
1980	96,138	38	42,212	32	4,063	26
1990	136,041	41	70,995	36	6,453	32
1997	157,695	42	94,607	38	9,303	34
All Developing Regions						
1970	312,756	43	84,772	35	6,956	29
1980	449,192	44	159,399	39	16,858	32
1990	570,308	45	209,496	43	29,125	39
1997	579,371	46	283,081	44	43,437	40

Source: Adapted from UNESCO 1999, II-13 and II-14.

them women, has not been able to go to school. Ironically, these countries include Ghana and Uganda, often cited by the World Bank as "success stories" in terms of dealing with SAPs (Muyale-Manenji 1998).

Yielding to the pressure of neoliberalism to shrink state expenditures and beset by the economic hardships generated in part by uncontrolled free trade, many governments in developing countries tend to acknowledge the importance of gender in education but assign limited funds to the implementation of pertinent programs. Much of what is done in this regard is funded by international assistance agencies. Further reducing support for gender programs is the fact that international agencies have reduced their overall aid by one-third between 1986 and 1997, shifting from an average gross national product of 0.35 percent in 1985 to 0.22 percent in 1997(*Washington Post,* 1999). Bilateral agency support for education has also shown decrements in recent years (Mundy 1999).

Educational assistance from development agencies focusing on girls and women in developing countries is usually framed as education for *poor* girls and women. While this group certainly has the most severe needs, conceptualizing gender interventions in terms of a specific subset misses the complexity and pervasive nature of the gender problem.

Valuable insights about the role of the state and the silencing of ideological issues can be gained from one recent document expected to have widespread and free distribution. A publication on gender issues by the Strategies for Advancing Girls Education (SAGE) Project, funded by USAID, proposes "multisectoral support" for basic and girls' education. A reading of the booklet's content reveals that these "sectors" are not government ministries or agencies but rather business, religious, and media institutions. The document makes some unsupported and patently distorted claims about the willingness of these three social groups to be mobilized for the purposes of influencing public education policy, raising public awareness of education issues and services, and providing educational services (Tietjen 2000). A summary of actions taken by the business sector on behalf of girls' education exaggerates the amount and degree of its support by failing to identify the specific monetary amounts and duration of its contribution in the various country case studies. For instance, the report claims that business involvement in Guatemala was characterized by "robust business sector support of girls' education" (Tietjen 2000, viii); however, a formal evaluation of such programs (conducted by Stromquist et al. 2000 at the request of USAID itself) found reasonable involvement by only three firms, one engaged for a very short time, the other two benefiting considerably from the exploitation of their "voluntary" involvement.

Advancing arguments curiously devoid of a theoretical understanding and recognition of existing research on the topic, the same report maintains that "the religious sector stands out as the most stable and committed to girls' education, with a long history of support," while the media is said to possess the "skills, tools and technologies needed to promote girls' education" (Tietjen 2000, viii, 201).[10] There is no mention of how, for instance, the television broadcasters' profit requirement might run counter to other, more altruistic objectives. The purpose of this USAID/Academy for Education Development document is clear. By stressing the "successful" action of the business, religious, and media institutions, it seeks "to orient program planners and implementers who may wish to involve private sector actors in their activities" (Tietjen 2000, 9). This can be taken as a subtle effort to seek support for social welfare, particularly for girls, from other than state sources. In line with the principle of depoliticization of issues, the report makes no reference to the possible involvement of women's organizations in efforts to provide an education more sensitive to gender issues.

The salience and treatment of gender issues in public education policy is not much better in the industrialized world. Even in Australia, one of the most advanced countries in gender policy, girls are no longer identified as a specific "equity target group," as the principle of "mainstreaming" gender has had the effect of moving gender "off the agenda" by assuming it is now being considered in all areas (Henry 2001). Before the advent of what most people now know as globalization (which began to be recognized as a trend in the 1980s), public policy efforts in the United States to address gender problems did not consider to any satisfactory degree the lived experiences in schools and classrooms, the content of the curriculum, or the need for teacher training and retraining. *A Nation at Risk* (U.S. National Commission on Excellence in Education 1983), a publication that started the national debate on the quality of schooling in the United States, did not contain a single reference to gender inequalities in schools (Weis 2000). The basic approach since then has not changed, except for the provision of funds for experimental projects in science and technology.

In most schools systems in the United States, sex education tends to address "hormonally charged boys who cannot help what they do," leaving for girls training in how not to be provocative "so as not to arouse the boys and men in their midst" (Weis 2000). This situation long existed and thus is not a function of globalization; however, the introduction of neoliberal perspectives, in making the state less responsible for the well-being of its subjects, is introducing a new set of actors whose tasks may operate in regressive ways toward women. As education is conceived in mostly technical terms, the ideological components of education become invisible, and any possible discussion of their role is replaced by the notion that education is merely a means to obtain high-paying jobs and to respond to the needs of the new economy. Without a revision of the formal educational content and the lived experience in schools, it is unlikely that women and men will move toward a new social order. Without new understandings of their forms of subordination, women will not identify problems, much less know how to solve them. As Egan (1998) wisely comments, women's "unfamiliarity with norms of the policy process can reduce bargaining power and leverage" (45).

At the level of higher education, there has been an increase in the number of women as both students and faculty members throughout the world. In fact, this increase has been aided by the increasing differentiation of institutions of higher learning. New private institutions, being cheaper and more numerous, tend to provide more access to women than do elite universities. At the same time, there is little evidence that women's (and men's) access to higher education is becoming less clustered along gender-typed fields of study.

Some observers predict that the increase in the number of women in higher education, regardless of the status of the university or institution, will pose a challenge to the status quo, especially in countries where the state upholds a policy of sexual apartheid, such as Saudi Arabia, the Persian Gulf states, and Iran (Mojab 2000). As larger numbers of women acquire professional skills that are well remunerated in the labor force, they will make demands for changes in the jobs and roles women can adopt.

For women, the expansion of institutions of higher education comes with a sweet-sour taste. While women have increased their representation in universities as faculty members, this growth has been mostly as part-time faculty. Data from the United States show that overall part-time faculty employment in 1970 was 22 percent of all faculty employment; in 2000, it grew to 42 percent (Benjamin 2000). Since social norms about women's domestic work have not been substantially modified, women academics find themselves making sacrifices in their family lives (Currie et al. 2000). Women hold one-third of all full-time appointments but half the part-time appointments. Further, female part-time employment is more common in the community colleges, where two-thirds are part time compared to less than one-third in four-year institutions (Benjamin 2000). It is possible that similar trends obtain in developing countries, but relevant studies have yet to be conducted.

In certain Asian countries (Singapore, Malaysia, and Hong Kong), women constitute the majority of university graduates, so one would expect to find a large number also in high positions, yet this is not the case. Luke's (2000) research shows that the absence of a pool of qualified women cannot be considered the primary cause for women's underrepresentation in senior management in either academia or the public sector. The cause lies in cultural norms that set psychological ceilings and that are not contested. Luke (2000) observes that women still bear "disproportionate family and cultural maintenance and continuity"; they provide "the emotional support and care of husbands and family elders, and they are responsible for developing their own abilities and potential as a family asset" (12). It would seem, then, that even university education does not help develop contesting minds.

With the increased efforts by universities to move into technical rationality rather than reflexivity, feminist production in the academic world is likely to suffer. Leonard (2001) has observed that many of the feminist theoretical contributions in the 1970s and 1980s in the United Kingdom came from doctoral dissertations. Today, doctoral dissertations tend to be more instrumental and pragmatic.

Parallel to the previously noted developments, gender studies programs are sprouting up all over the world. This is a positive event and signals the spread of questioning and emancipatory ideas in the university. Yet, as noted earlier, changes to align the university with economic production are drawing resources away from less revenue-producing fields; this has resulted in reduced, stagnant, or unstable budgets for departments such as those focusing on gender studies (Stromquist 2001a).

In a world increasingly characterized (at least according to the prevailing discourse) by a clear link between human capital and monetary reward, one would expect to see women benefiting from greater income and better social conditions. The statistics suggest otherwise. During 1990–1997, women's participation in the global labor force rose from 34 to 40 percent, but nearly 340 million women are not expected to survive to age forty, and a quarter to half of all women have suffered physical abuse by an intimate partner (United Nations Development Program 1999a, 22).

GLOBALIZED PROBLEMS WITH A GENDER DIMENSION

Three serious conditions can be identified as stemming from a clear gender bias. First, public sector enterprises and agencies have been found to be more tightly bound by equality legislation than private-sector firms. This occurs because governments are more vulnerable to public opinion, visibility, and international pressure for human rights, including salaries proportionate to skills and knowledge regardless of gender. Although this is an issue that has not attracted great attention, the reduction of the state machinery in many countries has generated less access by women to equal pay.

Second, the promise of a better financial situation in the wealthier or more dynamic economies of the world, combined with the increased mobility of individuals, is producing migratory situations that, though not new, are occurring on a much greater scale under times of globalization. In this new migration process, it is estimated that about thirty million people are victims of human traffic from and within Southeast Asia for sexual purposes and sweatshop labor. According to UN sources, human trafficking is the "fastest-growing criminal market in the world." About 500,000 women and girls from developing countries and transition economies enter the slave trade each year in western Europe alone (United Nations Development Program 1999a, 42). Reportedly, an estimated 5,000 Brazilian women are working as prostitutes in Europe against their will. The U.S. Department of Justice estimates that 50,000 to 100,000 women and children have been trafficked into the United States in the past few years (Hall 2001).

Third, now that it is cheaper and easier to communicate with anyone than ever before, the Internet is contributing to the sexual exploitation of women. It is estimated that the cyber-sex industry constitutes 60 percent of the current Internet economy (Gómez-Peña 2001).[11] The Internet is facilitating worldwide prostitution by creating a global market where women (and children) can be bought around the world. The Internet is also facilitating consensual sex via chat rooms, which make it possible to identify new customers easily and in which sexual workers often comprise young women (Hall 2001).

THE WOMEN'S MOVEMENT AND RESISTANCE

There is a consensus that one of the most significant emancipatory movements in recent times has been feminism. The relative success of feminism can be understood as the result of two sets of forces: the work of the women's movement and the spaces opened by intergovernmental agencies, primarily the United Nations, that have created opportunities for both reflection and action.

The feminist movement faces a major struggle. Women, who have endured some form of subjugation by most of the other half of the population since time immemorial, have themselves absorbed and internalized the ideological messages that justify the dominant position of men and often do not see the limiting conditions imposed by this situation. Men, for their part, being the direct and indirect beneficiaries, tend to minimize the nature of women's subordination, either stating that "cultural" values dictate those norms or arguing that women are much better off than critics would lead one to believe.

From modest beginnings involving small, scattered, and often ideologically isolated groups of women who were aware of their circumscribed condition and sought to change it, the feminist movement has evolved into a very global type of social action. With the decrease in the cost of travel and the ease and speed of communications, women have now been able to participate in world forums and to disseminate new ideas gained from these meetings among an increasingly large audience. Typically, these forums are UN-sponsored gatherings of representatives of most of the world's governments with a nongovernment version held simultaneously nearby. The benefits from participation in these world forums have been multiple. First, women have had access to new role models and learned from them which gender strategies worked and which did not. Second, the acceptance in principle by their respective governments of well-designed, forum-generated measures has provided women with the grounds on which to mobilize and lobby for ratification and implementation. Third, they have learned the discourse suitable to engage in dialogue with other institutions, including governments and international agencies. Fourth, they have adopted innovations successfully implemented elsewhere with great potential for women's advancement.

Access to networks of organized women's groups at these forums and subsequently through Internet communication has permitted women's groups in many countries to refine their ideas and then build these ideas into coherent plans of action. According to Dorsey (1997), the World Social Summit held in Copenhagen (March 1995) reflected a shift from an approach that sought to increase awareness of the oppression of women to one that emphasized the implementation of plans for women's empowerment. Dorsey also considers that the Fourth World Women's Conference held in Beijing (August 1995) marked a shift from silence about violence against women to incorporating this topic as a major agenda item. The Beijing forum is considered by many as an example of a sophisticated use of the UN system by women's NGOs, as many of those attending made a concerted effort to ensure that the new agreements contained specific guidelines for implementation by signatory governments and that the gains of each separate issue (later called "consecrated language") would not be set back (Dorsey 1997).

One example of the new ideas emanating from global forums is the use of quotas to promote women as candidates to public office and thus to increase their representation as formal representatives. This innovation, attempted first in Sweden, is now at work in many countries in Asia, Africa, and Latin America. In places as varied as Brazil, India, and the Philippines, women are serving in city councils and in national legislatures as a result of a requirement that a certain proportion of candidates for office be women.[12] As more experience is gained from access to public positions, women are becoming more alert to their current limitations. Many organized groups of women realize that the movement has to improve its analysis and proposals in economic areas and to increase its understanding of the impacts of the massive participation of women in the informal sector of the economy. So far, it is clear only that women face serious problems, that these are derived from social inequalities (and from the deteriorating ecological environment, as is becoming increasingly apparent), and that they cannot be resolved without a solid analysis of the development models imposed by central countries (Blandon and Montenegro 2000).

In contrast to the dominant globalization accounts disseminated by either the media or international organizations that see the world as constituted by market players in atomistic, gender-neutral ways (Bakker 2000), the women's movements in developing countries have been able to sharpen the understanding of their economic and political subordination and to advance and legitimize women's rights to equal economic and political opportunities. This has been done primarily through the constitution of organized groups of women who, through various forms of action, from nonformal education (workshops) to the organizing of grassroots groups and to political lobbying, have attempted to modify the way gender structures operate in daily life. Women have often utilized their traditionally ascribed gender roles to confront the institutionalized gender system. Examples are the actions by Mothers of Plaza de Mayo in Argentina (during 1977–1983) and the massive protests by women against neoliberal reforms that raised the cost of living in Ecuador and the Dominican Republic in the early 1980s.

Organized women have been fighting not only for reasons of survival but also for the construction of new political positions vis-à-vis the state and the prevailing development model. According to several observers (Alvarez 1990, 1992; Lind 1997; Stromquist 2001b), the women's struggles have enabled them to cross the boundaries of gender, class, race, and nation and to create new political subjects. One of their main strategies is based on the global targeting of formal political and economic institutions as well as on detrimental social practices (Dorsey 1997). Women have made human rights more inclusive and stronger by involving more people in the struggle (Bunch 2000; Darnovsky et al. 1995). The action by women-led groups is not always recognized, however. Some argue that women's NGOs are "hybrid cultures: trying to get what they want out of a new international community of funding agencies, foreign [international] NGOs and NGOs" (Townsend et al. 1999, 22–23). But this characterization substantially underplays the gender-emancipatory objectives and actions that many of these organizations have evinced.

When considering the impacts of globalization on gender, it is necessary to be sensitive to local reactions to global trends. The case of the state of Michoacan in Mexico is informative to our understanding the impacts and potential of appropriating global social symbols to specific community conditions. According to Pérez-Prado (1996), by using political and cultural symbols drawn particularly from the United States and other countries, women in that region of Mexico are challenging men for access to *ejido* (communal) land to support themselves. They are also organizing to fight against male violence. These efforts are occurring through discourse and actions by which women challenge the state.

Today, agendas have been carefully devised by the global women's movement. The most recent documents emanating from the International Conference on Population and Development (1994), the World Social Summit (1995), and the Fourth World Women's Conference (1995) clearly identify specific areas for action. At the same time, globalization trends seem to be causing social issues to appear anachronistic and unimportant. While one finds examples of women questioning current oppressive gender conditions, there is also evidence that younger generations of women are becoming less political than their predecessors. Many women's groups are experiencing problems renewing their cadre. So, we must ask ourselves, What kinds of politics to advance women's issues are possible today? What aspects of globalization can feminists use to strengthen their claims for social equity?

TOWARD A NORTH–SOUTH ALLIANCE?

A transnational feminist alliance is very much in evidence at present, but there still exist some major contradictions and conflicts between North and South to be resolved.

Some feminists from the South, such as Chandra Mohanty (1988), consider that Western feminist accounts excessively attribute a position of victimization and passivity to Third Women in accounts of global restructuring. Feminists question such a depiction since it negates the substantial amount of work that women in developing countries are undertaking to modify the negative consequences of globalization and neoliberalism. Highlighting some of the tensions between feminists of the North and those of the South is the observation by a key African feminist organization: "While patriarchal views and structures oppress women all over the world, women are also members of classes and countries that dominate others and enjoy privileges in terms of access to resources. Hence, contrary to the best intentions of 'sisterhood,' not all women share identical interests" (Association for African Women on Research and Development, cited in O'Brien et al. 2000, 35).

There may be not only a lack of fit between some North and South interests and concerns but also a lack of congruence between the interests of rich and poor women. This is well captured in a statement by Wilson (1993):

> Women's class interests are enmeshed in other forms of oppression: just as the creation of a middle class of women depended on a class of domestic servants in the nineteenth century, so today the domestication and consumerism of women in the First World calls for a new class of women producers in the Third. (351)

The existence of divergent interests is reflected in the priorities that have been identified by both worlds. For the women's movement in the United States, these issues comprise abortion, affirmative action in employment and education, requirements to consider women in awarding federal contracts, breast cancer research, contraceptive education, shelters for victims of domestic violence, and the international trafficking of women. Gender issues in developing countries tend to focus on basic needs, such as access to health, education, employment, and credit. The dramatic impact of SAPs on the well-being of poor people compels feminist groups in the Third World to direct much of their concern toward macroeconomic policies advanced by central countries. For the most part, the women's movement in the North has avoided this.

While economic measures linked to SAPs have hit women across social classes, global economic coalitions by women are still incipient. A nascent feminist economic rights coalition does exist: the Women's Global Alliance for

Development Alternatives. But at present it has no structure, secretariat, or address, and it lacks financial resources. Its membership includes the three strongest feminist regional networks (DAWN, WEDO, and WIDE).[13] So far, the alliance has been primarily reactive rather than proactive in setting an agenda for global change from the perspective of the women's movement (see O'Brien et al. 2000). If this alliance is able to define a common agenda and critique around global economic issues, it will be a force to be reckoned with.

An important issue for the women's movement in the Third World is the struggle against domestic violence, now seen as a form of human rights. This is an issue in which both North and South coincide and may be one on which to base stronger alliances and strategies. There already exist various global and regional coalitions on human rights, such as the International Women's Right Action Watch; the Asia-Pacific Forum on Women, Law and Development; Women in Law and Development in Africa; and the Latin American Committee for the Defense of Women's Rights.

CONCLUDING CONSIDERATIONS

So far, the complex globalization process presents a mixed picture for women. On the one hand, there are more opportunities than ever before for individual and social action in the economic, educational, and political spheres. At the same time, there are serious constraints for emancipatory action, both because of the weakening welfare responsibilities of the state and because of the depoliticization of culture. The sexual division of labor has not been altered under globalization, and the feminization of poverty continues unabated.

To counteract the vagaries of the market, nonmarket safety nets are needed. These include kin, community, and state provision. But in the neoliberal present, state provision is not forthcoming, leaving kin and community as the most common sources of strategies. Yet these, though necessary, result in trapping in the inequities of the status quo. A further complication is the neoliberal process that hides the political and social choices that shape organizational culture, making it difficult to consider alternative ways of being. As Currie et al. (2000) note, neoliberalism emphasizes the distinction between the private and public worlds and, in doing so, "undermines any movement toward the greater participation of males in families" (289).

As countries position themselves for economic competitiveness, attention to social justice policies, including those concerning gender, receives less importance. Paradoxically, the nature of the effort has become more transparent through the work of women's organizations and the increasingly explicit global agreements endorsed by most governments. The struggle ahead is far from easy. As Fraser (1998) advises, social justice today must be both a project of material redistribution and cultural recognition of oppressed groups. Both pillars of equity are highly contested by those fomenting globalization.

NOTES

1. The "second" movement followed the movement of the 1800s, which culminated in winning women's right to vote in 1920, with the Nineteenth Amendment to the Constitution.

2. Given the longer history of men's involvement in industrialized production, union organizing, and political negotiations, export-processing zones prefer women as the primary workforce, relying on cultural and social values as domesticating forces (Guttal 2000).

3. Ward (1984) predicted that the global assembly line would intensify, decompose (undermining the traditional family structure and delaying marriage/childbearing), or recompose gender subordination (placing men in managerial positions in the plants). Her prediction, which has became reality, has Fordist ways of production (assembly-line work with discrete and timed tasks) involving primarily women.

4. In the electronics industry, for instance, the design of software is highly paid, but the production of software is not. Women work in the manufacture of electronic chips that require keen eyesight and sensitive tactile skills. Costs of labor training are minimal, as nearly all production workers are unskilled and semiskilled. The work being done by women in Hong Kong, Taiwan, Singapore, and Malaysia earns particularly slim wages.

5. If women were to gain more than their husbands, they could also generate a condition in which they would dominate in the household. The point here is not who shall prevail but what conditions foster greater equality between domestic partners.

6. Simultaneous with the creation of an assertive but erotic femininity, globalized masculinities are also being promoted. Salient among these is what Connell (1998) calls the "transnational business masculinity," characterized by "egocentrism, very conditional loyalties (even to the corporation), and a declining sense of responsibility for others (except for the purposes of image making)" (16).

7. In some parts of Asia, notably Japan, women are subjected to very contradictory messages. The overall cultural imaginary is that Japanese women are gentle, submissive. At the same time, women as mothers are expected to behave assertively, obsessed with their children's education (Martinez 1998).

8. To have a policy focusing specifically on girls means making special efforts to offset the in-kind contributions they make to families or to persuade parents to send daughters to schools through media and community campaigns. Only a few countries (Bangladesh, Guatemala, and Mexico) have instituted measures to help girls financially. Countries such as Zambia and India have been running social campaigns to highlight the importance of educating girls. Most countries have increased the enrollment of girls in schools mainly through the establishment of more schools in a larger number of communities.

9. UNESCO statistics are well known for their inaccuracy. This is a product of the process used to obtain them, which depends on member countries to collect

the information. Ministries of education routinely ask regional units under them to report enrollment, and these lower units depend in turn on principals and teachers, who, given the situation of economic austerity, find it advantageous to report more students to obtain greater material resources.

10. For instance, the SAGE document under discussion acknowledges the contribution of the Opus Dei in countries such as Kenya, Mexico, El Salvador, and Peru. The Opus Dei, however, is a religious and secular order notoriously conservative regarding gender issues. The support provided to women in those countries by the Opus Dei was to "provide skills training to women in clerical, secretarial, administrative, hospitality, accounting work (often with childcare centers)" (Tietjen 2000, 282). This kind of support is not to be rejected, but more awareness should exist about the fact that this assistance tends to reproduce rather than transform gender relations.

11. A merger between AT&T Broadband and Comcast (a TV cable firm), proposed in May 2002, will create the largest pornographic conglomerate in the world, with 22 million subscribers.

12. The electoral reforms favoring women affirm their right to be *candidates* to public office; it does not mandate that a certain proportion of women be elected. The latter possibility exists in very few countries, notably India. Nonetheless, the presence of a larger number of women candidates has resulted in their election to public office.

13. DAWN stands for Development Alternatives with Women for a New Era, WEDO is the Women's Environment and Development Organization, and WIDE is the network on Women in Development in Europe. Other important women's organizations are REPEM (Women's Network on Popular Education, comprising Latin America) and the Women's International Coalition for Economic Social Justice.

8

Agency and Resistance in the Globalization Era

Venom—substance that currently prevails in the air, water, land, and soul

Galeano (1992)

In previous chapters, we described and analyzed a variety of incommensurable perspectives on the ongoing transformations at all levels of the educational system in many countries. These perspectives view transformations as both positive and negative in their consequences. The most positive consequence for education is notably the expansion of higher education and the increasing flexibility of this system in the provision of knowledge and skills linked to economic production needs. Another positive consequence might be the increased circulation of new ideas that render technological and scientific advances easier to reach by others.

The negative consequences are seen to be the narrowing of what is considered knowledge worth learning, the weakening of the social perception of education as a public good, and the growing presence in entrepreneurs concerned with profit and micro-focused knowledge instead of a broad and humanistic understanding of our surrounding world.

Linked to globalization processes today, there are increasing forms of resistance. Yet when we talk of resistance, we must make a 180-degree shift, for such resistance is seldom expressed against educational changes, despite several problematic developments in this area. Rather, the forces of resistance to globalization center on its consequences for tangible issues, such as the environment, democratic governance, jobs, indigenous groups, women, and social exclusion in general.

In a book of this type, focusing on education, the consideration of many of the emerging forms of resistance to globalization, even though they may not directly address education, is appropriate on two counts: to use education as a means to increase people's awareness of the impact on globalization on everyday life and to highlight how negative impacts on education itself can be attenuated.

Textual expressions of oppositional behavior have materialized at an increasing rate in recent years. They have caught the attention of the press only when these manifestations have taken the form of demonstrations against international meetings and of real and potential environmental disasters, especially when police have felt obliged to use force against some of the protesters. Steadily, these resistance forces are evincing an organized presence that is itself global.

Who are these protestors? Against what are they protesting? What do they seek to accomplish? How does education figure in these forms of resistance? Is schooling an arena in which protestation is taking place? This chapter explores these questions, piecing together literature existing mostly on the Internet. Curiously, while cybernetic space has been a major tool for the diffusion of the globalization of economic processes, at the same time it is proving to be a major resource for those seeking to introduce greater reflexivity in the immense whirl of globalization developments.

This chapter seeks to explain how the emerging global order is being perceived by groups in First and Third World countries. It highlights what the different groups consider to be the major negative outcomes linked to globalization and what forms their opposition to those globalization initiatives has taken.

WHAT IS THERE TO RESIST?

Various issues are acquiring a problematic character as time goes by. Some of them reach deeply into the meaning of life.

The environment is a major concern. The high levels of productivity reached by central countries have fostered an unprecedented amount of consumption. With it, greater demands are being made on Earth's natural resources, bringing many detrimental consequences to the environment, such as deforestation and soil and air pollution, and often social disruptions, such as encroachment on indigenous lands and rights.[1] Its role in global warming has been scientifically demonstrated, as have the high costs and rising frequency of climate-related disasters attributable to this production/consumption.[2]

The threat to the environment in many parts of the world has given impetus to the emergence of a variety of ecological movements, most of which see economic globalization as uninterested in preserving the fragile coexistence between humans and nature. While the notion of economic gain from increased consumption is an understandable goal, many in these movements view the gains as more transient than the environmental harm that accompanies the required increased production and as in need of some form of control. Concern for our deteriorating environment combines with issues of social justice, for the great share of those who face the negative ecological consequences are the poor, leading people to believe that climate change may become one of the greatest injustices in human history. While wealthy countries emit 80 percent of the world's greenhouse effects, 96 percent of the deaths from so-called natural disasters occur in poor countries. The United States, currently with 4 percent of the world's population, is responsible for 25 percent of greenhouse gas emissions (developed countries in general produce high levels of carbon dioxide and methane emissions) (Lynas 1999). Today, developing countries export industrialized products, especially those deriving from polluting industries, such as aluminum (De Oliveira 1996).

There are also concerns for the well-being of those likely to be losers in the globalization process. The landless in the Third World, workers in very low paying factories, and hidden forms of child labor are coming into the consciousness of people who seek greater economic and social equality across countries. So, a second group of globalization resisters is very much focused on addressing poverty and seeks to block the development of a homogenized mind that does not contest injustice and that does not even think about it (Sana, n.d.).

The obvious influence that transnational corporations (TNCs) and multilateral financial organizations exert on states in developing countries is a source of concern for those interested in citizen participation in governance. Transnational corporations can, to a great extent, control the production of goods and services, the movement of workers, action by ecologists, and activities by unions. The International Monetary Fund (IMF) can force cuts in public expenditure and devaluation of currencies; it can diminish with great ease governments' expenditures on welfare policies. Intellectual property rights are perceived as further contributing to the poverty of people in the Third World since these rights cover not only patents for highly advanced technologies but also foods consumed by all social groups, such as rice, wheat, and cheese. Indian groups, for instance, successfully contested in 2001 the use of the word "basmati" for similar rice produced in the United States. Since intellectual property rights limit the ownership of essential goods to certain people living in developing areas, in many ways these issues "epitomize the struggle of the local versus the cosmopolitan views of the world and the long-standing presence of the human as a local creature" (Lee 2000, 199).

The threat to democracy and human rights posed by dubious utopias predicated on consumerism and profit triggers reactions from idealist groups, reactions that question the evolving decision-making venues, notably the global gatherings of members of influential multinational organizations and representatives of the wealthiest countries in the world, such as the WTO, the IMF, and G-8 meetings, venues in which the presence of developing nations is weak or nonexistent but in which important decisions affecting them are made.

Some resistance also arises in central countries from the loss of jobs to labor in the Third World, as globalization, seeking highest profit, follows lowest cost. This response is guided by the protection of self-interest; unsurprisingly, it takes place mostly in the First World as workers there fear the deindustrialization of their economies.

Yet another problematic issue derives from the incursion into previously untouched indigenous areas of ownership, regarding both lands and knowledge. As will be seen later in this chapter, indigenous movements have come alive in numerous countries in recent years.

One of the key challenges of globalization is "to find the rules and institutions for stronger governance—local, national, regional and global—to preserve the advantages of global markets and competition, but also to provide enough space for human, community and environmental resources to ensure that globalization works for people—not just for profits" (United Nations Development Program 1999a, 2). The reasons for resisting globalization are far from equally shared by all those who oppose it. This chapter explores in greater detail the causes and problems affecting specific groups and how they see—and have expressed—united contestation of unfolding globalization developments.

WHO IS RESISTING?

Nearly all of those who oppose globalization would readily admit that they do not oppose globalization as a form of increasing interconnection between and among countries. What they reject is the growing inequality between countries and the concomitant asymmetry of economic and political power and the accompanying cultural homogenization.

There are, of course, multiple forms of individual resistance. Here we focus on collective and organized forms of resistance. Nonetheless, it may be pertinent to observe some individual manifestations. One such example is reflected in a letter to the editor of a major U.S. newspaper questioning the values to accumulate wealth being inculcated through the *Who Wants to Be a Millionaire* television program:

> I don't want to be a millionaire. No, Regis [in reference to the master of ceremony of the program]. I don't want to be a millionaire. Though I could proba-

bly answer most of the academic questions, I know not and care less about who won which sports contest or which "Friends" character is currently sleeping with Joey or Monica. Nor do I want to be on an island eating rats in order to vote the other rat-eaters off so that I can win a million dollars.

No, I am not missing the "I want to be rich" gene. I do want to be rich—rich with a loving family, caring friends, rich in a healthy community in balance with nature, rich in rewarding work that improves the human prospect for the next generation. I want to be able to earn a living through meaningful work that provides me with enough money to take care of my family, own a comfortable home, drive a safe car, send my children to college and have health care until the end of my life. And I want this for everyone else. (Villagran 2000, 9B)

Another form of individual resistance (one that involves more organization but functions at the individual level) occurs through such activities as the International Day Against Consumption (or Buy-Nothing Day in the United States, the day after Thanksgiving, which has traditionally been one of the biggest shopping days of the year). A third manifestation of resistance is reflected in the rejection of cash awards for improving student test scores by hundreds of California teachers; they oppose such bonuses because they wish to protest the "drill and practice" climate that has been created in the schools in order to prepare for the multiple-choice testing; they also consider that cash awards create unhealthy competition among teachers (Asimov 2001).[3]

Such forms of individual agency are extremely important, yet they are not sufficient. Collective forms of response have a greater likelihood of impact. The emerging antiglobalization movement comprises a diverse set of groups, with different levels of sophistication in knowledge and organization: labor unions, environmentalists, intellectuals, young anarchists, cyber-activists, indigenous groups, and small farmers (Gómez-Peña 2001).

Within schools, forms of individual resistance have also been detected. Lipman (2000) reports resistance against neoliberal policies at all levels of the educational system in her case study of Chicago: teachers who complain about the testing of students, students who call for dropping the testing procedures and resist police roundups and youth programs imposed from above, and parents who seek waivers from test-based evaluations.

Civic Groups and Social Movements

Since the 1960s, there have been a growing number of movements organized around grievances not merely based on economic and class interests but focused instead on "less 'objective' elements such as identity, status, humanism, and spiritualism" (Johnston et al. 1994, 21).[4] The existence of these groups, notably nongovernmental organizations (NGOs), has reflected concerns with the well-being of individuals and environments in broader ways than previously and perhaps with stronger emphasis on the transformation of our societies—beyond marginal internal improvements. As globalization has unfolded, some of the already existing groups have re-acted more visibly, and many new ones come into being. In recent years, the world has seen an explosion of civic organizations of varying size and scope. During the 1990s, international NGOs grew from 6,000 to 26,000 (Keohane and Nye 2000); as they have grown in numbers, they have also grown in organizational complexity. The Continental Social Alliance, which actively monitors trade issues, comprises about 240 NGOs, networks, labor unions, and study and research centers from the entire North and South American continent.

The presence of NGOs has been accompanied by both satisfaction and discomfort. Sana (n.d., 70–71) sees NGOs as instances of a modified left whose objectives "fit well within bourgeois ideology: protection and diffu-sion of human rights as a precondition to the gradual path toward an inter-national civil society." In Sana's view, civil society is an abstract concept that skillfully avoids direct treatment of class issues or concrete sociopolitical problems—an abstraction beyond suspicion; a similar view is held by Simp-son (1998). Sana refers specifically to certain German NGOs that, while seek-ing to help developing countries and conducting good deeds, do not con-tribute to any significant change. Sana calls this work at most "social therapy." Another observer of the globalization process (Mato 1996b) charges that NGOs are absorbing responsibilities that should be discharged by the state; he sees them as a consequence of unattended social welfare measures brought about by structural adjustment programs (SAPs) in many developing countries.

The range of action by NGOs, both in developing countries and in the First World, is extensive. While not always successful, civic organizations and their larger expressions—the social movements—decenter power and poli-tics by demonstrating how forces from the margin can influence the state. They decenter power also by contesting the state's assertion to be the single rational actor.

Recent years have seen the emergence of an educational interest among international NGOs, which are now pressing governments and multilateral and bilateral organizations for greater support of basic education. Groups such as ActionAid and Oxfam have played a substantial role in promoting universal access to primary education, especially for girls, who are seriously underenrolled, particularly in Africa and southern Asia. They have also forged alliances with other groups, notably teacher unions throughout the world (Mundy and Murphy 2001). The size and experience of these interna-tional NGOs have enabled them to engage in transnational advocacy of ed-ucation and lobbying of governments, efforts that show great promise for positive developments in the years ahead.

Some of the major contributions of the civil groups and social movements to the critique of globalization revolve around the production of alternative ways of interpreting the world via discourses that counter dominant perceptions of globalization. These discourses have been effective because they have had destabilizing effects on the received social order. Declarations by civic groups have called attention to poverty, social exclusion, and the diminution of well-being for a number of underrepresented populations, ranging from farmers to young children. The groups behind these discourses have not only sought to critique but have also been proposing alternative ideas, norms, and identities (Alvarez 1992). In only one case has a social movement succeeded in becoming a political party—that of the Workers' Party in Brazil.

In the North, large international NGOs have begun to act to protect the environment, especially that of developing countries, where TNC activity has shown considerably less concern for environmental damage than if it had been carried out in their home-base country.

In response to concentration of power in the media (i.e., the dominance by the three media giants today: AOL Time Warner, The News Corporation, and Disney), a loose coalition has been formed of more than eighty nonprofit organizations that "favor democratic, localized, and ecologically sound alternatives to globalization, democracy, cultural diversity" (Turning Point 2000). Calling itself the Turning Point Project, it seeks to counter the action of the "conglomerate of global TV, films, newspapers, books, cable systems, music, theaters, advertising" (Turning Point 2000).

An important strategy by civic organizations to reduce global inequalities is to have the Bretton institutions and central countries to forgive the external debt of poor countries. As noted in chapter 2, SAPs have required the imposition of austerity measures from many Third World governments as a means to generate the financial resources to pay back the debt, producing in their wake a substantial shift of public allocation away from such fundamental services as health and education. It is well known that many developing countries spend far more on debt repayment than on health and education each year.

Jubilee 2000, a coalition of charities and religious groups, celebrities, and NGOs, carried out a four-year campaign seeking write-offs of the debts of fifty-two heavily indebted poor countries (HIPCs) (all of them African countries, except for four Latin American nations: Bolivia, Guyana, Honduras, and Nicaragua), which totaled U.S.$375 billion.[5] This campaign also highlighted the hypocrisy of foreign aid, noting that for every dollar flowing out as aid to poor countries each year, eight dollars returned in debt payments. By 2000, twenty-two poor nations got debt relief from the United States, Japan, Europe, and other countries; so far, about U.S.$20 billion have been relieved (Kahn 2000).

Actions of resistance to globalization best known to people in general are those that took place in the cities of Seattle (1999), Washington, D.C. (1999), Quebec (2000), Göteborg (2001), and Genoa (2001). Such demonstrations take advantage of meetings held by powerful organizations that set international economic policies, such as the World Bank, the IMF, the WTO, and the G-7 or G-8, to call world attention to the undemocratic nature of their decisions—they exclude most of the world's countries. The demonstrations condense the wide array of issues that create discontent among those who fear or have experienced the negative consequences of globalization.

The mainstream press does not always report accurately on the purpose and nature of the demonstrations. The Seattle demonstration, which attracted between 20,000 and 50,000 participants, was not covered in the news until violence broke out (McChesney 2000). The demonstrators succeeded in interrupting WTO decisions, particularly those concerning trade-related aspects of intellectual property rights (TRIPs). The WTO is a central target because it is considered to be a "set of treaties on agriculture, service, property rights that put the right of capital over the rights of nature and poor people" (Shiva 2001). The demonstration in Quebec took place to question the third meeting of the Americas, which was to discuss the possibility of a free-trade agreement encompassing the entire continent (the Free Trade Area of the Americas [FTAA]).[6] The Quebec event, in which trade unions were heavily involved, expressed concern for the loss of jobs in the United States and Canada, inadequate or nonexisting workers' rights in the other countries of the Americas, and damage to the environment. Demonstrators also expressed concern that TRIPS would benefit the large chemical companies involved in agricultural genetic engineering, seen as a threat to the environment as well as to small farmers.

Demonstrations in Göteborg and Genoa have sought to render more transparent the negotiations of the G-8, whose decisions greatly affect developing countries and in which the representation of the latter is simply absent. The Genoa demonstration engaged some 100,000 protesters and about 25,000 police.

Workers' Unions

As mentioned previously, trade unions are participating in actions against globalization. Unions in the North feel that as manufactures and industries move from core to peripheral countries, many such jobs will disappear. Further, they fear that as wages are low in the South, this will have repercussions on wages in the North, thus creating an overall reduction in living standards.

In addition to participating in demonstrations and alliances with other groups, labor unions are also developing programs to educate its members. An example can be seen in the courses provided by the AFL-CIO, in one of which, titled "Common Sense Economics," the student is asked, "What's the difference between Tanzania and Goldman Sachs?" The reply: "One is an African country that makes US$2.2 billion a year and shares it among 25 million people. The other is an investment bank that makes US$2.6 billion and shares most of it between 161 people" (Salt et al. 2000, 23–24).

Observers have noted that while mergers of firms are occurring across national borders, a similar process is not taking place with the labor unions of the same firms. When Dander (Germany) merged with Chrysler (United States), the *Wall Street Journal* facetiously wondered whether this could mean a merger between the United Auto Workers (UAW) and IG Metall, the German labor union (Salt et al. 2000).

During the 1980s and 1990s, SAPs had considerable negative impacts on national educational budgets, particularly on teacher salaries (Carnoy 1995; International Labor Organization 1996; Tiramonti 2001). Teachers' unions are aware of this influence and have resisted, in consequence, efforts to effect educational reforms that do not address their financial situation.

Women's Groups

It was noted in chapter 6 that globalization has had positive impacts on women, notably the diffusion of democratic principles calling for the equality of opportunity for women and men in education, work, political life, the family, and so on. Feminism is a movement that has been nurtured by global ideas and international solidarity. So why is the women's movement engaged in resistance to globalization? Its concerns focus on economic consequences linked to the influence of TNCs and their growing power over land, TRIPS, and working conditions.

The expansion of agro-industries is reducing the amount of communal lands in which women could and do work. The engagement of men in industries away from home is leaving women in the precarious condition of having to take care of their families while maintaining their production levels. Mies and Shiva (1993; the best-known exponents of ecofeminism) discuss the replacement of local seeds by genetically modified seeds and the imposition of monocultures in the agricultural sector by TNCs, both of which have negative, albeit unintended, consequences for rural women. Shiva (2001) reports on the increasing shift from informal to industrial production in foods in India, where, in 1999, 1 percent of its food was bought processed (compared to 70 percent in the United States), and 99 percent of that processing was being done by women at micro levels (cottage and home). The stakes for profits are great for a country with a large population such as India. It is estimated that there is a U.S.$4 billion flour market to be exploited if only packaged flour were to be sold in India. The food market is making inroads; at present, Indian laws already make it illegal to sell open cooking oil (Shiva 2001). The fundamental issue linking women and globalization in agriculture is the displacement of women without any clear understanding of how their position will be improved or even protected.

Related to both agricultural and technological production under globalization is the likely fate of indigenous knowledge. As knowledge becomes protected by patents and must be purchased in the marketplace, many women will lose their status as repositories of local knowledge.[7]

Women-led NGOs are making significant contributions to a better understanding of contemporary globalization events by analyzing current trends and proposing policies and actions to deal with the negative aspects of globalization. Instances of resistance by women include nationwide campaigns on food rights run by Indian women (Shiva 2001). In 2000, women protesting world poverty and the inevitably concomitant mistreatment of women organized a "World March of Women," culminating the event by protesting in front of the World Bank and the IMF in Washington, D.C. Women groups were also present at the demonstrations in Genoa in 2001. Additionally, women's groups have presented to Kofi Annan, the current secretary-general of the United Nations, petitions signed by two million people seeking an end to violence against women; women activists see a link between violence against women and globalization because of the increase in prostitution, the growth of poverty that results in greater domestic disputes, and the competitiveness among states that reduces the importance of gender justice.

Indigenous Groups

Actions of contestation by indigenous groups offer the strongest instance of globalized resistance, insofar as it involves the collaboration of many different groups throughout the world. Indigenous groups receive much attention because their issues blend the condition of women, intellectual property rights (associated with the emergence of several genetically modified staple foods), environmental conditions, and ultimately issues of democracy and social inclusion/exclusion.

The destruction of the environment in forests and other territories populated by indigenous groups has attracted attention from groups in the North and met with resistance from groups in the South. The use of genetically modified organisms (GMOs) and the possible impact on food security of indigenous populations are other issues that have generated concern.

The main issue in the North is the possible negative effects of GMOs on the health of consumers. The issues in the South are different. First, there is the displacement of farmers from their lands, which they are increasingly unable to keep, primarily because now they are being forced to use new forms of production that require buying new seeds, equipment, and then the fertilizers needed to cultivate the seeds. The new seeds have to be bought regularly, thus forcing farmers to enter the cash economy.[8] According to Shiva (2001), TNCs are major creditors of farmers in India, sometimes charging 200 percent annual interest rates. There have also been displacements of indigenous groups through the challenging by private interests of indigenous land titles, especially in forested areas throughout the Amazon region, as some lands become targeted for the logging of mahogany or for large-scale cultivation of soy (Menotti 2000).[9]

Second, there is a gradual loss of indigenous knowledge concerning agriculture and medicine.[10] Several groups contend that a number of "scientific discoveries" in both fields are but appropriations of existing indigenous knowledge of certain plants, for example, the medical uses of turmeric in India and the Hoodia plant (a cactus found to be a powerful weight reducer) in southern Africa. Current technological developments are permitting much greater productivity in agriculture than ever before: better technologies for animal husbandry, fertilization, irrigation, crop rotation, and disease control and agricultural tools and better varieties of seed designed for improved resistance, annual yields, and nutritional value. At the same time, the threat to indigenous knowledge (likely to occur through the creation of patents that appropriate traditional plants) and thus the survival of indigenous technologies have not received careful consideration in the North. Another issue of concern regards the potential loss of variation in seeds and plants as hybrid varieties invade large cultivation areas and become dominant.

A third globalization development affecting indigenous groups is the ownership and use of ancestral lands. As extraction technologies of fuels and minerals become more sophisticated, new areas are being discovered or found to be more cost effective for exploitation. Rauch (2001) affirms that "technology is stretching the bounds of finitude" (35); examples of this occur in the extraction of oil, gold, and diamonds in some parts of the world.

The role of GMOs is under great debate. Those in favor of the new seeds assert that these scientific developments will permit greater agricultural productivity and thus the improvement of nutritional diets throughout the world. This group considers that the negative effects of such seeds, mostly the possibility of creating allergic reactions on consumers, are being carefully tested and controlled by pertinent government agencies. They see the opposition to GMOs as being either ill-informed or derived from the need that antiglobalizers have for greater access to information in general.[11] Those against GMOs underscore the fact that the new seeds do not operate to benefit the poorest farmers,[12] whose efficiency can be easily surpassed by larger farm owners or agro-industrial complexes. They believe that GMOs will deprive farmers from the use of traditional crops by patenting seeds that indigenous populations have long used; they further argue that many consequences of using GMOs on human beings are not completely known. In the case of some seeds, by design, these have to be replaced on a yearly basis (as opposed to using seeds from the new plants in traditional agriculture), forcing farmers to buy them in the monetarized economy under unsustainable conditions.

The major resistance group by farmers is Via Campesina, a movement founded in 1996 comprising more than eighty peasant and farm organizations in some thirty-seven countries (Osava 2001). Its motto is "Globalize the struggle, globalize the hope." According to its members, which include Zapatistas, they "are not against globalization but against globalizing oppression and marginalization." Via Campesina favors protecting women's contributions to food production, implementing agrarian reform to return territories to indigenous people, and granting landless and farming people ownership and control of the land they work as a means to avoid dislocation, forced urbanization, and repression of peasants; it opposes GMOs. In 1999, Via Campesina launched a "Global Campaign for Agrarian Reform."[13] Another instance of farmers' resistance can be seen in a number of villages in India that declared themselves "biodiversity republics" (Shiva 2001).

Improved communications and transportation have facilitated contact among indigenous groups as well as new supportive action by certain church groups and many NGOs. Globalization is said to have promoted differentiation in the case of indigenous groups by enabling these groups to rescue their identities and traditions to defend themselves against encroachment.[14] It has been observed that indigenous people in Latin America and in North America are trying to rescue the meaning of "nation," taking it out of the monopoly of the nation-state. According to Brysk (2000), who has been closely following political action by indigenous groups in Latin America, their efforts to regain rights can be taken as evidence that globalization is capable of promoting local identities, which can then get wide circulation. She remarks, however, that such "symbolic appeals generate ephemeral and episodic attention which cannot always be translated into concrete resources"; further, she astutely underscores that "land rights, a key issue for indigenous people, are not addressed in any existing agreement or venue" in the region (Brysk 2000, 289). While it is undeniable that indigenous groups are recovering their specificity and seeking ways of strengthening their identity, it must also be acknowledged that their actions have arisen primarily as a *defensive* response to external situations.[15]

University Students

The participation of students in opposing the detrimental impacts of globalization has taken two major forms, one in the First World and another in the Third World. Here we present only sketches of what seems to be taking shape.

On U.S. university campuses, students have acted to oppose the growing number of university contracts with corporations known to permit sweatshop conditions for their workers in developing countries and administrative decisions to subcontract basic campus services, thus creating deteriorating conditions for many university workers.

Students have actively worked against certain university–TNC connections, deploring relations with corporations that, in seeking to maximize profits, give little or no evidence of concern for either workers or the environment. Students at Stanford University, for instance, objected in 2001 to a U.S.$2 million contract with Nike permitting that company to use commercial logos on garments of athletes. The students' opposition was based on the poor labor reputation Nike has had in developing countries, particularly in Southeast Asia. The university prevailed, holding that Nike now ascribes to the College Licensing Company Code of Conduct and the Fair Labor Association Code of Conduct, both of which recognize important workers' rights. Critical of the labor conditions of workers in the university facilities and grounds themselves, students have demanded that they be given "livable wages." In institutions from the University of Southern California to Harvard University, student mobilizations against neoliberal economic models (which, as noted earlier, accompany today's globalization trends) have obtained significant victories.

University students have also been active in various mobilizations to demonstrate against globalization in cities where major official meetings on trade and related globalization topics have taken place.

In the Third World, student opposition to globalization and neoliberalism has taken form primarily in demonstrations against policies to institute tuition fees in public universities, the best-known case being that of Mexico, where a student strike in 2000 lasted nine months, only to achieve meager results.

As a whole, youths are becoming organized around issues of labor conditions, the environment, and what they perceive to be student rights.

The United Nations

Elements of civil society are not the only ones evincing reaction to some of the negative consequences of globalization; governments of Third World countries are also seeking collective protection. This is suggested by an initiative pursued by the secretary-general of the United Nations, Kofi Annan, in 2000. On the occasion of the UN Millennial Celebrations (welcoming the twenty-first century), Annan proposed a "Global Compact" to commit TNCs to respect human, labor, and environmental rights.[16] The compact has been signed by forty-four TNCs, which will now use the UN logo as a seal of corporate responsibility.

Several civic groups monitoring this UN initiative believe that it might be "one of the biggest blunders of the UN" since it creates "global corporate citizenship" and gives legitimacy to corporations such as Nike, Rio Tinto, Shell, Novartis AG, and BP Amoco, known to persist in actions that damage the environment and create abusive labor conditions. Moreover, these critics note, a compact is not a legally binding instrument (Corporate Watch 2001).[17]

FORMS OF ONGOING AND FUTURE RESISTANCE

Those who oppose globalization constitute, not surprisingly, a much smaller number than those who accept it with or without understanding all its consequences and including those who associate it primarily with technological advances. Critics of globalization located outside formal institutions have a small repertoire of actions to influence political decisions. Salient among them are public demonstrations (or the politics of disruption) and lobbying of political figures deemed to be potentially sensitive to their concerns.

Since 1998, there have been several demonstrations, primarily in cities serving as venues for meetings of core country representatives, financial institutions such as the World Bank and the IMF, and organizations with a direct focus on globalization, such as the WTO. The Seattle demonstrations, popularized in the press as the "Battle of Seattle," was the first to bring awareness to the general public about the "antiglobalization" movement. It is estimated that between 25,000 and 50,000 persons representing a wide variety of groups participated in this November 1999 event against the WTO. About 20,000 to 40,000 protesters gathered in demonstrations in Prague, followed by demonstrations with a similar number of participants in Washington, D.C., against a World Bank/IMF meeting. Reportedly, this meeting was preceded by "protest training" courses organized by some of the groups. Other demonstrations have followed in Quebec, Göteborg, and Genoa. The first two meetings had the participation of about 30,000 protesters and 6,000 police. The Genoa meeting engaged over 100,000 demonstrators and 25,000 police.[18]

The current generation of activists opposing the negative features of globalization characterizes itself with new forms of political action. While activist communication is constantly circulated through the Internet, many of the coalitions that emerge for city demonstrations are of brief duration and adopt names based on the date of the event, such as J-18, N-30, and A-16. After the demonstrations, the organizers leave "virtually no trace behind, save for an archived website" (Klein 2000).

Among those opposing the negative effects of globalization, there are also groups that engage in more drastic forms of action. One such group is the Earth Liberation Front, referred to in the press as the "eco-terrorists." The Front has inflicted more than U.S.$37 million in damages since it appeared in the United States in 1996; it has "declared war" on urban sprawl, loggers, genetic engineering of seed, the fur industry, and the use of animals for research. Organizationally, the Front moves primarily through the Internet. The FBI has been unsuccessful in identifying the Front's members because they use encrypted e-mail that bounces around the world before reaching the intended recipients (*60 Minutes,* 2001).

The majority of groups opposing globalization pursue pacific means and have attained some incremental victories. Actions by peasants revolving around the Global Campaign for Agrarian Reform have included sending open letters to presidents and government offices of several countries as well as setting up an information network for regional and internal communication among members of this initiative. Via Campesina seeks to remove all negotiation in the areas of food production and marketing from the WTO and make this a more nation-based decision, to cancel a current WTO obligation for countries to import at least 5 percent of its food consumption, and to prohibit "biopiracy" and patents on life (animal, plants, and parts of the human body), including the development of sterile varieties through genetic engineering.[19] Women farmers have also been active participants, as reflected in the First Rural and Indigenous Women's International Assembly held in Bangalore, India, in September 2000.

The Jubilee 2000 campaign to cancel the unpayable debts of developing countries by the end of 2000 obtained only a small amount of debt cancellation, but it succeeded in giving the debt issue prominence on the international agenda. Jubilee 2000 has now started another campaign, "Drop the Debt," which was presented in public demonstrations at the G-8 summit in Genoa (July 2001).

The student involvement in antiglobalization actions has evolved from engaging in protest to presenting proposals for action. Thus, the student movement in the United States, which started as an anti-sweatshop reaction, has moved into drafting an alternative code of conduct and proposing a quasi-regulatory body to monitor it, the Workers Rights Consortium.

In response to the Global Compact proposed by the United Nations, globalization watchers have proposed instead a "Citizens Compact" and asked the United Nations and corporations to participate in it. The Citizens Compact is endorsed by more than seventy human rights and environmental groups from around the world. It emphasizes the need for monitoring and the enforcement of a legal framework for corporate behavior.

After realizing that a World Economic Forum attended by more than 1,000 TNCs had been meeting informally in Davos, Switzerland, for the past thirty years, numerous groups working against globalization excesses organized the First World Social Forum (WSF) in Porto Alegre, Brazil, in 2001. Topics dealing with the environment, youth, labor, gender, and education were frequently represented in the workshops of the forum. The WSF seeks to "radicalize democracy," and there are plans to continue meeting on an annual basis.

THE INTERNET IN OPPOSITIONAL POLITICS

Current forms of resistance are characterized by a large number of grassroots groups and NGOs, "coordinated by a tidal wave of information" (Klein 2000). For such diverse sources as manifestos, academic papers, and Web diaries, the Internet prevails.

Ironically, the Internet, which has been one of the main technologies contributing to the impact of globalizing forces throughout the world, is also one of the key tools used to combat it. In fact, in many efforts to develop "globalization from below," or the creation of solidarity networks throughout the world, the Internet is a major device. Thanks to the Internet, environmentalists in one country are quickly reporting on the behavior of a multinational in that country to environmentalists in other countries. Women's groups are sending detailed accounts of what they have learned in regional or international forums to other members in their network. The Internet has demonstrated that it is capable of developing a sense of community despite geographic distance and even language differences. It has also shown that it can be effective in the launching and coordination of regional and global citizens' campaigns.

Writing of the emergence of a transnational indigenous movement, Brysk (2000) notes that information technologies (particularly the Internet) have facilitated the formulation of international appeals as well as data collection, the processing of such data, and the creation of affective bonds and collective identities over broader networks. Many would agree that the Zapatista movement is the first one to have utilized the power of the Internet. However, observers of events such as the WSF are aware of the limits of cybernetic venues. In the opinion of Maria de Conceicao Tavares, a Brazilian economist and professor, global networking is effective for sharing experience and knowledge and promoting civic consciousness but much less so for creating economic solidarity (World Social Forum 2000). Tavares maintains that to combat the problems of poverty and hunger, it is more effective to work on the local and national levels of public politics.[20] The strategy of networks is excellent for sharing experiences and knowledge globally, but it does not serve well for public politics and political struggles within national states because tighter forms of organization are needed. Recognizing the need for concrete institutions, the WSF has called for the creation of organizations for credit, health, and education to replace the IMF and the World Bank (World Social Forum 2000).

IMPLICATIONS OF RESISTANCE FOR EDUCATION

As mentioned throughout this book, globalization produces both positive and negative consequences. We have seen that globalization affects education directly through the creation of diverse and larger numbers of educational institutions and the adoption of new objectives and instructional procedures. The preference for an instrumental role of education over more critical and humanistic endeavors is a particular trend that merits questioning.

From the review of the actors engaged in resistance to globalization and the focus of their opposition, we have seen that most resistance is not aimed at changes in the educational arena, despite the enormous consequences that formal education has on a society's ideology and the social stratification being created by globalization. There is a desperate need for more critical examination by educators of current developments related to globalization.

A substantial implication for education is its role in the transmission of information and knowledge regarding various economic and political actors engaged in globalization practices. This is an education that would occur not only through the formal education system but also through nonformal education, working with distinct groups of adults. Here education would have a role to play in (1) raising awareness among scattered citizen groups about the impact of globalization and possible actions to alter its negative impacts and (2) the more difficult task of redefining globalization so that its exclusionary practices are better understood and more effectively corrected. We agree strongly with the assertion by Gonzalez Casanova (1996) that finding "the alternative to neoliberalism is a moral, political, and social problem requiring urgent solution. It is also the most important intellectual problem confronting the social sciences of our time" (47).

NOTES

1. Some 65 million hectares of forest were lost in the developing world between 1990 and 1995 because of overharvesting, conversion into agricultural land, disease, and fire (Annan 2000, 62). High demand for timber in the industrialized countries is a major factor behind this depletion.

2. In July 2001, the Intergovernmental Panel on Climate Change, comprising hundreds of scientists and established by the United Nations in 1988, presented a report identifying mankind as responsible for global warming rather than other factors. The study concluded that the Earth's average temperature could rise by as much as 10.4 degrees over the 100 years, more than 60 percent higher than the panel's prediction less than six years ago. This temperature change was anticipated to create droughts, floods, and violent storms throughout the world (Pan 2001). Despite the categorical findings by this prestigious panel, the U.S. government chose to call the conclusions "ambiguous."

3. An analysis of the California schools rewarded for registering academic improvement by students showed that the wealthiest 10 percent of schools received grants as a higher rate than the statewide average school (Bell 2001).

4. Santos (1995) identifies three types of civil society: The first represents private economic interests, the second represents the social movements (ecological, antinuclear, pro-peace, and feminist), and the third he sees as that which functioned during the final phase of the socialist regimes in eastern Europe and were characterized by dissident theoretical reflection.

5. To qualify for debt relief, countries must have a "poverty reduction strategy in place" and agree to spend the money they would have allocated to debt repayments on specific antipoverty projects.

6. The FTAA would link thirty-four nations comprising 800 million people, or 15 percent of the world's population. Its mandate is currently under discussion, with the intention of becoming effective by 2005.

7. In this respect, Mooney (cited in Parker 2000, 5) argues that education in the form of literacy contributes to the destruction of local knowledge: He found that the knowledge and experience of local healers, herbalists, and farmers decreased considerably when "literacy campaigns derided community knowledge systems in favor of the North's technology and culture."

8. According to Shiva (2001), patents deny nature's creativity; they also negate the amount of work that farmers have conducted through many years in the development of seeds and are "antithetical to any notion of food security." One example of such appropriation comes from the effort by several U.S. scientists to patent the word "turmeric" as a wound-healing agent. Apparently, the WTO made a decision in their favor, but it was overturned when India showed that the use of the spice as a healing agent had existed as common knowledge for millennia (Lee 2000).

9. In an interesting instance of technology helping indigenous movements, a decision by the Inter-American Court of Human Rights in September 2001 favored the Awas Tignis Indians in Nicaragua. The court recognized the indigenous community's current and historical use and the occupancy of its territory through ethnographic research and computer-generated maps using geographic information systems or GIS (Macdonald 2002).

10. Parker (2000) proposes to use the term "non-indigenous local knowledge" to refer to the knowledge of relatively recent settlers in a community about the local effects of globalization. In his view, this recent local knowledge can easily develop into theories about the universal effects of globalization, particularly those of environmental degradation.

11. Studies, however, have shown that in the pressure to sell GMOs, some corporations have not told farmers to take the proper precautions to avoid that the modified seeds invade lands with regular seeds (Flora 2001).

12. According to Novartis AG (2001), the countries most vulnerable to the new technologies are those of sub-Saharan and the Caribbean, who exports consist of potentially substitutable agricultural products.

13. How a specific agrarian reform is actually implemented is a crucial issue. In Brazil, 90 percent of land reform is taking place through settlements in the Amazon region (often colonized by those expelled from lands now taken over by export-oriented agro-industries). The new settlers burn the land and cause forest fires, contributing (no less than some TNCs) to the problems of deforestation and pollution (Menotti 2000).

14. According to the Inter-American Development Bank and the Instituto Indigenista Interamericano, there are 400 indigenous peoples in Latin America, amounting to a population of forty million, an amount that represents 10 percent of the region's population. In the case of Bolivia and Guatemala, the indigenous population represents more than half, in Peru and Ecuador about half, in Mexico and Honduras about 15 percent, in Chile 8 percent, and in the rest of the region between 1 and 7 percent, except in Brazil, where it constitutes 0.2 percent (cited in Mato 1996b, 38).

15. Some observers call Indian rights movements "postmodern" because they are increasingly identity based, internationally focused, composed of networks as well as organizations, and culturally oriented. In my view, it is not accurate to call them postmodern since variation and transnational features are not the monopoly of postmodernity.

16. The Global Compact consists of nine principles drawn from existing environmental, labor, and human rights agreements. It seeks to gain a commitment from some fifty corporations to these principles and to implement them in three ways: (1) including them in their mission statements and annual reports, (2) providing specific examples of progress made or lessons learned in putting the principles into practice, and (3) participating in partnerships with the United Nations both at the policy level and "on the ground" in developing countries and "helping villagers link up to the Internet" (for additional details, see Corporate Watch's Web page at <http://www.corpwatch.org>).

17. About seventy human rights and environmental groups that oppose the Global Compact are arguing instead for a "Citizens Compact," which would establish the basis for cooperation between the United Nations and nonbusiness, nongovernmental groups that together would try to determine a proper relationship between the United Nations and business groups.

18. The Genoa demonstration, unfortunately, produced the first death of a protester—the son of a well-known union organizer.

19. Shiva (2001) describes biopiracy as "the false claim to biodiversity that already exists." It is seen as extremely dangerous because the proliferation of such patents will alter the nature of relations in the countryside. For instance, the informal sharing by farmers of hybrid seed (since it is now bought in the market rather than set aside from a previous harvest) will be treated as theft.

20. In areas less susceptible to economic and political controversy, the Internet may be sufficient. The Land Mines Campaign, which won the 1997 Nobel Peace Prize, accomplished its goals of information sharing and shaping of public opinion primarily through the use of this information/communication technology.

9

Reframing the Future

> We serve our use as analysts and as critics—but as involved critics in the
> process of the transformation of the world.
>
> Wallerstein (1999)

This chapter begins with a synthesis of our earlier discussions as a spring-
board toward a presentation of suggested forms of constructive response
that one can present to globalization. It then moves to an identification of a
feasible set of actions within the educational arena.

Summarizing the main features of globalization, it can be said to be a
process characterized by many simultaneous events in multiple arenas of social life, moving at very fast speeds, and usually producing mutually reinforcing causation or "circular causation."[1] This process, guided by specific
economic interests, is creating a strong connectivity between the economy,
technology, culture, and politics.

A significant feature of globalization is the increasing polarity between
North and South and between social groups. It can be readily seen that the
world is becoming more corporatized (through the solidification of a sur-
prisingly small number of increasingly large transnational corporations
[TNCs]), while the functions of the state are at the same time narrowing.
There is a simultaneous process of concentration of economic power, first by
organizations that are active across countries and second by individuals in
Northern countries.

Education is heavily implicated in the globalization process. It is part of
the official means to become citizens in the "knowledge society." It is also
the vehicle for the new value traits required by the prevailing economic

world. It is a major target for the conduct of economic enterprises themselves. Linked to the corporatization of society, is the positioning of education as one consumer good among others that people can either sell or buy
indiscriminately. The monopoly of education by public schools is being dis-
solved, usually through attacks charging that current structures do not work
either because they are centralized or because there are no powerful incentives to make schools perform more efficiently. Guidance by the efforts of
international lending and development organizations and business firms is
creating new consensus on such matters as the desirability of privatization
and decentralization in education.

With these simultaneous transformations, education is losing considerable
ground in its traditional social acceptance as a "common" or "public good,"
a resource open to all as a human right and to be collectively shared. Levin
(1987) concedes that "public education stands at the intersection of two legitimate rights" (3). One right calls for parents to decide what educational
environments they want for their children, and the other right requires a
democratic society to ensure a common set of values and norms. With globalization, however, education has become a commodity that, like any other,
is to be determined and bought on the market. Will the reduced role of the
state in running schools and conversely the privatization of schooling improve the academic quality or merely destroy one of the few stable unifying
experiences increasingly distinct social classes have?

Parallel to the increasing accumulation of wealth is the consolidation of a
value system in which worthiness is assigned almost exclusively to material
production and consumption. In the production of new value structures,
the role of the mass media, also in private hands and with little government
guidance, is perhaps the main determinant. In this value system, those who
create tangible wealth are rewarded much more than those who are concerned with spiritual abundance or those who question the unbridled
attention to competition and excellence to the detriment of solidarity and
satisfactory conditions for the largest groups.[2] Advanced communication
technologies, such as the Internet and cable television, are promoting the
dissemination of cultural values from the North. As in cases of broad and
widespread exposure, there are good and negative aspects in the consumption of contemporary cultural good, yet little assessment is being made
of the balance of these messages and representations. Moreover, it remains
unclear to what extent these values will have any variability and depth since
the global media reside in the hands of nine mutually emulating corporations with very little government monitoring.

Developing countries around the world recognize a public responsibility
for education, but this is limited largely to basic education. Moreover, this
recognition (in part because of insufficient state funding) has not been accompanied by the substantial financial support needed to attain it, beyond

reforms that seek to instill accountability. It is interesting that the acknowl-edgment of this minimum level of educational responsibility has a counter-part in the economic world, where the state recognizes also a minimum of responsibility—essentially, that needed to maintain a stable, law-abiding so-ciety to permit market forces to function.

Unquestionably, there exists today a much stronger linkage between educa-tional systems and business, some explicitly fostered by regional organizations and international development institutions. Regional and national variability in the new forms and content of education, of course, exists. The more encom-passing a phenomenon is, the more possibilities there are for local reaction and thus differentiation. We are not ignoring that some "divergence" and local forms of expression have emerged, but we are firmly asserting that the forces for "con-vergence" are much more numerous and stronger.

Information technologies are increasing the connectivity between people and helping the dissemination of information that can, in some cases, help transform undesirable situations. In crucial instances, however, the informa-tion that is being accessed is limited and still determined by the North. As the Global Development Gateway proposed by the World Bank becomes a real-ity, chances are that the information will be based primarily on cognitive and political criteria from the North.

Many changes are discernable in higher education, the level most likely affected by globalization given its focus on more complex scientific and tech-nological knowledge. Moving higher education into private hands and diver-sifying its programs makes it possible for a larger number of young people to attend than before. Yet this possibility occurs at the cost of increasing differ-ential statuses within the educational system, creating new patterns of dis-tinction based on the type of institution attended and the prestige and rank-ing of such an institution. Educational entrepreneurs respond quickly to market needs for instrumental knowledge; this contributes to the creation of a better fit between education and the labor market. An unintended effect of the private role in tertiary education is the narrowing of the curriculum from liberal and humanities coverage to pragmatic knowledge and skills. Pri-vate forces in education are also modifying the governance of education, par-ticularly in research universities. Contributing to these changes is the growing presence of educational technologies, which are modifying forms of delivery and at the same time promoting a certain kind of content (also pragmatic), pushing other knowledge aside.

Women are encountering positive and negative scenarios with global-ization. The labor market is incorporating them into jobs that enable them to have access to independent incomes, and women are increasing their levels of participation in higher education. But increased poverty in devel-oping countries drives women into survival modes rather than into creat-ing coalitions for social change. The imposing ethos of competition also reduces possibilities of alliances across social classes and ethnicities. In all, however, important political victories are being obtained by women in many parts of the world, even though the educational system per se has played a modest role in this.

The strategies employed by the processes of globalization to bring greater convergence in education and culture constitute a wide mix. Some influences are direct, as in the case of policies being advocated by lending institutions, budgetary reductions affecting public education imposed under the conditions of structural adjustment programs (SAPs), and the transmission of educational programs designed abroad with little adaptation to local context and needs. Many are indirect; these include the growing exposure to media content, the privatization of university education that facilitates the consumption of Northern products, and the networking of groups with similar interests. The market, of course, is a prime source of indirect influences.

We live in a gradually emerging and very changed new world. Yet some things remain the same. Communication crosses boundaries constantly, but geopolitics dividing the North and the South continue. Pluralism and the open society, both required and fostered by the market, are constantly invoked ideals; nonetheless, the power concentration of TNCs and the hegemonic position of the North in areas of high technology and culture remains. Access to education and some material goods has expanded, yet the process of social exclusion is patent, particularly in the Third World.

So far, globalization has yielded an explosion of new technological ideas, abundant production of goods and services, and, in a few geographical areas, increasing levels of wealth. The dispersion of all these positive attributes has been limited, with the North being the greatest beneficiary. The Third World's persistent poverty and inability to catch up with the North under the present form of globalization represents the strongest deterrent to a relaxed and unproblematized acceptance of the globalization process.

Countries are expected to attain a state of well-being on the basis of what they produce and subsequently sell. However, there is increased understanding in certain academic and international circles that the reduction of poverty will be assisted much more by social and economic reforms to increase the capabilities of the poor than by simple economic growth. Moreover, historic evidence demonstrates that trade per se does not create wealth. Wealth depends on what is being traded and at what price, and prices of goods—though influenced by supply and demand—are greatly determined in central markets. According to the United Nations Development Program (1999a), there has been an elevenfold increase in world trade since 1950. At the same time, there has been an increasing gap between rich and poor countries. To repeat a disturbing fact, the 225 richest individuals in the world have assets greater than the combined annual income of 2.5 billion people (or 47 percent of the world's population). At present, 40 percent of the world's population is below the age of twenty. Many of these young people are, or are about to start, having children of their own. Most of the resulting youth bulge, nearly 98 percent, will be in the developing world (Annan 2000).

Education is invoked as a means to prevent the expansion of poverty and to enable countries to enter the "knowledge society." Technology-based production, heavily dependent on educated populations, will unquestionably generate the greatest revenues, yet it will not generate the largest employment. The largest employer in the United States is not one of the TNCs but the temporary employment agency Manpower. In many developing countries, the growing sector of the economy is the informal labor sector, where academic knowledge takes second place to ingenuity in daily survival.

The economist Lynn Ilon (1997) predicts that there will be a five-layer stratification of jobs in terms of their articulation with the global economy: world-class, internationally linked, locally supported, community supported, and nonparticipatory jobs. She believes that this will be mapped onto the demand and provision of education, with the consequence that education will become also highly stratified, notably between private provision of internationally comparable quality and state provision of much more variable quality.

Are some observers unduly pessimistic? Perhaps envious of the wealth emerging elsewhere? This could be. But to be concerned about disparities is not a misplaced jealousy; it is rather the product of a reflection on how major human needs will be satisfied.

DEGLOBALIZATION

Though a possibility in terms of logical argumentation, in reality the return to a pre-1970s world is remote and not even desirable. It is also true that globalization has not affected the entire world. In many African countries, tribalism, often ignored in contemporary accounts, continues to be the only dependable entity providing local government for many people (Rideout 2001).

Given the development of technologies, the dominance of large economic enterprises, and the growing power of a few central countries, it is difficult to imagine a world characterized by dispersed and benevolent forms of power. Nonetheless, it is imperative to consider alternative structures, processes, and cultures. Social scientists such as Johann Galtung and Samir Amin have recognized the urgent need for other types of social organization and development—new forms of relating in the social world without exploiting others.

REGLOBALIZATION THROUGH GLOBALIZATION FROM BELOW

Happiness and progress are conditions most of us want to attain. The major question today is, Where can they be reached with reduced levels of consumerism and growth? A corollary of this is whether the search for profit and accumulation can be diminished under a viable international economic system.

Is it possible to restructure globalization so as to maximize benefits for all? Some believe that it is and are calling for a globalization "from below." This concept is defined as constituting "an array of transnational forces animated by environmental concerns, human rights, hostility to patriarchy, and a vision of a human community based on the unity of diverse cultures seeking an end to poverty, oppression, humiliation, and collective violence" (Falk 1993, cited in Henry 2001, 96).

Groups from civil society seeking economic and social justice have succeeded, through their demonstrations and public pressure, to put on negotiating tables issues that were being slighted: the environment, debt forgiveness, and awareness of negative effects of free trade. They have been giving visibility to issues and introducing among formal representatives of the North a sense of shame, reflected in the adoption of a new position toward sub-Saharan Africa and a willingness to explore unintended negative effects of trade at the 2001 World Trade Organization (WTO) meeting in Genoa.

In the following paragraphs, we present a distillation of the most critical requirements for the creation of a new, alternative globalized world as expressed by various groups representing civil society.

1. In reglobalization, we should be moving not only to global institutions but also to those of a more democratic nature that would reflect no longer national interests but global society (Held and McGrew 2000), what Held (1995, 239–286) calls a "cosmopolitan" democracy. This means reclaiming the power of the more representative institutions, the United Nations being the key governance body (Elmandrja, ca. 1999; Held 1995; Khor 2000). Some thought has already been given to this possibility. In its 1999 report, the United Nations Development Program (1999a, 12) calls for a "broader UN including two chambers in the General Assembly to allow for greater civil society representation, and a global central bank and lender of last resort." Elaborating on this notion, Annan (2000, 74) refers to the United Nations as a "catalyst for collective action, both among its Member States and between them and the vibrant constellation of new non-state actors." Changes in the UN would also include the transforming of the Security Council and, thus, the veto power of certain countries, although great powers would retain permanent membership (Camillieri et al. 2000).

2. Concomitant with this, there should be a transfer of power and authority from international bodies representing powerful coalitions of central states (such as the G-8 and the Organization for Economic Cooperation and Devel-

opment) to the United Nations. In the new scheme, the role of international financial institutions, such as the World Bank, should be evaluated. In this respect, the conclusions of the Meltzer Commission, appointed by the U.S. Congress to examine the performance of the World Bank and the International Monetary Fund (IMF), are extremely important. The Meltzer Commission found that 70 percent of the nonaid resources provided by the Word Bank flowed to eleven countries that already enjoy substantial access to private resource flows. In each of the main developing regions (Asia, Latin America, and Africa), four to six of the most creditworthy borrowing countries receive most nonaid resource flows from the regional banks: 90 percent in Asia, 80 to 90 percent in Africa, and 78 to 85 percent in Latin America (Meltzer et al. 2000, 7). Development banks in general are known to decide primarily in terms of the bottom line (economic returns) rather than promoting more humanitarian development efforts that may incur risk but ultimately improve conditions. Some thought has been given by academicians and researchers to the creation of a World Financial Authority (to be created under UN auspices) that would oversee the functioning of a stable and comprehensive world financial framework (Camillieri et al. 2000).

Efforts by U.S. citizens to modify practices by the World Bank have centered on lobbying Congress to use its leverage to release funds from the U.S. Treasury to the World Bank in exchange for compliance with certain points. This strategy was used successfully by environmental groups in the mid-1980s (O'Brien et al. 2000). Both the IMF and the World Bank recently abandoned the term "structural adjustment," applying instead the notion of "poverty reduction." Both institutions have produced a number of poverty reduction strategy papers since 2000, but several observers see this as a change in vocabulary, not in objectives.[3] In keeping with the creation of new international institutions, a positive step has been the establishment of the International Criminal Court in July 2002. In a surprising move, however, the United States, after having given it presidential signature, decided to renounce the treaty.

3. Once the United Nations begins functioning in a more autonomous and democratic manner, it should prioritize funding for sustainable development, human rights, health, labor standards, and ecological protection over commercial interest. Part of human dignity is not only to recognize needs of others but also to have the courage and will to address them. UN Secretary-General Kofi Annan (2000) stated in his millennium speech, *"I challenge the foremost experts in the world to think through the barrier of low agricultural productivity in Africa. I implore the great philanthropic foundations—which have stimulated so much good and practical research on agriculture—to rise to this vital challenge"* (31). This statement correctly highlights the severe crisis that Africa is undergoing today. At the same time, it reflects a sorry condition that the request for improvement should be made on the basis of charity, as an appeal to "philanthropic foundations." Many people, particularly Annan, are aware that

modifications to social and political structures are needed. The time should come to make such requests on the basis of the common good and human progress rather than as special favors that the North (home of the philanthropic foundations) should grant the South.

4. Related to the previous points, there is consensus that as the world becomes globalized in multiple arenas, a body is needed to establish a just basis for free trade and monitor its activities. As Held (1995), puts it,

> The corporate capitalist system requires constraint and regulation to compensate for the biases generated by the pursuit of the "private good." At issue is the establishment of an economic system that is neither simply planned nor merely market orientated but, rather, open to organizations, associations and agencies pursuing their own projects, subject to the constraints of a common structure of political action and democratic processes. (251)

Demands have been presented to reconstitute the WTO as such a body to ensure free and fair international trade. Demands have been made also for a world environmental agency to avoid the current conflict between low-cost production and high environmental damage (United Nations Development Program 1999a). Additional suggestions to improve financing, commercial, and monetary structures were presented at the UN-sponsored International Conference on Financing for Development (Monterey, Mexico, March 2002). These included the reestablishment of the Unit on Transnational Corporations within the UN, the creation of an International Compensatory Fund to facilitate the debt servicing of middle-income countries, special economic considerations for small island-states, and the reformation of the current international financial system through the creation of a World Financial Authority to monitor the global financial market, and an International Tax Organization to supervise cooperation in transnational taxation and thus create new mechanisms for the extraction of financial resources to eradicate poverty.

5. There is strong consensus as well regarding the impossibilities that many developing countries have encountered in their efforts to pay their external debts. Two counterproposals have been presented. One, under the motto "instead of poverty reduction, let's have wealth reduction," calls for the immediate and comprehensive debt cancellation.[4] It calls also for taxation on TNCs in all countries and at all points of production, taxes on currency transactions (to inhibit speculation and to raise resources; this is the Tobin tax mentioned in chapter 5), and elimination of tax havens (Bello 2000). The other calls for Northern countries to pay the "ecological debt" they owe to the South for the pollution of rivers and oceans, decimation of forests, and so on by TNCs.

6. There have also been proposals for developing countries to engage in more endogenous development, moving away from the mirage of export-led

growth. Such proposals are calling for agrarian reform to generate more economic activity and for greater domestic savings. The latter is seen as possible, provided that increases in the minimum wage occur, as citizens then would be able to generate capital through savings. Increased taxation, particularly on personal consumption of luxury goods and on inheritance property, is seen as fundamental to the elaboration of a new economy (Gomes and Mangabeira Unger 1998; Mangabeira Unger 2000).

On the basis of these main proposals, broad coalitions of individuals and groups in civil society continue to organize and press their respective governments for reconsideration of the ongoing globalization process. Their work reveals that they are not blindly opposed to globalization but rather favor "politics and economics for the common good" (Rete Lilliput 2001).

How civil society responds to globalization tendencies is crucial to the educational system. Economic globalization, and particularly neoliberal economic thought, tends to limit the degrees of freedom of the state and public schools. Technological advances, added to the expanded economic globalization, carry with them great positive and negative consequences for education as we know it. If the poverty of the world continues to grow unabated, technological inventions will not reach many in the Third World, and their marginalization will deepen.

A NEW BASIS FOR GLOBALIZATION

It is evident that capitalism is a structure that tends to maintain inequality and poverty as the way to accumulate wealth and power. Efforts to enact change from mainstream politics rather than from the margins have been termed the "Third Way," which seeks to avoid the polarization between neoliberalism and Marxism. The Third Way is an approach endorsed by progressive political parties, such as the current Labor Party in the United Kingdom; it seeks to promote democracy and public welfare services with the help of private-sector partnerships and the modernization of public institutions. Another take of the Third Way is present in the more radical alternatives proposed by Third World scholars (presented as points 1 to 6 in the previous paragraphs). Will the Third Way proposed by the North be possible, or will the self-regulating market continue to displace the will of elected governments?

From the margins, efforts by the women's movement, the ecological movement, indigenous rights movements, and the human rights movements are bringing new dimensions to a new global politics. Their ideas, at odds with the socially modifying, freewheeling activities of the TNCs, deserve more prominence in the international discourse as well as at local levels, where their efforts are felt.

TASKS AHEAD FOR EDUCATIONAL RESEARCHERS

The complexity and multidimensionality of globalization phenomena require concomitant modifications in our approach to their understanding. Education has long been accepted as an eclectic field that does not hesitate to borrow contributions from the behavioral sciences. Yet at any one time, educational research efforts have emphasized one particular discipline over others. Globalization is such that it will press beyond its limits efforts of any single discipline to reach an understanding of unfolding human affairs. More than ever, we need to conduct more interdisciplinary research to better understand these affairs. In the future, the field of comparative education might engage in truly interdisciplinary research by incorporating team members with solid and extensive expertise in a variety of domains. More than ever, we need descriptions of contexts and settings that capture significant features, that weave events in the educational arena with those taking place in other arenas (be they economic, technological, cultural, or political), and that provide insightful interpretations of an otherwise chaotic world. Under conditions of increasing inequality among countries, we need to connect issues of poverty and wealth with markers such as gender, ethnicity, and urban/rural location to transcend local and national settings. Likewise, we need to provide detailed and careful attention to issues of proximal and distal causation. Direct influences through school reforms, curricular contents, and family socialization will continue under our analytical lens, but powerful indirect influences—such as international and internal migration, access to jobs, funding to public education, the role of international funding and development agencies, and the pervasive nature of the mass media—may be elements that need to figure prominently in future analyses of education.

TASKS FOR EDUCATORS

With minor exceptions, there is an ongoing globalization of educational policy and practice, and it is the Western paradigm of what constitutes good educational practice that prevails. Often, the adoption of practices in effect in central countries occurs with little evidence of their effect on application in peripheral and semiperipheral social and cultural contexts.

Educators have remained relatively complacent amid dramatic changes in form, content, and process introduced by globalization. Yet education has a major role to play: internally vis-à-vis the knowledge to be disseminated to students and externally vis-à-vis the awareness it should bring to citizens at large. As Bamyeh (2000) notes, "Life in the global era requires a particular kind of action: integrally informed rather than fragmented; intelligent and effective in its application" (158). This applies centrally to educators.

Educators have an obligation to understand the impact of capitalism around the world and to link it to the local conditions that are manifested in their schools and communities (Darder 2001; Mangabeira Unger 2000). Citizenship is being de facto redefined by the very high levels of migration and by cultural globalization: Are the schools recognizing this? What are the implications for education and society when educators consider globalization theories that recognize the role of TNCs, mass movements, and multilateral aid agencies? Global economics is exerting an impact on education and on how some populations are treated. For instance, the use of state-mandated testing in the United States is having the effect of retaining (as repeaters) children of African American, Latino, and poor families in general (Darder 2001). An unavoidable challenge for educators will be to become familiar with educational systems in other countries to detect ways in which similarities and differences may exist and to establish to what extent variability may signify difference and exclusion for some groups.

Educators, more than most other social actors (and more than they and others are often willing to recognize), are faced with heavy responsibilities in the era of globalization. A formidable concern for all progressive educators will be to defend those principles that make real democracy possible— a sense of solidarity and constant effort toward the reduction of social inequalities—and to engage in serious discussion of when and how principles of "efficiency," "client choice," "flexibility," and "competitiveness" work against the construction and maintenance of democratic societies.

In particular, adult educators must evince social and political commitment and must enable others to understand the forms of oppression and solidarity in the world (Allman and Mayo 1997). As UN sources affirm, the key task we all face is not to stop expansion of world markets but rather to find new rules and institutions for stronger governance with ethical principles, equity (less disparity), inclusion (less marginalization of people and countries), human security, sustainability (with less environmental destruction), and development (less poverty and deprivation) (United Nations Development Program 1999a).

At least three challenges can be identified for educators: First, they should recognize how globalization is changing the nature of schooling and universities, the growing interconnection between knowledge and power, and the cases in which education has become either a silent partner or a conscious opponent. The key connections between globalization and education may be less visible than the economic and ecological challenges, but they both must be underscored and faced. Second, they should examine formal education (schooling and university teaching), nonformal education (with adult groups), and informal education (particularly through the production of alternative media) as key venues in which to provide understanding about the various positive and negative consequences of globalization. For example, courses in such topics as ecology and consumerism and critical reading of the mass media could be provided. Third, they should use education as a means to create active citizens, moving people from passively observing the actions of others to undertaking action themselves. Educators should play a central role in moving minds from "globalization," with its emphasis on expansion of markets and competition, to "internationalism," which Jones (1998) defines as "the promotion of global peace and well-being through the development and application of international structures, primarily but not solely of an intergovernmental kind" (143). In this manner, the positive promise of globalization—ensuring a better world for *all*—stands a good chance of being realized.

Finally, although educators need to become key players in a globally democratizing transformation, the time for solitary protagonistic roles has passed. Their work will be more effective in alliance with other groups of civil society, establishing bridges that go beyond school and community, reflecting and planning with organized groups in other areas of our contemporary world, not only within the confines of the nation-state but also in venues of transnational action.

NOTES

1. The concept of "circular causation" was first formulated by Gunnar Myrdal (1957) to describe situations in which a change in one factor would affect a number of other factors, which in turn would influence the first factor.

2. The situation of health throughout the world is perhaps the strongest indicator of the low levels of human solidarity today. Although more than U.S.$56 billion a year is spent globally on health research, less than 10 percent is aimed at the health problems affecting 90 percent of the world's population. Pneumonia, diarrhea, tuberculosis, and malaria receive less than 1 percent of global health research budgets (Annan 2000, 26). Some fifty million people have been infected with HIV since the early 1970s, and sixteen million have already died from AIDS. In 1999 alone, 5.6 million people were newly infected with HIV, half of them under twenty-five years old. Of the nearly thirty-six million now living with HIV/AIDS worldwide, more than twenty-three million reside in sub-Saharan Africa (Annan 2000, 26).

3. In another indication of concern, the World Bank focused its 2000–2001 *World Development Report* on the theme of poverty and development, for which it held interviews with 60,000 poor women and men from sixty countries, later compiled in a document called *Consultations with the Poor* (World Bank 1999a).

4. Critics of the current form of globalization are calling for the cancellation by central countries, and particularly by the World Bank and the IMF, of 100 percent of the debt in the most-indebted poorest countries as opposed to the 30 percent currently offered. They also seek a commitment from lending institutions not to force poor countries to pay more in servicing the debt than they do in servicing health needs (Rete Lilliput 2001).

Appendix A

Table A1.   Top 100 Economies, 1999 (millions of dollars)

	Country/*Corporation*	GDP/*sales*		Country/*Corporation*	GDP/*sales*
1	United States	8,708,870.0	51	Colombia	88,596.0
2	Japan	4,395,083.0	52	*AXA*	87,645.7
3	Germany	2,081,202.0	53	*IBM*	87,548.0
4	France	1,410,262.0	54	Singapore	84,945.0
5	United Kingdom	1,373,612.0	55	Ireland	84,861.0
6	Italy	1,149,958.0	56	*BP Amoco*	83,556.0
7	China	1,149,814.0	57	*Citigroup*	82,005.0
8	Brazil	760,345.0	58	*Volkswagen*	80,072.7
9	Canada	612,049.0	59	*Nippon Life Insurance*	78,515.1
10	Spain	562,245.0	60	Philippines	75,350.0
11	Mexico	474,951.0	61	*Siemens*	75,337.0
12	India	459,765.0	62	Malaysia	74,634.0
13	Korea, Rep.	406,940.0	63	*Allianz*	74,178.2
14	Australia	389,691.0	64	*Hitachi*	71,858.5
15	Netherlands	384,766.0	65	Chile	71,092.0
16	Russian Federation	375,345.0	66	*Matsushita Electric Ind.*	65,555.6
17	Argentina	281,942.0	67	*Nissho Iwai*	65,393.2
18	Switzerland	260,299.0	68	*ING Group*	62,492.4
19	Belgium	245,706.0	69	*AT & T*	62,391.0
20	Sweden	226,388.0	70	*Philip Morris*	61,751.0
21	Austria	208,949.0	71	*Sony*	60,052.7
22	Turkey	188,374.0	72	Pakistan	59,880.0
23	*General Motors*	176,558.0	73	*Deutsche Bank*	58,585.1
24	Denmark	174,363.0	74	*Boeing*	57,993.0
25	*Wal-Mart*	166,809.0	75	Peru	57,318.0
26	*Exxon Mobil*	163,881.0	76	Czech Republic	56,379.0
27	*Ford Motor*	162,558.0	77	*Dai-Ichi Mutual Life Ins.*	55,104.7
28	*Daimler Chrysler*	159,985.7	78	*Honda Motor*	54,773.5
29	Poland	154,146.0	79	*Assicurazioni*	53,723.2
30	Norway	145,449.0	80	*Nissan Motor*	53,679.9
31	Indonesia	140,964.0	81	New Zealand	53,622.0
32	South Africa	131,127.0	82	*E.On*	52,227.7
33	Saudi Arabia	128,892.0	83	*Toshiba*	51,634.9
34	Finland	126,130.0	84	*Bank of America*	51,392.0
35	Greece	123,934.0	85	*Fiat*	51,331.7
36	Thailand	123,887.0	86	*Nestle*	49,694.1
37	*Mitsui*	118,555.2	87	*SBC Communications*	49,489.0
38	*Mitsubishi*	117,765.6	88	*Credit Suisse*	49,362.0
39	*Toyota Motor*	115,670.9	89	Hungary	48,355.0
40	*General Electric*	111,630.0	90	*Hewlett-Packard*	48,253.0
41	*Itochu*	109,068.9	91	*Fujitsu*	47,195.9
42	Portugal	107,716.0	92	Algeria	47,015.0
43	*Royal Dutch/Shell*	105,366.0	93	*Metro*	46,663.6
44	Venezuela	103,918.0	94	*Sumitomo Life Insurance*	46,445.1
45	Iran, Islamic Rep.	101,073.0	95	Bangladesh	45,779.0
46	Israel	99,068.0	96	*Tokyo Electric Power*	45,727.7
47	*Sumitomo*	95,701.6	97	*Kroger*	45,351.6
48	*Nippon Tel & Tel*	93,591.7	98	*Total Fina Elf*	44,990.3
49	Egypt, Arab Rep.	92,413.0	99	*NEC*	44,828.0
50	*Marubeni*	91,807.4	100	*State Farm Insurance*	44,637.2

Note: Data drawn from *Fortune*, July 31, 2000 and World Bank, *World Development Report 2000*.
Source: Anderson and Cavanaugh 2000.

Table A2. Changing Profile of the Top 200 Transnational Corporations, various years (billions of dollars)

Country	1983			1995			1999		
	No. of firms	Sales $billion	% of Top 200	No. of firms	Sales $billion	% of Top 200	No. of firms	Sales $billion	% of Top 200
United States	90	1,370.6	47.4	59	1,994.6	28.0	82	3,267.2	39.3
Japan	37	635.2	22.0	58	2,760.8	38.7	41	2,034.4	24.5
Germany	13	158.3	5.5	22	715.3	10.0	20	948.3	11.4
France	13	137.5	4.8	22	579.2	8.1	17	613.7	7.4
United Kingdom	16	230.5	8.0	13	364.9	5.1	11	439.1	5.3
Netherlands	4	83.1	2.9	6	209.4	2.9	7.5	313.2	3.8
Switzerland	2	20.3	0.7	7	170.6	2.4	6	212.9	2.6
Italy	4	67.3	2.3	4	124.8	1.8	4	169.2	2.0
South Korea	5	36.2	1.3	4	88.7	1.2	5	140.9	1.7
Spain	1	11.3	0.4	0	0.0	0.0	3	78.1	0.9
Sweden	1	12.9	0.4	3	57.1	0.8	1	26.0	0.3
Belgium	1	8.7	0.3	1	11.3	0.2	0.5	21.8	0.3
Canada	6	43.7	1.5	1	17.9	0.3	1	21.3	0.3
Finland	0	0.0	0.0	0	0.0	0.0	1	21.1	0.3
Brazil	2	24.0	0.8	2	34.6	0.5	0	0.0	0.0
Israel	2	22.1	0.8	0	0.0	0.0	0	0.0	0.0
South Africa	1	9.3	0.3	0	0.0	0.0	0	0.0	0.0
India	1	9.3	0.3	0	0.0	0.0	0	0.0	0.0
Austria	1	9.8	0.3	0	0.0	0.0	0	0.0	0.0

Note: Data ranked by sales in 1999. Corporations owned by interests in two countries are counted as one half.
Source: Anderson and Cavanaugh 2000.

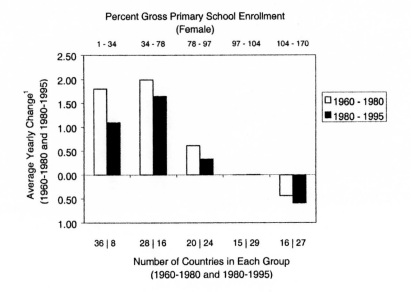

Figure A1.   Average Yearly Change in Female Primary School Enrollment

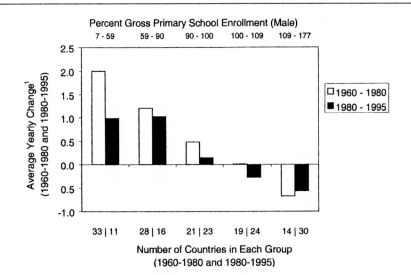

Figure A2.   Average Yearly Change in Male Primary School Enrollment

194

Appendix A

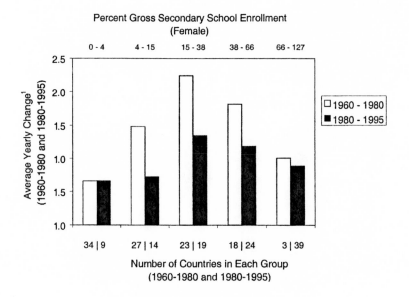

Source: World Bank, World Development Indicators, 2000

[1] In percentage points

Figure A3.   Average Yearly Change in Female Secondary School Enrollment

---

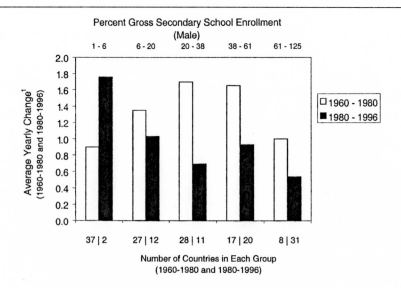

Source: World Bank, World Development Indicators, 2000

[1] In percentage points

Figure A4.   Average Yearly Change in Male Secondary School Enrollment

References

Abate, Tom. 2001. Scientists' "Publish or Perish" Credo Now "Patent and Profit." *San Francisco Chronicle,* August 11, pp. D1, D4.

Acker, Sandra, and Johanna Wyn. 2001. Gender, Change, and Leadership in Faculties of Education in Australia and Canada. Paper presented at the annual meeting of the American Education Research Association, Seattle, April 10–14.

Aghion, Philippe, Cecilia Garcia-Penalosa, and Peter Howitz. 2000. Knowledge and Development: A Schumpeterian Approach. Paper presented at the ABCDE Conference organized jointly by the World Bank and the Conseil d'Analyse Economique, Paris, June 27.

Allman, Paula, and Peter Mayo. 1997. Freire, Gramsci and Globalisation: Some Implications for Social and Political Commitment in Adult Education. 27th annual SCUTREA conference proceedings.

Altbach, Philip. 2000. The Crisis in Multinational Higher Education. *International Higher Education,* no. 21 (fall): 3–5.

———. 2001. Higher Education and the WTO: Globalization Run Amok. *International Higher Education,* no. 23 (spring): 1–4.

Altbach, Philip, and Patti Peterson. 1998. Internationalize American Higher Education? Not Exactly. *International Higher Education,* no. 11 (spring): 15–17.

Alvarez, Sonia. 1990. *Engendering Democracy in Brazil: Women's Movements in Transition Politics.* Princeton, N.J.: Princeton University Press.

———. 1992. *The Making of Social Movements in Latin America.* Boulder, Colo.: Westview Press.

Amin, Samir. 1997. *Capitalism in the Age of Globalization.* London: Zed Books.

Anderson, Sarah, and John Cavanagh. 2000. *The Rise of Corporate Global Power.* Washington, D.C.: Institute for Policy Studies. <http://corpwatch.org>

Annan, Kofi. 2000. *We the Peoples: The Role of the United Nations in the 21st Century.* New York: United Nations.

196   *References*

Appadurai, Arjun. 1990. Disjuncture and Difference in the Global Cultural Economy.
  In Mike Featherstone, ed., *Global Culture: Nationalism, Globalization and Moder-
  nity.* London: Sage, pp. 295–310.
———. 1996. *Modernity at Large: Cultural Dimensions of Globalization.* Minneapo-
  lis: University of Minnesota Press.
Apple, Michael. 1986. *Teachers and Texts: A Political Economy of Class and Gender
  Relations in Education.* New York: Routledge & Kegan Paul.
Arrighi, Giovanni, and Beverley Silver. 2000. Globalization and the Persistence of the
  North-South Divide. Paper presented at the Center for International Studies, Uni-
  versity of Southern California, Los Angeles, November 16.
Asimov, Anette. 2001. Teachers Rejecting Test Score Bonuses. *San Francisco Chron-
  icle,* July 30, p. A1.
Bakker, Isabella. 2000. Restructuring Discourse and its Gendered Underpinnings: To-
  ward a Macro-Analytical Framework. In Stephen McBride and John Wiseman, eds.,
  Power in the Global Era: Grounding Globalization. New York: St. Martin's, pp.
  24–36.
Ball, Stephen. 1998. Big Policies/Small World: An Introduction to International Per-
  spectives in Education Policy. *Comparative Education* 34, no. 2: 119–30.
Bamyeh, Mohammed. 2000. *The Ends of Globalization.* Minneapolis: University of
  Minnesota Press.
Bazeley, Michael. 2000. Dissension Threatens Voucher Movement. *San Jose Mercury
  News,* October 16, pp. 1A, 12A.
Bazeley, Michael, and Kate Folmar. 2000. 2 School Initiatives Close to Attracting $100
  Million. *San Jose Mercury News,* October 28, A1.
Beaverstock, J. V., and J. T. Boardwell. 2001. Negotiating Globalization, Transnational
  Corporations and Global City Financial Centres in Transient Migration Studies.
  <http://info.lut.ack.uk/departments/gy/research/gawc/rb/rb22.html>
Beaverstock, J. V., R. G. Smith, and P. J. Taylor. 2000. Geographies of Globalization:
  U.S. Law Firms in World Cities. *Urban Geography* 21, no. 2: 95–120.
Bell, Elizabeth. 2001. State's Cash Rewards for Testing Reach Rich, Poor Schools
  Equally. *San Francisco Chronicle,* May 22, pp. B1, B6.
Bello, Walden. 2000. From Melbourne to Prague: The Struggle for a Deglobalised
  World. *Focus on Trade,* no. 53 (September). <http://www.focus.org>
Benjamin, Ernst. 2000. Overreliance on Part-Time Faculty: An American Trend. *In-
  ternational Higher Education,* no. 21 (fall): 7–9.
Benson, C. S. 1978. *The Economics of Public Education.* Boston: Houghton Mifflin.
Benveniste, Luis. 2002. The Political Structure of Assessment: Negotiating State Power
  and Legitimacy. *Comparative Education Review* 46, no. 1: 89–118.
Blackmore, Jill. 1999. *Troubling Women: Feminism, Leadership, and Educational
  Change.* Buckingham: Open University Press.
Blandón, María Teresa, and Sófia Montenegro. 2000. La Corta Primavera de la De-
  mocratización. *Perspectivas,* no. 19 (July–September): 13–17.
Boshier, Roger. 2000. How the "Free Market" Destroys a Good Idea: The Rise and Fall
  of Lifelong Learning in New Zealand. Paper presented at the annual conferences
  of the Comparative and International Education Society (Western Region), University of California, Los Angeles, November 16–18.
Bourdieu, Pierre. 1996. *On Television.* New York: The New York Press.

————. 1998. L'Essence du Neoliberalisme. *Le Monde Diplomatique.* March.

Bowles, Samuel, and Herbert Gintis. 2000. Schools in Capitalist America Revisited. *Sociology of Education* 73: no. 1: 1–18.

Brooks, David. 2001. The Organization Kid. *Atlantic Monthly* 287, no. 4 (April): 40–54.

Brysk, Alison. 2000. *From Tribal Village to Global Village: Indian Rights and International Relations in Latin America.* Stanford, Calif.: Stanford University Press.

Buenfil, Rosa Nidia. 2000. Globalization and Educational Policies in Mexico, 1988–1994: A Meeting of the Universal and the Particular. In Nelly P. Stromquist and Karen Monkman, eds., *Globalization and Education: Integration and Contestation across Cultures.* Boulder: Rowman & Littlefield, pp. 275–97.

Bunch, Charlotte. 2000. Promises to Keep: Beijing and Beyond (Interviews by Mary Thom). *Ford Foundation Report,* winter, pp. 30–33.

Burton, Diana, and John Robinson. 1999. Cultural Interference—Clashes of Ideology and Pedagogy in Internationalizing Education. *International Education* 28, no. 2: 5–30.

Camillieri, Joseph, Kamal Malhotra, and Majid Tehranian, eds. 2000. *Reimagining the Future. Towards Democratic Governance.* Melbourne: La Trobe University, Department of Politics.

Cardoso, Fernando, and Enzo Faletto. 1970. *Dependencia y Desarrollo en América Latina.* Mexico City: Siglo XXI Editores.

Carnoy, Martin. 1974. *Education as Cultural Imperialism.* New York: D. McKay.

————. 1995. Structural Adjustment and the Changing Face of Education. *International Labor Review* 13, no. 6: 653–73.

————. 2000. Globalization and Educational Reform. In Nelly P. Stromquist and Karen Monkman, eds., *Globalization and Education: Integration and Contestation across Cultures.* Boulder: Rowman & Littlefield, pp. 43–61.

Castells, Manuel. 1996. *The Rise of the Network Society.* Malden, Mass.: Blackwell.

————. 1997. *The Power of Identity.* Malden, Mass.: Blackwell.

————. 2000. The Internet and the Network Society. Presentation at the University of Southern California, Los Angeles, October 26.

Champlin, Dell, and Paulette Olson. 1999. The Impact of Globalization on U.S. Labor Markets: Redefining the Debate. *Journal of Economic Issues* 33, no. 2: 443–51.

Chaudhuri, Maitrayee. N.d. The Concept of Culture in Globalized Times and in My Classroom. New Delhi: Jawaharlal Nehru University. <http://members.tripod.com/~csssjnu/culture.html>

Cole, Mike, ed. 2000. *Education, Equality and Human Rights.* London: Routledge.

Compaine, Benjamin, and Douglas Gomery. 2000. *Who Owns the Media? Competition and Centration in the Mass Media Industry.* 3rd ed. Mahwah, N.J. Lawrence Erlbaum Associates.

Connell, Robert. 1998. Masculinities and Globalization. Men and Masculinities 1: no 1: 3–23.

Cooper, Phillip. 2000. Approaching Rio+10: Institutional Capacity Building for the Twenty-First Century. Paper presented at the annual meeting of the Comparative and International Education Society, San Antonio, March 8–12.

Corporate Watch. 1998. The Education Industry. Case Study: Channel One. July 8.

————. 2000–2002. <http://corpwatch.org>

Cuban, Larry. 2001. The Convenient Fallacy of Education. *San Jose Mercury News*, January 7, pp. 1C, 3C.

Currie, Jan, Patricia Harris, and Bev Thiele. 2000. Sacrifices in Greedy Universities: Are They Gendered? *Gender and Education* 12, no. 3: 269–91.

Cvetkovich, Ann, and Douglas Kellner. 1997. Introduction: Thinking Global and Local. In Ann Cvetkovich and Douglas Kellner, eds., *Articulating the Global and the Local: Globalization and Cultural Studies*. Boulder: Westview Press, pp. 1–30.

Dahl, Stephan. 1998. Communications and Culture Transformation. <http://stephweb .com/capstone>

Dale, Roger, and Susan Robertson. 2002. The Varying Effects of Regional Organizations as Subjects of Globalization of Education. *Comparative Education Review* 46, no. 1: 10–36

Darder, Antonia. 2001. Education in the Age of "Globalization" and Difference." Paper presented at the Rossier School of Education, University of Southern California, Los Angeles, April.

Darling-Hammond, Linda. 2001. Educational Research and Educational Reform: Drawing the Connections between Research, Policy, and Practice. Presentation by the 2000 Winner of the AERA Relating Research to Practice Award at the annual meeting of the American Education Research Association, Seattle, April 10–14.

Darnovsky, Mary, Barbara Epstein, and Richard Flacks, eds. 1995. *Cultural Politics and Social Movements*. Philadelphia: Temple University Press.

David, Paul. 2000. A Tragedy of the Public Knowledge "Commons"? Global Science, Intellectual Property and the Digital Technology Boomerang. Oxford and Stanford University Press: 10 September. Draft.

Davies, Scott, and Neil Guppy. 1997. Globalization and Educational Reforms in Anglo-American Democracies. *Comparative Education* 41, no. 4: 435–59.

DeAngelis, Richard. 1996. Globalization and Recent Higher Education Reform in Australia and France: Different Constraints, Differing Choices in Higher Education Structures, Politics and Policies. Paper presented at the IX Congress on Comparative Education, Sydney, July. <http://www.ssn.flinders.edu.au/politics/staff/ ethos.htm>

Deem, Rosemary. 2001. Globalization, New Managerialism, Academic Capitalism and Entrepreneurialism in Universities: Is the Local Dimension Still Important? *Comparative Education* 37, no. 1: 7–20.

Deen, Thalif. 1999. Globalisation Threatens Third World Cultures. July 12. <http://www.globalpolicy.org/globaliz/cultural/hdrpoor.htm>

De Oliveira, Antonio, Jr. 1996. Reestruturação Económica Global e Questão Energética: Identidade e Integração Latino-Americana no Liminar do Século XXI. In Daniel Mato, Maritza Montero, and Emanuele Amodio, eds., *América Latina en Tiempos de Globalización: Procesos Culturales y Transformaciones Sociopolíticas*. Caracas: Centro Regional para la Educacion Superior en America Latina y el Caribe, pp. 173–85.

DiMaggio, Paul. 2000. Social Structure, Institutions, and Cultural Goods: The Case of the United States. In Gigi Bradford, Michael Gary, and Glenn Wallach, eds., *The Politics of Culture: Policy Perspectives for Individuals, Institutions and Commu-*

nities. New York: The New York Press and the Center for Arts and Culture, pp. 38–62.

Dobuzinskis, Laurent. 2000. Global Discord: The Confusing Discourse of Think-Tanks. In Stephen McBride and John Wiseman, eds., *Power in the Global Era: Grounding Globalization.* New York: St. Martin's Press, pp. 11–24.

Dorsey, Ellen. 1997. The Global Women's Movement: Articulating a New Vision of Global Governance. In Paul Diehl, ed., *The Politics of Global Governance: International Organizations in an Interdependent World.* Boulder, Colo.: Lynne Rienner, pp. 335–59.

Dos Santos, Teotonio. 1973. The Crisis of Development Theory and the Problem of Dependence in Latin America. In H. Bernstein, ed., *Underdevelopment and Development: The Third World Today.* Harmondsworth: Penguin, pp. 57–80.

Dowling, Anne. 2000. Case Study: Preserving Cultural Heritage. *Washington Quarterly* 23, no. 2: 164–65.

Drucker, Peter. 1993. *Post-Capitalist Society.* New York: Harper.

Egan, Michelle. 1998. Gendered Integration: Social Policies and the European Market. *Women and Politics* 19, no. 4: 23–52.

Ehrenreich, Barbara. 2001. *Nickel and Dimed: On (Not) Getting by in America.* New York: Metropolitan Books.

Eisenstein, Zillah, ed. 1979. *Capitalist Patriarchy and the Case for Socialist Feminism.* New York: Monthly Review Press.

Elmandjra, Mahdi. 1999. Need for a Reglobalization of "Globalization." Invited presentation at the 49th annual conference of the UK Political Studies Association, Nottingham, March. <http://www.elmandjra.org/conference.htm>

Elson, Diane, and Rosemary McGee. 1995. Gender Equality, Bilateral Program Assistance and Structural Adjustment: Policy and Procedures. *World Development* 23, no. 11: 1985–94.

Engberg, David. 2001. Attitudes about International Education in the United States. *International Higher Education,* no. 22 (winter): 8–9.

Evans, Tom, Jackie Lyons, Adam Newman, and Katherine Rymearson. 2000. *Eduventures.* Boston: Eduventures.com, Inc.

Fallon, Daniel, and Mitchell Ash. 1999. Higher Education in an Era of Globalization. In Carl Lankowski, ed., *Responses to Globalization in Germany and the United States.* Washington, D.C.: American Institute for Contemporary German Studies, pp. 67–78.

Featherstone, Mike, Scott Lash, and Roland Robertson, eds. 1997. *Global Modernities.* London: Sage.

Feenberg, Andrew. 1980. The Political Economy of Social Space. In Kathleen Woodward, ed., *The Myths of Information: Technology and Postindustrial Culture.* Madison, Wis.: Coda Press, pp. 111–24.

Finkelstein, Neal, and W. Norton Grubb. 2000. Making Sense of Education and Training Markets: Lessons from England. *American Educational Research Journal* 37, no. 3: 601–31.

Finn, Chester, Bruno Manno, and Gregg Vanourek. 2000. *Charter Schools in Action: Renewing Public Education.* Princeton: Princeton University Press.

Firebaugh, Francille, and Julia Miller. 2000. Diversity and Globalization: Challenges, Opportunities, and Promise. *Journal of Family and Consumer Sciences* 92, no. 1: 27–36.

Fischman, Gustavo, and Nelly P. Stromquist. 2000. Globalization Impacts on the Third World University. In John C. Smart, ed., *Higher Education: Handbook of Theory and Research*. Bronx: Agathon Press, pp. 501–21.

Fitz, John, and Bryan Beers. 2001. Education Maintenance Organizations and the Privatization of Public Education: A Cross National Comparison of the USA and the UK. Paper presented at the annual meeting of the American Education Research Association, Seattle, April 10–14.

Flora, Gabriela. 2001. *Aventis: Global Compact Violator.* Institute for Agriculture and Trade Policy. <www.corpwatch.org/campaigns/PCDjsp.articleid=621>

Fossaert, R. 2001. World Cities in a World System. *Research Bulletin,* no. 38 (January). <www.boro.ac.uk/department/gy/research/gawc.html>

Franzway, Suzane, Diane Court, and R. W. Connell. 1989. *Staking a Claim: Feminism, Bureaucracy, and the State.* Oxford: Polity Press.

Fraser, Nancy. 1989. *Unruly Practices: Power, Discourse, and Gender in Contemporary Social Theory.* Minneapolis: University of Minnesota Press.

———. 1998. A Future for Marxism. *New Politics* 6, no. 4: 95–98.

Friedman, Milton. 1962. *Capitalism and Freedom.* Chicago: University of Chicago Press.

Friedman, Thomas L. 1999. *The Lexus and the Olive Tree.* New York: Farrar, Strauss & Giroux.

Fritzberg, Gregory. 2001. Opportunities of Substance: Reconceptualizing Equality of Educational Opportunity. *Journal of Thought* 36, no. 1: 43–54.

Galeano, Eduardo. 1992. *Ser Como Ellos y Otros Artículos.* Madrid: Siglo Veintiuno de Espana Editores.

Gamage, David. 2000. Australian Higher Education: Current Issues and Policy Directions. *International Higher Education,* no. 21 (fall): 20–21.

Giddens, Anthony. 1990. *The Consequences of Modernity.* Stanford: Stanford University Press.

Gidley, Jennifer. 2000. Unveiling the Human Face of University Futures. In Sohail Inayatullah and Jennifer Gidley, eds., *The University in Transformation: Global Perspectives on the Futures of the University.* Westport, Conn.: Bergin and Garvey, pp. 235–45.

Goff, Patricia. 2000. Invisible Borders: Economic Liberalization, Identity, and the Postmodern Polity. Paper presented at the Center for International Studies, University of Southern California, Los Angeles, October.

Gomes, Ciro, and Roberto Mangabeira Unger. 1998. *Una Alternativa Práctica al Neoliberalismo.* Mexico, D.V.: Oceano.

Gómez-Pena, Guillermo. 2001. The New Global Culture: Somewhere Between Corporate Multiculturalism and the Mainstream Bizarre (a Border Perspective). *The Drama Review* 45, no. 1: 7–30.

González, Martín, and Alicia Menéndez. 2001. Higher Education Subsidies in Argentina, *International Higher Education,* no. 22 (winter): 19–21.

González Casanova, Pablo. 1996. Globalism, Neoliberalism, and Democracy. *Social Justice* 23, nos. 1–2: 39–49.

Graham, Edward. 2001. The Cause of Antiglobalists in Wrong in the Aggregate: Debate with Lori Wallach. <http://www.iie.com/papers/graham0301.htm>

Gramsci, Antonio. 1971. *Selections from the Prison Notebooks.* Edited by Q. Hoare and G. Nowell Smith. New York: International Publishers.

Green, R. H. 1998. A Cloth Untrue: The Evolution of Structural Adjustment in Sub-Saharan Africa. *Journal of International Affairs* 52, no. 1: 207–32.

Gumport, Patricia. 2000. Presentation at Panel on the Organizational Structure of the University: Its Impact on Epistemological Diversity. Paper presented at the annual meeting of the American Education Research Association, New Orleans, April 24–28.

Guttal, Shalmali. 2000. Women and Globalisation—Some Key Issues. Presentation at the Conference on Strategies of the Thai Women's Movement of the 21st Century, Bangkok, March 28–29. <http://www.focus.org>

Hall, Kevin. 2001. Web Sites Feed Boom in Sex Trade and Slavery. *San Jose Mercury News,* January 3, pp. 1A, 8A.

Hannaway, Jane. 1999. *Contracting as a Mechanism for Managing Education Services.* Philadelphia: CPRE Policy Briefs, November 28.

Hanson, Mark. 1986. *Educational Reform and Administrative Development: The Cases of Colombia and Venezuela.* Stanford: Hoover Institution Press.

Harvey, David. 1989. *The Condition of Postmodernity.* Cambridge: Blackwell.

Harvey, Keith. Ca. 2000. A Marxist Analysis of Globalisation Theories. <http://destroyimmf.org/afterprage/ideas/globalisationharvey.tmml>

Hegedus, Zsuzsa. 1990. Social Movements and Social Change in Self-Creative Society: New Civil Initiatives in the International Arena. In Martin Albrow and Elizabeth King, eds., *Globalization, Knowledge and Society.* London: Sage, pp. 263–80.

Held, David. 1995. *Democracy and the Global Order: From the Modern State to Cosmopolitan Governance.* Stanford: Stanford University Press.

Held, David, and Anthony McGrew. 2000. *The Global Transformation Reader: An Introduction to the Globalization Debate.* Cambridge: Polity Press.

Heller, Dana. 2000. Fields of Miracles: The New Russian Television. Paper presented at the Third International Crossroads in Cultural Studies Conference, Birmingham, United Kingdom, June 21–25.

Henry, Miriam. 2001. Globalisation and the Politics of Accountability: Issues and Dilemmas for Gender Equity in Education. *Gender and Education* 13, no. 1: 87–100.

Hentschke, Guilbert, and Ira Krinsky. 2000. Emerging Educational Enterprises: Schools, Colleges, and Universities as Economic Organizations. Course syllabus. Los Angeles: Rossier School of Education, University of Southern California, August.

Heron, Katrina. 20001. Rewriting the Future: Journalism and the Internet. Public presentation at Stanford University, May 15.

Heubert, Jay, and Robert Hauser, eds. 1999. *High Stakes: Testing for Tracking, Promotion, and Graduation.* Washington, D.C.: National Academy Press.

Heyneman, Stephen. 1997. Economic Growth and the International Trade in Educational Reform. *Prospects* 27, no. 4: 501–30.

Holton, Robert. 1997. Some Myths about Globalization. *Advancing International Perspectives: HERDSA '97.*

Hufbauer, Gary, and Tony Warren. 1999. The Globalization of Services: What Has Happened? What Are the Implications? Paper presented at the International Conference of Private Business Organization, Dresden, June 3–4.

Ilon, Lynn. 1997. Educational Repercussions of a Global System of Production. In William Cummings and Noel McGinn, eds., *International Handbook of Education and Development.* Oxford: Pergamon, 609–29.

Inter-American Development Bank. *Development beyond Economics.* Baltimore: The Johns Hopkins Press for the Inter-American Development Bank.

International Forum on Globalization. 1999. Beyond the WTO: Alternatives to Economic Globalization. November. <http://www.ifg.org/beyondwto.html>

International Labor Organization. 1996. *Incidencia del Ajuste Structural en el Empleo y la Formación del Personal Docente.* Geneva: International Labor Organization.

———. 2000. IFGers Respond: Is Globalization Inevitable? <http://www.ifg.org/inevitable.html>

International Society for Ecology and Culture. 2001. Interview with Paul Hellyer: Global to Local. <http://www.isec.org.uk/ISEC/core.html>

Jarvis, Peter. 1997. Adult Education and the University. *Educazione Comparata* 7, nos. 26–27: 101–10.

Jenson, Jane, and Boaventura de Sousa Santos. 2000. Introduction. In Jane Jenson and Boaventura de Sousa Santos, eds., *Globalizing Institutions: Case Studies in Regulation and Innovation.* Aldershot: Ashgate, pp. 9–26.

Johnston, Hank, Enrique Larana, and Joseph Gusfield. 1994. Identities, Grievances, and New Social Movements. In Enrique Larana, Hank Johnston, and Joseph Gusfield, eds., *New Social Movements: From Ideology to Identity.* Philadelphia: Temple University Press, pp. 3–35.

Jones, Glen. 2000. The Canada Research Chairs Program. *International Higher Education,* no. 21: 22–23.

Jones, Phillip. 1992. *World Bank Financing of Education: Lending, Learning, and Development.* London: Routledge.

———. 1998. Globalisation and Internationalism: Democratic Prospects for World Education. *Comparative Education* 34, no. 2: 143–55.

———. 2000. Globalization and Internationalism: Democratic Prospects for World Education. In Nelly P. Stromquist and Karen Monkman, eds., *Globalization and Education: Integration and Contestation across Cultures.* Boulder: Rowman & Littlefield, pp. 27–42.

Kachur, Jerrold. 1999. Privatizing Public Choice: The Rise of Charter Schooling in Charter Schools. In Trevor Harrison and Jerrold Kachur, eds., *Contested Classrooms: Education, Globalization, and Democracy in Alberta.* Edmonton: University of Alberta Press and Parland Institute, pp. 107–22.

———. 2001. The Postmodern Prince: Gramsci and Anonymous Intellectual Practice. Paper presented at the Comparative and International Education Society meeting, Washington, D.C., March 14–17.

Kachur, Jerrold, and Trevor Harrison. 1999. Public Education, Globalization, and Democracy. Wither Alberta? In Trevor Harrison and Jerrold Kachur, eds., *Contested Classrooms: Education, Globalization, and Democracy in Alberta.* Edmonton: University of Alberta Press and Parland Institute, pp. xiii–xxxv.

Kahn, Joseph. 2000. 22 Poor Nations Get Debt Relief. *San Francisco Chronicle,* December 14, p. A14.

Kamen, Paula. 2001. *Her Way: Young Women Remake Social Revolution.* Albany: New York University Press.

Keith, Kent. 1998. The Responsive University in the Twenty-First Century. In William Tierney, ed., *The Responsive University: Restructuring for High Performance.* Baltimore: The Johns Hopkins University Press, pp. 162–72.

Kelly, Patricia. 2000. Internationalizing the Curriculum: For Profit or Planet? In Sohail Inayatullah and Jennifer Gidley, eds., *The University in Transformation: Global Perspectives on the Futures of the University.* Westport, Conn.: Bergin and Garvey, pp. 161-72.

Kenway, Jane, and Peter Kelly. 2000. Local/Global Labor Markets and the Restructuring of Gender, Schooling, and Work. In Nelly P. Stromquist and Karen Monkman, eds., *Globalization and Education: Integration and Contestation across Cultures.* Boulder: Rowman & Littlefield, pp. 173–95.

Keohane, Robert, and Joseph Nye Jr. 2000. Introduction. In Joseph Nye Jr. and John Donahue, eds., *Governance in a Globalizing World.* Washington, D.C.: Brookings Institution Press, pp. 1–41.

Kerr, Clark. 2001. Shock Wave II: The 21st Century in American Higher Education. *International Higher Education,* no. 23: 10–11.

Khor, Martin. 2000. The United Nations and Globalization. *Corporate Watch,* May.

King, Anthony, ed. 1991. *Culture, Globalization and the World System.* London: Macmillan.

Kirby, Carrie. 2000. Politicians Ponder How Best to Use Web in Education. *San Francisco Chronicle,* December 20, pp. B1, B5.

Klein, Naomi. 2000. Does Protest Need a Vision? *New Statesman* (London), July 3, pp. 23–25.

Kovel-Jarboe, Patricia. 2000. The Changing Contexts of Higher Education and Four Possible Futures for Distance Education. <http://www.horizon.unc.edu/projects/issues/papers/kovel.asp>

Langman, Jimmy. 2000. Chile's Socialist President Wooing Capitalist Kings in Silicon Valley. *San Francisco Chronicle,* November 28, pp. A16, A17.

Lash, S., and J. Urry. 1994. *Economics of Signs and Space.* London: Sage.

Lee, James. 2000. *Exploring the Gaps. Vital Links between Trade, Environment, and Culture.* West Hartford, Conn.: Kumarian Press.

Lee, Molly. 1999. *Private Higher Education in Malaysia.* Penang: School of Educational Studies, University Sains Malaysia.

Leed, Eric. 1980. "Voice" and "Print": Master Symbols in the History of Communication. In Kathleen Woodward, ed., *The Myths of Information: Technology and Postindustrial Culture.* Madison, Wis.: Coda Press, pp. 41–61.

Leonard, Diana. 2001. Transforming Postgraduate Education in the U.K.: The Impact of Globalization. Paper presented at the annual meeting of the American Education Research Association, Seattle, April 10–14.

Levin, Henry. 1987. *Education as a Public and Private Good.* Stanford: Center for Educational Research, Stanford University.

———. 2000. Economic Consequences of High-Stakes Testing. Paper presented at the annual meeting of the American Education Research Association, New Orleans, April 24–28.

Lind, Amy. 1997. Negotiating Boundaries: Women's Organizations and the Politics of Restructuring in Ecuador. Paper presented at the 20th conference of the Latin American Studies Association, Guadalajara, April 24–28.

Lipman, Pauline. 2000. Toward an Analysis of the Political Economy of Chicago School Policy. Paper presented at the annual meeting of the American Education Research Association, New Orleans, April 24–28.

López de la Roche, Fabio, ed. 1999. *Globalización: Incertidumbres y Posibilidades.* Bogota: Tercer Mundo, S.A.

Luke, Carmen. 2000. Globalization and Women in Higher Education Management in Southeast Asia. Paper presented at the annual meeting of the American Education Research Association, New Orleans, April 24–28.

Lull, James. 2000. Superculture for the Communication Age. Paper presented at the Third International Crossroads in Cultural Studies Conference, Birmingham, United Kingdom, June 21–25.

Lynas, Mark. 1999. Storm Warning. *Training and Development* 53, no. 11: 38–39.

Macdonald, Theodore. 2002. Inter-American Court Decision Internationalizing Indigenous Community Land Rights. *ReVista*, winter, p. 27.

Magnier, Mark. 2000. Economic Reform Comes at a Price: Signs of Strain Show as Firms Struggle to Compete Globally by Focusing on Consumer. *Los Angeles Times,* September 27.

Malhotra, Kamal. 1997. Globalisation and Its Implications for ActionAid. Paper prepared for the Focus on the Global South Meeting, Chulalongkorn University Social Research Institute, Bangkok, November. <http://www.focus.org>

———. 1998. Vietnam at the Crossroads: Globalisation and the Implications of the East Asian Crisis for Sustainable Development. Paper presented at the workshop on Asian Finance and Currency Crisis and Policy Implications for Vietnam, Hanoi, March 6. <http://www.focus.org>

Mangabeira Unger, Roberto. 2000. *La Segunda Vía: La Alternativa Progresista.* Mexico, D.F.: Grupo Editorial Miguel Angel Porrua.

Maquieira, Virginia, and María Jesús Vara, eds. 1997. *Género, Clase y Etnia en los Nuevos Procesos de Globalización.* Madrid: Instituto Universitario de Estudios de la Mujer, Universidad Autonoma de Madrid.

Marginson, Simon, and Marcela Mollis. 2001. "The Door Opens and the Tiger Leaps": Theories and Reflexivities of Comparative Education for a Global Millennium. *Comparative Education Review* 45, no. 4: 581–615.

Martinez, D. P. 1998. Gender, Shifting Boundaries and Global Cultures. In D. P. Martinez, ed., *The Worlds of Japanese Popular Culture: Gender, Shifting Boundaries and Global culture.* Cambridge: Cambridge University Press.

Masemann, Vandra. 2000. Deconstructing the World Bank Education Sector Strategy Report. Paper presented at the annual conference of the Comparative and International Education Society, San Antonio, March 8–12.

Mato, Daniel. 1996a. On the Theory, Epistemology, and Politics of the Social Construction of "Cultural Identities" in the Age of Globalization: Introductory Remarks to Ongoing Debates. *Identities* 3, nos. 1–2: 61–72.

———. 1996b. Procesos Culturales y Transformaciones Sociopolíticas en América "Latina" en Tiempos de Globalización. In Daniel Mato, Maritza Montero, and Emanuele Amodio, eds., *América Latina en Tiempos de Globalización: Procesos Culturales y Transformaciones Sociopolíticas.* Caracas: Centro Regional para la Educacion Superior en America Latina y el Caribe, pp. 11–47.

Mazarr, Michael. 1996. Culture in International Relations. *Washington Quarterly*, spring. <http://www.globalpolicy.org/globaliz/cultural/cultur2.htm>

Mazumdar, Ranjani. 2000. Hindi Film Songs on TV: Globalization, Youth and the Circulation of "Electronic Catalogs." Paper presented at the Third International

Crossroads in Cultural Studies Conference, Birmingham, United Kingdom, June 21–25.

McCollum, Charlie. 2001. MTV@20: Revolution Was Televised as Cable Pioneer Evolved into a Youth Powerhouse. *San Jose Mercury News,* July 28, pp. 1A, 20A.

McEwan, Patrick. 2000. The Potential Impact of Large-Scale Voucher Programs. *Review of Educational Research* 70, no. 2: 103–49.

McMurria, John. 2000. "Feeding" Youth Culture: Global Channel Branding and the "Customization" of Music Television. Paper presented at the Third International Crossroads in Cultural Studies Conference, Birmingham, United Kingdom, June 21–25.

Meltzer, Allan, et al. 2000. Report from the International Financial Institution Advisory Commission presented to the Senate Banking Committee in March 2000. <http://csf.colorado.edu/roper/if.Meltzer-commission-mar00/>

Menotti, Victor. 2000. Globalization and the Acceleration of Forest Destruction since Rio. *International Forum on Globalization.* <www.ifg.org/forest.html>

Messner, Dirk. 1999. Towards a New Bretton Woods: Globalization and the New Challenges Facing Politics. *D+C,* no. 1: 4–5, 19.

Messner, Michael. 1995. "Changing Men" and Feminist Politics in the United States. In Michael Kimmel, ed., *The Politics of Manhood: Profeminist Men Respond to the Mythopoetic Men's Movement (and the Mythopoetic Leaders Answer).* Philadelphia: Temple University Press, pp. 97–111.

Meyer, John, and Michael Hannan. 1979. *National Development and the World System: Educational, Economic, and Political Change.* Chicago: University of Chicago Press.

Mies, Maria, and Vandana Shiva. 1993. *Ecofeminism.* London: Zed Books.

Minow, Martha. 2000. Our Separate Ways: The Hidden Consequences of Not Hanging Together. *Civilization,* August/September, pp. 68–69.

Mittelman, James, ed. 2000. *The Globalization Syndrome: Transformation and Resistance.* Princeton: Princeton University Press.

Mittelman, James, and Ashwini Tambe. 2000. Global Poverty and Gender. In James Mittelman, ed., *The Globalization Syndrome: Transformation and Resistance.* Princeton: Princeton University Press, pp. 74–89.

Mohanty, Chandra. 1988. Under Western Eyes: Feminist Scholarship and Colonial Discourses. *Feminist Review* 30, pp. 61–88.

Mojab, Shahrzad. 2000. Civilizing the State: The University in the Middle East. In Sohail Inayatullah and Jennifer Gidley, eds., *The University in Transformation: Global Perspectives on the Futures of the University.* Westport, Conn.: Bergin and Garvey, pp. 137–48.

Mok, Joshua. 2001. From State Control to Governance: Decentralization and Higher Education in Guangdong, China. *International Review of Education* 47, no. 2: 123–49.

Mok, Ka Ho. 2000. Impact of Globalization: A Study of Quality Assurance Systems in Higher Education in Hong Kong and Singapore. *Comparative Education Review* 44, no. 2: 148–74.

Mollis, Marcela, and Simon Marginson. 2000. The Assessment of Universities in Argentina and Australia: Between Autonomy and Heteronomy. Paper presented at the annual conference of the Comparative and International Education Society, San Antonio, March 7–12.

Molloy, Maureen. 1999. Women's Studies/Cultural Studies: Pedagogy, Seduction and the Real World. In Michael Peters, ed., *After the Disciplines: The Emergence of Cultural Studies*. Westport, Conn.: Bergin and Garvey, pp. 143–56.

Monterey Peninsula Review. 2001. 'Tis the Season to Go Whale-Watching. January 10, pp. 1, 10.

Morley, Louise. 1999. *Organising Feminisms: The Micropolitics of the Academy*. New York: St. Martin's.

Morris, David. 2000. International Forum on Globalization. IFGers Respond: Is Globalization Inevitable? <http://www.ifg.org/inevitable.html>

Morse, Jodie. 2001. Do Charter Schools Pass the Test? *Time*, June 4, pp. 60–62.

Mucchielli, Jean-Louis. 1998. *Multinationales et Mondialisation*. Paris: Editions du Seuil.

Muller, Jerry Z. 2001. The Mind and the Market: Capitalism in Modern European Thought. Washington, D.C.: Catholic University of America. Draft.

Mundy, Karen. 1999. Educational Multilateralism in a Changing World Order: UNESCO and the Limits of the Possible. *International Journal of Educational Development* 19: 27–52.

Mundy, Karen, and Lynn Murphy. 2001. Transnational Advocacy, Global Civil Society? Emerging Evidence from the Field of Education. *Comparative Education Review* 45, no. 1: 85–126.

Muyale-Manenji, Fridah. 1998. The Effects of Globalization on Culture in Africa in the Eyes of an African Woman. Geneva: World Council of Churches. <http://www/wcc-coe.org/wcc/what/jpc/effglob.html>

Myrdal, Gunnar. 1957. *Economic Theory and Underdeveloped Regions*. London: Duckworth.

Nelson, Howard, Edward Muir, and Rachel Drown. 2000. *Venturesome Capital: State Charter School Finance Systems*. Washington, D.C.: U.S. Department of Education, December.

Newby, Howard. 1999. Higher Education in the Twenty-First Century. *New Reporter* 16, no. 14 (March 22). <http://www.soton.ac.uk/~newrep/vol16/no14future.html>

Novartis AG. 2001. The Socio-Political Impact of Biotechnology in Developing Countries. <http://www.foundation.novartis.com/biotechnology-developing countries .htm>

Oakes, Jeannie. 2000. The Lens of Social Theory. Paper presented at the annual meeting of the American Education Research Association, New Orleans, April 24–28.

Oberle, Christoph. 1998. The African Virtual University Project of the World Bank: Solution for African Universities? Some Preliminary Ideas on Achievements and Alternatives. *NORRAG News*, October, pp. 55–56.

O'Brien, Robert, Anne Marie Goetz, Jan Aart Scholte, and Marc Williams. 2000. *Contesting Global Governance: Multilateral Economic Institutions and Global Social Movements*. Cambridge: Cambridge University Press.

Offe, Claus. 1984. *Contradictions of the Welfare State*. Cambridge: MIT Press.

Okuni, Akim. 2000. Higher Education through the Internet. *D+C*, no. 2 (March/April): 23–25.

O'Meara, KerryAnn. 2001. The Impact of Consumerism, Capitalism, and For-Profit Competition on American Higher Education. *International Higher Education*, no. 22: 3–5.

Opfer, V. Darleen. 2001. Beyond Self-Interest: Educational Interest Groups and Congressional Influence. *Educational Policy* 15, no. 1: 135–52.

Oplatka, I. 2000. The Emergence of Educational Marketing: Lessons from the Experiences of Israeli Principals. Tel Aviv: University of Tel Aviv. Draft.

Orfield, Gary, and Mindy Kornhaber, eds. 2001. *Raising Standards or Raising Barriers? Inequality and High-Stakes Testing in Public Education.* New York: Century Foundation Press.

Orzack, Louis. 1992. *International Authority and Professions: The State beyond the Nation-State.* Florence: European University Institute.

Osava, Mario. 2001. Brazil: Farmers Demand Agrarian Reform. *Corporate Watch,* April 17. <http://www.ifg.org>

Pan, Philip. 2001. Global Warming Disasters Predicted. *San Francisco Chronicle,* January 23, p. 2A.

Pannu, R. S. 1996. Neoliberal Project of Globalization: Prospects for Democratization of Education. *Alberta Journal of Educational Research* 42, no. 2: 87–101.

Parker, Jenneth. 2000. Indigenous, Local and Traditional Knowledges: Issues for Higher Education in a Period of Rapid Globalization. *New Era in Education* 82, no. 2: 2–12.

Pelton, Joseph. 1996. Cyberlearning vs. the University: An Irresistible Force Meets an Immovable Object. *The Futurist* 30 (November–December): 17–20.

Pérez-Prado, Luz Nereida. 1996. Sueños Globales, Oportunidades Locales: Conmoción de Identidades de Género en la Tierra Caliente de Michoacán. In Daniel Mato, Maritza Montero, and Emanuele Amodio, eds., *América Latina en Tiempos de Globalización: Procesos Culturales y Transformaciones Sociopolíticas.* Caracas: Centro Regional para la Educacion Superior en America Latina y el Caribe, pp. 201–9.

Petras, James. 1999. Globalization: A Critical Analysis. *Journal of Contemporary Asia* 29, no. 1: 3–37.

Pitt, Leyland, Pierre Berthon, and Matthew Robson. 1997. The Internationalization of Management Knowledge Dissemination: A Dialectic. *Journal of World Business* 32, no. 4: 369–85.

Power, Sally, and Geoff Whitty. 1999. Market Forces and School Cultures. In Jon Prosser, ed., *School Culture.* London: Paul Chapman Publishing, pp. 15–29.

Probyn, Elspeth. 1993. *Seeing the Self: Gender Positions in Cultural Studies.* London: Routledge.

Prosser, Jon. 1999. Introduction. In Jon Prosser, ed., *School Culture.* London: Paul Chapman Publishing, pp. xi–xvii.

Quebec Network on Continental Integration. 2001. Globalization of What, How, and for Whom? Quebec Network on Continental Integration. <http://attac.org/fra/toil/doc/rqicen.htm>

Quesada Monge, Rodrigo. 1998. *Globalizacion y Deshumanizacion: Dos Caras del Capitalismo Avanzado.* Heredia, Costa Rica: Editorial de la Universidad Nacional de Costa Rica.

Rampton, Sheldon, and John Stauber. 2001. *Trust Us, We're Experts: How Industry Manipulates Science and Gambles with Your Future.* New York: Penguin Putnam.

Rauch, Jonathan. 2001. The New Old Economy: Oil, Computers, and the Reinvention of the Earth. *Atlantic Monthly* 287, no. 1: 35–49.

Ravela, Pedro, ed. 2000. *Los Próximos Pasos: Hacia Dónde y Cómo Avanzar en la Evaluación de Aprendizajes en América Latina?* Lima: GRADE/PREAL, March.

Rebhun, Uzi, and Chaim Waxman. 2000. The "Americanization" of Israel: A Demographic, Cultural, and Political Evaluation. *Israel Studies* 5, no. 1: 65–91.

Reich, Robert. 2000. The Choice Fetish. *Civilization*, August/September, pp. 64–66.

Reinalda, Bob. 2000. The International Women's Movement as a Private Actor between Accommodation and Change. In Karsten Ronit and Volker Schneider, eds., *Private Organizations in Global Politics*. London: Routledge, pp. 165–86.

Rete Lilliput. 2001. Per Una Politica ed Un'Economia del Bene Comune. <http://www.retelilliput.org/g8/docG8-it.asp>

Richardson, Julie Ann, and Anthony Turner. 2001. Collaborative Learning in a Virtual Classroom. *National Teaching and Learning Forum* 10, no. 2. <http://www.ntlf.com>

Rideout, William. 2001. Tribalism and Globalization in Sub-Saharan Africa. *International Connection* 17, no. 4 (March): 1–3.

Roberts, Peter. 2000. Knowledge, Information and Literacy? *International Review of Education* 46, no. 5: 433–453.

Robertson, Roland. 1992. *Globalization*. London: Sage.

Robinson, William. 1997. A Case Study of Globalization Processes in the Third World: A Transnational Agenda in Nicaragua. *Pensamiento Propio* 1, no. 3 (January–April): 161–92.

Rooney, David, and Greg Hearn. 2000. Of Minds, Markets, and Machines: How Universities Might Transcend the Ideology of Commodification. In Sohail Inayatullah and Jennifer Gidley, eds., *The University in Transformation: Global Perspectives on the Futures of the University*. Westport, Conn.: Bergin and Garvey, pp. 91–103.

Rowan, Brian. 2000. Presentation at Panel on the Organizational Structure of the University: Its Impact on Epistemological Diversity. Paper presented at the annual meeting of the American Education Research Association, New Orleans, April 24–28.

Rothkopf, David. 1997. In Praise of Cultural Imperialism? Effects of Globalization on Culture. <http://www.globalpolicy.org/globaliz/cultural/globcult.htm>

Rudra, Nita. 2000. Globalization and the Decline of the Welfare State in Less Developed Countries. Paper presented at the Center for International Studies, University of Southern California, Los Angeles, November.

Ruggie, Mary. 1984. *The State and Working Women: A Comparative Study of Britain and Sweden*. Princeton: Princeton University Press.

Salt, Ben, Ronald Cervero, and Andrew Herod. 2000. Workers' Education and Neoliberal Globalization: An Adequate Response to Transnational Corporations? *Adult Education Quarterly* 52, no. 2: 9–31.

San Francisco Examiner. 2000. "Study: California Leads Nation in Dead-End Jobs." September 3, p. C7.

San Jose Mercury News. 2001. "Video Games Take on New Dimension." May 16, pp. 1A, 18A.

Sana, Heleno. N.d. *Imperialismo en acción (I)*. Madrid: Libreria DERSA.

Sandler, Michael. 2000. Talk at class on Emerging Educational Enterprises. University of Southern California, Los Angeles, October 19.

Santos, Boaventura de Sousa. 1995. *Pela Mão de Alicia: O Social e O Polítíca na Pos-Modernidade*. São Paulo: Cortez Editora.

Sassen, Saskia. 1999. The Spatiality and Temporality of Globalization. GaWC Annual Lecture. <http://www.lboro.ac.uk/fawc/rb/all.html>

Schevitz, Tanya. 2001. UCLA among Schools on 3 Continents Joining in Net Venture. *San Francisco Chronicle,* January 19, p. C9.

Schmidt, Kathleen. 2000. Outlook 2000: Globalization. *Marketing News* 34, no. 2 (January 17), pp 9–18.

Schugurensky, Daniel. 2000. Adult Education and Social Transformation: On Gramsci, Freire, and the Challenge of Comparing Comparisons. *Comparative Education Review* 44, no. 4: 515–22.

Sen, Gita. 1998. *Los Desafíos de la Globalización.* Montevideo: DAWN and REPEM.

———. 2001. Globalization and Its Challenges for Women in the South. <http://attac.org/planet/doc/doc03.htm>

Shain, Farzana, and Jenny Ozga. 2001. Identity Crisis? Problems and Issues in the Sociology of Education. *British Journal of Sociology of Education* 22, no. 1: 109–20.

Shiva, Vandana. 2000. The World on the Edge. In Will Hutton Will and Anthony Giddens, eds., *On the Edge: Living with Global Capitalism.* London: Jonathan Cape, pp. 112–29.

———. 2001. Globalization, Women, and Agriculture. Radio talk, KQED (FM), January 3.

Simpson, Christopher. 1998. An Introduction. In Christopher Simpson, ed., *Universities and Empires: Money and Politics in the Social Sciences during the Cold War.* New York: The New Press, pp. i–xxxvii.

60 Minutes. 2001. Television program. January 14.

Sklair, Leslie. 1996. Australia in the Global Capitalist System. *Social Alternatives* 15, no. 1: 14–17.

Stromquist, Nelly P. 2001a. Gender Studies: A Global Perspective of Their Evolution and Challenges to Comparative Higher Education. *Higher Education* 41, no. 4: 373–87.

———. 2001b. Knowledge and Power in Feminist Politics: The Experience of CIPAF. University of Southern California, Los Angeles. Manuscript.

Stromquist, Nelly P., Steven Klees, and Shirley J. Miske. 2000. USAID Efforts to Expand and Improve Girls' Primary Education in Guatemala. In Regina Cortina and Nelly P. Stromquist, eds., *Distant Alliances: Promoting Education for Girls and Women in Latin America.* New York: Routledge Falmer, pp. 239–60.

Stromquist, Nelly P., and Joel Samoff. 2000. Knowledge Management Systems: On the Promise and Actual Forms of Information Technologies. *Compare* 30, no. 3: 323–32.

Sweetland, Scott. 1996. Human Capital Theory: Foundations of a Field of Inquiry. *Review of Educational Research* 55, no. 3: 3341–59.

Taylor, P. J. 2001a. Regionality within Globalization: What Does It Mean for Europe? <http://info.lut.ac.uk/departments/gy/research/gawc/rb/rb35.html>

———. 2001b. Specification of the World City Network. *Research Bulletin* 23. <http://info.lut.ac.uk/departments/gy/research/gawc/rb/rb35.html>

Taylor, P. J., D. R. F. Walker, and J. V. Beaverstock. 2001a. Introducing GaWC: Researching World City Network Formation. *Research Bulletin* 6. <http://info.lut.ac.uk/departments/gy/research/gawc/rb/rb6.html>

Taylor, P. J., M. J. Watts, and R. J. Johnston. 2001b. Geography/Globalization. <http://info.lut.ac.uk/departments/gy/research/gawc/rb/rb40.html>

The Economist. 2000. Pros and Cons of Globalisation. October 12.

————. 2001. March.

The Revolutionary Worker. 2002. The Rise and Fall of Enron: Bloodsucking as Usual. Vol. 23, no. 37: 7, 14.

Thurow, Lester. 1980. *The Zero-Sum Society: Distribution and the Possibilities for Economic Change.* New York: Basic Books.

Tietjen, Karen. 2000. *Multisectoral Support of Basic and Girls' Education.* Washington, D.C.: Academy for Educational Development, October.

Tikly, Leon. 2001. Globalization and Education in the Postcolonial World: Towards a Conceptual Framework. *Comparative Education* 37, no. 2: 151–71.

Tikly, Leon, and Michael Crossley. 2001. Teaching Comparative and International Education: Separation, Integration or Transformation? *Comparative Education Review* 45, no. 4: 561–80.

Tiramonti, Guillermina. 2001. *Sindicalismo Docente y Reforma Educativa en la America Latina de los '90.* Washington, D.C.: PREAL.

Townsend, Janet, Emma Zapata, Joanna Rowlands, Pilar Alberti, and Marta Mercado. 1999. *Women and Power: Fighting Patriarchies and Poverty.* London: Zed Books.

Townsend, Peter. 1993. *The International Analysis of Poverty.* New York: Harvest Wheatsheaf.

Tsing, Anna. 2000. The Global Situation. *Cultural Anthropology* 15, no. 3: 327–60.

Turning Point. 2000. Monocultures of the Mind. <http://www.turningpoint.org>

Turpin, Tim, Robyn Iredale, and Paola Crinnion. 2001. Globalization and Higher Education: Implications for Developing Economies and the Transformation of Knowledge Systems. Wollongong, New South Wales: University of Wollongong. Draft.

United Nations Development Program. 1996. *Human Development Report 1996.* New York: United Nations Development Program.

————. 1998. *Overcoming Human Poverty.* New York: United Nations Development Program.

————. 1999a. *Human Development Report 1999.* New York: United Nations Development Program.

————. 1999b. *World Economic and Social Survey.* New York: United Nations Development Program.

————. 2000. *Human Development Report 2000.* New York: United Nations Development Program.

United Nations Development Program, UNESCO, UNICEF, and World Bank. 1990. *World Declaration on Education for All.* New York: United Nations Development Program.

UNESCO. 1999. *UNESCO Statistical Yearbook 1999.* Paris: UNESCO.

United States Department of Education. 2000. *Internet Access in Public Schools and Classrooms, 1994–99.* Washington, D.C.: National Center of Education Statistics.

United States National Commission on Excellence in Education. 1983. *A Nation at Risk: The Imperative for Education Reform.* Washington, D.C.: National Commission on Excellence in Education.

Valdés, Adriana. 1991. *Women, Cultures, and Development: Views from Latin America.* Santiago: Economic Commission for Latin America and the Caribbean, May.

Van Damme, Dirk. 2001. Quality Issues in the Internationalisation of Higher Education. *Higher Education* 41, no. 4: 415–41.

Van Reisen, Mirjam. 1999. *EU "Global Player": The North-South Policy of the European Union*. Utrecht: International Books.

Veltmeyer, Henry, and James Petras. 2000. *The Dynamics of Social Change in Latin America*. Houndmills: Macmillan.

Viesca, Victor. 2000. Straight from the Barrio: Chicano/a Popular Culture and Underground. Paper presented at the Third International Crossroads in Cultural Studies Conference, Birmingham, United Kingdom, June 21–25.

Villagran, Gil. 2000. Letter to the Editor. *San Jose Mercury News,* June 24, p. 9B.

Viviano, Frank. 2001. New Face of Mafia in Sicily. *San Francisco Chronicle,* January 8, pp. A1, A4, A5.

Volkova, Elena. 2000. American Televangelism and the Russian Preaching Tradition. Paper presented at the Third International Crossroads in Cultural Studies Conference, Birmingham, United Kingdom, June 21–25.

Wainer, Howard. 2000. CATs: Whither and Whence. *Psicológica* 21, no. 1: 121–33.

Walby, Sylvia. 1990. *Theorizing Patriarchy*. Oxford: Basil Blackwell.

Wallerstein, Immanuel. 1999. Interview by Anand Kumar and Frank Weltz. Paris: Maison de Sciences de l'Homme, June 25. Manuscript.

Ward, Kathryn. 1984. *Women in the World System: Its Impact on Status and Fertility*. New York: Praeger.

Washington Post. 1999. Giving Less: The Decline in Foreign Aid. November 25, p. A1.

Watson, Keith. 1998. Memories, Models and Mapping: The Impact of Geopolitical Changes in Comparative Studies in Education. *Compare* 28, no. 1: 5–31.

Watson, Sophie, ed. 1990. *Playing the State: Australian Feminist Interventions*. London: Verso.

Weis, Lois. 2000. On *Closing the Gender Gap* by Madeleine Arnot, Miriam David, and Gaby Weiner. Paper presented at the annual meeting of the American Education Research Association, New Orleans, April 24–28.

Weisbrot, Mark, Dean Baker, Egor Kraev, and Judy Chen. 2001. The Scorecard on Globalization 1980–2000: Twenty Years of Diminished Progress. Briefing Paper. Washington, D.C.: Center for Economic and Policy Research.

Weisbrot, Mark, Robert Naiman, and Joyce Kim. 2000. *The Emperor Has No Growth: Declining Economic Growth Rates in the Era of Globalization*. Briefing Paper. Washington, D.C.: Center for Economic and Policy Research, September.

Wheeler, Mark. 2000. Globalization of the Communications Marketplace. *Harvard International Journal of Press/Politics* 5, no. 3: 27–44.

Will, George. 2001. Don't Be Too Quick with Warnings of Doom. *San Jose Mercury News,* January 1, p. 7B.

Williams, Christopher. 2000. Education and Human Survival: The Relevance of the Global Security Framework to International Education. *International Review of Education* 46, nos. 3/4: 183–203.

Willis, Paul. 2002. Comments to Homage: Panel on "25 Years after *Learning to Labour*." Paper presented at the annual meeting of the American Education Research Association, New Orleans, April 1–5.

Wilson, John. 1993. The Subject Women. In Paula England, ed., *Theory on Gender/Feminism on Theory*. New York: Aldine de Gruyter, pp. 343–57.

Wilson, Mary, Adnan Qayyum, and Roger Boshier. 1998. World Wide America? Think Globally, Click Locally. *Distance Education* 19, no. 1: 109–23.

Winkler, Donald, and Alec Ian Gershberg. 2000. *Los Efectos de la Descentralización del Sistema Educacional Sobre la Calidad de la Educación en América Latina*. Washington, D.C.: Inter-American Dialogue and CINDE, April.

Wirpsa, Leslie. 2001. When the Market Is Not the Norm: The Impact of Neo-Liberal and Indigenous Rights Regime Collision on Democracy and the State in Latin America. University of Southern California, Los Angeles. Manuscript.

Woodward, Kathleen. 1980. Introduction. In Kathleen Woodward, ed., *The Myths of Information: Technology and Postindustrial Culture*. Madison, Wis.: Coda Press, pp. xiii–xxvi.

World Bank. 1999a. *Consultations with the Poor*. Washington, D.C.: World Bank.

———. 1999b. *Poverty Trends and Voices of the Poor*. Washington, D.C.: World Bank, December 2.

———. 1999c. *World Development Report 1998/1999: Knowledge for Development*. Washington, D.C.: World Bank.

World Social Forum. 2000–2001. <http://www.forumsocialmundial.org.br./ingles/journal/index.php3?arqNoticia=20010>

Wren, Christopher. 1999. U.N.: Hunger Worsened with War, Poverty. *New York Times*.

Zipes, Jack. 1980. The Instrumentalization of Fantasy: Fairy Tales and the Mass Media. In Kathleen Woodward, ed., *The Myths of Information: Technology and Postindustrial Culture*. Madison, Wis.: Coda Press, pp. 88–110.

Index

A Nation at Risk, 42, 147
academic freedom, 97
accountability, 21, 40, 41–44, 57, 59, 61, 96, 131n3; in universities, 112, 113
adolescents, 68, 69
Adorno, Theodor, 72
advertising, 66, 81, 95; and women, 141
affirmative action, 136; in universities, 114
African Americans, 32, 58, 187
African Virtual University, 124
AIDS. *See* HIV/AIDS
agency, 32, 34, 79, 92, 157–75
agrarian reform, 167, 174n13
agriculture, 164, 166, 167; traditional, 168
agro-industries, 11, 139, 165; and TNCs, 174n13
anarchists, 15
apartheid, 12
artificial intelligence, 108
Asian Pacific Economic Conference (APEC), 56
Asian tigers, 9
assembly line, 6, 10, 17n6; and women, 139, 155n3
assessment, 16, 41, 111, 112, 123; culture of, 115; programs, 107; schools, 16, 41; student, 112

bachelor's degrees, 121, 124, 126
basic needs: and women, 153
bilingual education, 39, 60
binary categories, 32
biodiversity, 168
biopiracy, 171, 175n19
bonds, 7, 86; school bonds, 39
books, 31; and English, 110; publication of, 65
branding: of MTV programs, 68; of products, 97; of universities, 120
Bretton Wood institutions. *See* International Monetary Fund; World Bank
business, vii, 85; academies, 105; firms, 10, 43, 51, 107, 146; influence, 104, 110–19; norms, 40; values, 38
Buy-Nothing Day, 161

capitalism, 19, 21, 27, 72; and education, 187; global, 63, 85, 88; transition to capitalism, 138; variants of, 23; venture, 49
Carnegie Foundation, 109
Catholic Church, 12
central countries. *See* core countries
centralization, 92, 109
citizens, 93

citizenship, 83
civic organizations, 90, 102n9, 160
civil society, 8, 69, 97, 133, 174n4, 187
chaebols, 27
Channel One, 50–51, 67
charter schools, 45, 46–47, 53, 55
chat rooms, 64
child labor, 159
collectivism, 27
comics industry, 74
communication, vii, 5, 6, 10, 17n2, 20, 24, 25, 48, 49, 63–82; innovations, 5; telecommunications, 5, 35n2, 51
communism/communist countries, 4, 5, 24
community participation, 30
comparative: advantage, 138; education, 186
competition, 6, 27, 43, 70, 101n7, 107, 111, 161; among universities, 111; economic, 139; foreign, 102n7; within universities, 112–15
competitiveness, 10, 39, 90, 95, 154, 187
computers, 2, 69; in classrooms, 50
connectivity, 3, 16
consumerism, 65, 85, 116
consumption, 6, 157
convergence trends, 1, 13, 17, 34, 41, 65, 125
copyrights, 127
core countries, viii, 8, 48, 85
critical theory, 34
critical thought, 71–72
culture, 2, 3, 4, 15, 16, 22, 24, 31, 33, 34, 64, 74, 76, 90, 180; American, 75; commodified, 31; defined, 66; f human rights, 23; linkage with media and business, 72; local, 75; mass, 63; organizational, 28; popular 20, 68, 73, 98
cultural: capital, 28; critics, 67; elite, 74; forms, 72; global, 74; homogenization, 66; local, 74; policies, 16; popular, 68, 73, 74; studies, 73
curriculum, 40, 43, 46, 51, 56, 59, 60, 61n2, 122, 124, 131n9, 147; and

gender content, 147; homogeneous, 60; innovations, 70; narrowing, 43; national, 56; tracks, 44; in universities, 106, 109, 112, 116, 122, 124, 131n7
cyberspace, 4

debt relief, 184
decentralization, 6, 16, 57, 61n1, 113, 131n3, 178
deglobalization, 181
democracy, 23, 182
Department for International Development (DFID), 75
dependency theory, 8, 9
deregulation, 26, 89, 91, 120; and gender, 137; of universities, 107, 120
deterritorialization, 3
Development Alternatives with Women for a New Era (DAWN), 156n13
distance education, 51. *See also* telecommuting
divergence trends, 1, 13
diversity, 16, 60

e-mail, 69, 72, 140, 171
ecofeminism, 165
ecological movements, 157
Edison Schools, 50, 54
education, 178, 186; informal, 187; nonformal, 138, 151, 187; primary, 1, 144; secondary, 16
Education for All (EFA), 58
educational: enrollment, 5, 30, 121, 126, 129, 132n12, 143, 144, 155n9; ideology, 147; primary, 16, 144; secondary, 16
efficiency, 14, 40, 41,46, 47, 48, 62n6, 96, 97, 115, 187; of farmers, 167
elites, 16, 95, 119, 123
emerging countries. *See* Third World
empowerment, 41, 62n6
English language, 114; knowledge exchange, 70
entertainment, 11, 68, 81
entrepreneurs, 55, 56, 122
environment, 157, 160

equality of opportunity, 135, 165
equity, 28, 60, 152, 155
ERASMUS, 105, 106
ethnic: minorities, 24; studies, 109
European Union (EU), 56, 70, 91, 124
evaluation. *See* assessment
export-based development, 11, 12

family, 140, 144, 148, 154, 155n3; care, 137; participation of men and women,118
femininity, 14
feminism, 165, 174n4
film, 31, 66, 85
financial flows, 87
Fulbright Program, 109
foreign direct investment (FDI), 22, 85, 86, 89
Foucault, Michel, 35n10
Fourth World Women's Conference (Beijing), 136, 151
Free Trade of the Americas (FTAA), 164
Freire, Paulo, 35n10
Friedman, Milton, 47, 130

gay/lesbians, 132n16
gender, 133–56; and communication, 134, 140–41; and culture, 141–43; and the economy, 137–40; and education, 143–49; inequalities, 147; and reality, 32; segregation, 115; studies, 149; subordination, 147
Gender Empowerment Measure (GEM), 133
genetically modified organisms (GMOs), 165, 166, 167, 174n11
geography, 8
global cities. *See* world cities
Global Compact, 169, 171, 175n16
Global Development Gateway, 78, 179
Globalization: "from above," 13; "from below," 13
governance, 44, 51, 56, 122, 128, 129, 159, 160; city, 93; democratic, 157; global, 94; local, 6
government, vii
Gramsci, Antonio, 18n7, 35n10

Group of Eight, 8, 25, 182
Group of Seven, 8, 25

Hayek, Friedrich, 26
health, 188n2
high school. *See* education
higher education, 96, 97, 103–32, 148
Hispanics, 58, 136, 187
HIV/AIDS, 25, 143, 188n2
Horkheimer, Max, 72
human rights, 132n16, 149, 159, 178
humanities, 179

identity, 19, 65, 75, 92, 114, 129, 142, 161; Chicano, 32; and culture, 65, 98; European, 57; and indigenous groups, 168, 175n15; local, 63, 68; national, 66; sexualized, 142; student, 111
ideology, viii, 27, 65
immigrants. *See* migration
imperialism, 19
indigenous: groups, 157, 165–67, 171, 172; knowledge, 138, 166; rights, 132n16, 158, 175n15; and women, 138
individualism, 6, 27, 70
industrialization, 20, 34, 98, 139
industrialized countries. *See* core countries
industry, 4, 39
inequality, 28, 33, 39, 160; in schools, 147
information, 77, 127
innovations, 48
intellectual property, 120, 124, 126–28, 159
Inter-American Development Bank, 20, 43, 174n14
Intergovernmental Panel on Climate Change, 173n2
international: assistance, 8; education, 129; students, 116
International Conference on Financing for Development, 184
International Conference on Population and Development (ICPD, Cairo), 158

International Monetary Fund (IMF), 8,
    21, 29, 33, 35n6, 88, 90, 166, 170, 183
internationalism, 132n15, 188
internationalization, 116, 132n12
Internet, 11, 45, 51, 64–70, 71, 78, 170,
    171, 175n16; cafes, 69; and
    cyberspace, 149, 150; investments,
    48, 60; and NGOs, 171; and
    organized crime, 24; and women,
    140, 149, 150

Jubilee 2000, 153, 171

knowledge, 2, 45, 62n5, 64, 67, 70, 80,
    110, 115, 119, 130nl, 157, 161, 168,
    174n7; acquisition, 109, 116;
    adaptation, 95; as commodity, 96;
    economy, 103; educational, 40, 43;
    local, 138, 166; mercantilization, 48,
    128; production, 104, 113;
    protection, 127, 128; scientific, 107;
    technical, 93;
    transmission/distribution, 1, 3, 41,
    119, 126
Knowledge Management Systems
    (KMS), 75–80
"knowledge society," 15, 103, 124, 126,
    140, 177

labor, 39: costs, 15; market, 3, 179;
    mobility, 34, 84
land reform. *See* agrarian reform
landless, 159
languages, 2, 172
Latinos. *See* Hispanics
liberalization, 22, 26, 29, 66, 122, 135,
    137
literacy, 54, 174n7
literature, 108
local vs. global, 2, 3, 11, 13, 15–16, 17,
    72–75, 138, 140, 152, 159, 174n10

magnet schools, 45
market, vi, 5, 6, 7, 9, 11, 13, 15, 18n7,
    21, 26, 31, 34, 38, 48, 107, 116, 119,
    120, 165, 175n19; economics, 16;
    educational, 106; export, 12;

financial, 20; forces, 8; free, 9, 11;
    global, 81, 120, 122, 160; reforms,
    135; value, 108
marketing of educational programs, 44,
    49, 120, 131n7
masculinity, 14, 142, 155n6
mass media, v, 7, 9, 10–11, 24, 63,
    80–81, 95, 141, 186; branding, 68;
    concentration, 64–65, 81; global, 81;
    industry, 10
master's of business administration
    (MBAs), 123
media. *See* mass media
Meltzer Commission, 183
men, 69, 140; work time, 118
mercantilism, vii
migration, 21, 22, 23, 60, 94, 149
minorities, 43, 58, 60, 96
modernity, 20
Mohanty, Chandra, 153
morality, 34
MTV, 64, 68
multiculturalism, 33, 116
Multilateral Agreement on Investment
    (MAI), 92, 100
multinational institutions, 88
music, 65, 68, 73, 74, 81

neoliberal: defined, 6; development
    model, 6, 25–31; philosophy, 137;
    theory, 47
neoliberalism, 25–31, 40
newspapers, 66, 82n2
nonformal education, 138, 151
nongovernmental organizations
    (NGOs), 11–13, 90, 101, 151, 152,
    168, 175n17; growth, 24; and
    international meetings, 151; and new
    knowledge, 141; normal curve
    equivalents (NCEs), 56, 62n5; and
    women, 141, 152
North, 3, 9, 12, 34, 35n3, 166
North American Free Trade Association
    (NAFTA), 56, 57, 100
North–South alliances, 141, 154
Norwegian Development Agency
    (NORAD), 75

objectivity, 32
off-shore educational programs, 121
on-line courses, 122, 123, 125, 126, 127
Opus Dei, 156n10
Organization for Economic Cooperation
and Development (OECD), 19, 25,
33, 92, 100, 182
Organization of Iberoamerican States, 43

parental choice, 40, 45, 47, 48
parents, 44
Partnership for Educational
Revitalization in the Americas
(PREAL), 57
partnerships, 41, 51, 57, 120, 124, 125,
129, 146; business-universities, 119;
private-public, 52
patriarchy, 134, 143, 153
performance: schools, 56; state, 10, 20,
29; student, 16, 30, 40, 61
peripheral states, 48. *See also* South
philanthropic foundations, 183–84
pluralism, 180
pollution, 184
popular culture. *See* culture
post-Fordist, 10, 139
postmodernity, 31–34, 175n15
poverty, 134, 137, 138, 159; asymmetric,
19; and domestic violence, 166; and
exclusion, 17n4; and HIV/AIDS, 143;
levels, 12, 61; line, 59; and low wages,
85, 136; reduction, 174n5, 175n16,
183, 188n3; and social market, 138,
154; and women, 136, 138, 166
power, 1, 13, 22, 24, 39, 104, 129;
economic, 3, 83, 177; political, 16,
80, 147
primary education. *See* education
private: financing, 53; schools, 47, 50,
55, 96; sector 146, 149; sphere, 154;
universities, 147
privatization, 6, 16, 26, 28, 39, 51, 54,
78, 106, 122, 137, 178; forms, 55–55;
of higher education, 122, 123, 180;
and telecommunications, 61; and
women, 137
productivity, 39, 115

profit, 8, 20, 49, 56, 85, 97, 128, 160
prostitution, 166
public good, 37, 178

quality, 42, 48, 60; control, 40
Quality Process Review (QPR), 112

Reglobalization: from below, 182
religious institutions, 146
reterritorialization, 3, 22
research, 105, 109, 114, 123; and
development
resistance, 11, 34, 73, 85, 99–101,
150–52, 157–75
robotics, 108

safety nets, 27, 154
satellites, 2, 51
schools, 9, 67, 173; enrollment (*see*
educational enrollment)
science, 4; and technology, 28, 147
secondary education. *See* education
sex education, 147
sexual: apartheid, 148; division of labor,
148, 154
Shiva, Vandana, 166, 167, 174n8
slave trade, 149
social: inequalities, 14; integration, 63;
justice, 11, 129, 132n16, 155;
movements, 130, 132n16;
regulation, 71; transformation, 34;
welfare, 8
socialism, 17n4, 24, 138
SOCRATES, 105, 106
South, 3, 9, 12, 34, 166
Soviet bloc. *See* communist countries
special education, 56
state, 9, 12, 13, 15, 27, 31, 38, 55, 85,
91–92, 113; expenditures, 145; and
family, 134; funding of universities,
103, 105, 106, 108, 113; and social
welfare, 135, 147; and women, 135,
136, 138, 152
stocks, 7
student: international travel, 109; loans,
107; movements (*see* university
student resistance)

structural adjustment programs (SAPs), 20, 29–30, 136, 145, 165, 180, 183
subjectivity, 32
sweatshops, 12

teachers, 28, 40–44, 56, 61n1, 61n3, 105; contracts, 46; living standards, 30; profession, 48, 61n3; resistance, 161; salaries, 30, 54; training, 42, 46, 54, 128, 147; unions, 61n1, 96, 185
technological development, 14, 61
technology, 1, 4, 22; in biology, 5, 108; in communications, 6, 14, 65, 103, 140, 178; in information, 22, 175n20; in telecommunications, 125; in transportation, 22
teenagers. *See* adolescents
television, 45, 65, 66, 67–68, 73, 85, 178
testing, 38, 41–44, 60, 161; high-stakes testing, 40, 42, 61, 95; standardized, 56
theory, viii, 19, 146; of globalization, 1–18
Third International Mathematics and Science Study (TIMMS), 62n4
Third Way, 185n4
Third World, 17n4, 21, 45, 57, 89, 124, 158, 159, 160, 163, 168–69
time and space compression, 63
Tobin tax, 101, 102n12, 184
Total Quality Management (TQM), 111, 112
tourism, 25, 31, 35n4
Trade-Related Intellectual Property Rights (TRIPS), 92, 98, 127, 164, 165
Trade-Related Investment Measures (TRIMS), 21
transnational corporations (TNCs), 4, 7, 10, 21, 23, 27, 71, 75, 83–102, 159, 177, 181; and agriculture, 165, 167; and culture, 97–99, 119; and Global Compact, 169; and taxation, 184
tuition fees, 116

UNESCO, 43, 143, 155n9
unions, 4, 155n2, 161, 164

unit of analysis, 4
universities, 9, 28; competition from private sector, 104, 108, 120; differentiation, 104, 106, 110; governance, 117, 122, 128, 129; instrumental ends, 108, 113, 121, 148; linkages to business, 119, 120, 128; marketing of programs, 113; performance assessment, 110, 117; ranking, 111; student resistance, 168–69; tenure 118
United Nations (UN), 133, 144, 150, 169-70, 182–84
United Nations Conference on Trade and Development (UNCTAD), 84, 90
United Nations Development Program (UNDP), 31, 180, 182
United States Agency for International Development (USAID), 43, 75, 146
urban centers, 58
user fees, 115

values, 5, 38, 55, 150, 178; homogenization, 81
Via Campesina, 168
video, 64, 66, 68, 73, 82n5
violence: physical, 15; symbolic, 15
voucher programs, 45, 47–48

Wallerstein, Immanuel, 4, 8, 17n3, 17n5
Web: pages, 51; sites, 69, 72, 78, 117, 170
women, 23, 32, 118, 139, 140, 147, 157, 166; in labor force, 138, 140; professors, 118; rural, 138; and university, 148; urban, 138; work time, 118
Women in Development in Europe (WIDE), 156n13
women's: movements, 133, 153, 160; networks, 154, 156n13; oppression, 142; organizations, 165–66; rights, 132n16, 141; subordination, 147; and university, 148
Women's Environment and Development Organization (WEDO), 156n13
workers' unions, 164–65

working poor, 73

World Bank, 8, 21, 25, 27, 29, 33, 43, 57, 70, 75, 78, 88, 90, 116, 124, 166, 170, 183

world cities, 57–60, 74, 92–95

World Economic Forum, 70, 90, 171

World Social Forum, 70, 171, 172

World Social Summit (Copenhagen), 136

World Trade Organization (WTO), 21, 92, 164, 170, 174n8, 182; and higher education, 96, 105; and TRIPS, 98

youth programs, 160

Zapatista movement, 172

zero-sum game, 14, 27

About the Author

Nelly P. Stromquist is professor of education at the Rossier School of Education and an affiliated scholar in the Center for Feminist Research, both at the University of Southern California, Los Angeles. She specializes in international development education, which she analyzes from a sociological perspective. Her research focuses on questions of gender, equity policies, educational innovations, and adult education in developing countries, particularly Latin America and West Africa. She has published widely. Her articles can be found in such journals as the *Comparative Education Review* (US), *Compare* (UK), and *Educação e Pesquisa* (Brazil). Her most recent work includes authoring the books *Literacy for Citizenship: Gender and Grassroots Dynamics in Brazil* and *Improving Girls' Participation in Basic Education*, and editing *Distant Alliances: Promoting the Education of Girls and Women in Latin America, Globalization, Education, and Culture: Integration and Contestation Across Countries* (Rowman & Littlefield 2000, with Karen Monkman), and *Women in the Third World: An Encyclopedia of Contemporary Issues*.